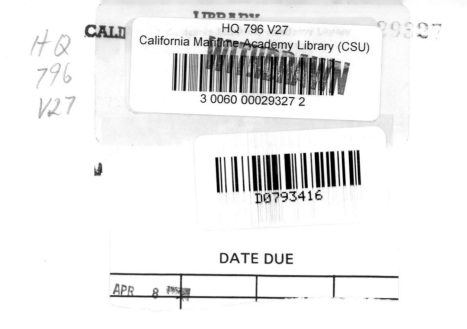

THE VALUE OF YOUTH

ARTHUR PEARL, DOUGLAS GRANT AND ERNST WENK

EDITORS

RESPONSIBLE ACTION · DAVIS · CALIFORNIA

The cover designs and illustrations
for all DIALOGUE BOOKS are created
by the well known Swiss artist Celestino Piatti

Library of Congress Card Number 78-65130
ISBN 0-931364-05-1

4843760

A CALL FOR
A NATIONAL YOUTH POLICY

ILLUSTRATIONS

COMING OF AGE 5
IN SEARCH OF A ROLE 61
CREATIVE EXPRESSION 95
SPORTS 131
AID TO THOSE IN NEED 149
HELP FOR THE HANDICAPPED 171
YOUNG AND OLD 187
ECOLOGY 221
YOUTH TEACHING YOUTH 245

EDITORS

ARTHUR PEARL is professor of Education at University of California at Santa Cruz and Vice President of Social Action Research Center. He was formerly at University of Oregon and Howard University. He served as Deputy Director of New York State Division for Youth 1961-63 and Research Director of California Governor's Special Commission on Minorities 1960-61. He is co-author of NEW CAREERS FOR THE POOR (with Frank Reissman), editor of MENTAL HEALTH OF THE POOR (with Frank Reissman and Jerome Cohen), and author of THE ATROCITY OF EDUCATION and LANDSLIDE.

DOUGLAS GRANT is president of the Social Action Research Center, a non-profit organization bringing together education and individual development through participation in social action approaches. He has contributed chapters to NEW CAREERS FOR THE POOR; MENTAL HEALTH OF THE POOR; AGENTS OF CHANGE: A STUDY IN POLICE REFORM; JUVENILE DELINQUENCY; and THE HANDBOOK OF EVALUATION RESEARCH.

ERNST WENK is president of Responsible Action, a non-profit organization. He was formerly the Director of the Research Center of the National Council on Crime and Delinquency and a faculty member of the California State University, Sacramento. He is author and co-author of THE YOUNG ADULT OFFENDER, DROPOUT (with Nora Harlow), PARTNERSHIP IN RESEARCH, DELINQUENCY PREVENTION: EDUCATIONAL APPROACHES (with Richard Carlton), and editor (with Nora Harlow) of SCHOOL CRIME AND DISRUPTION: PREVENTION MODELS.

CONTRIBUTORS

STEPHANIA ARNESS, Skills Specialist, Far West High School, Oakland, California

JOE BERNEY, Teacher, Soquel High School, Soquel, California

GERALD BLAKE, Professor of Urban Affairs, Portland State University, Oregon

DENNIE BRIGGS, Professor of Human Justice, Governor's State University, Park Forest South, Illinois; Project Coordinator, Social Action Research Center, San Rafael, California

RONALD BUCKNAM, Senior Associate, Education and Work Group, National Institute of Education, Washington, D.C.

RICHARD CAREY, Coordinator, Research and Program Evaluation, Palo Alto Unified School District, Palo Alto, California

JAMES S. COLEMAN, Professor of Sociology, University of Chicago

LEE CONWAY, Social Action Research Center, San Rafael, California

AMITAI ETZIONI, Professor of Sociology, Columbia University, and Director, Center for Policy Research

DOUGLAS GRANT, President, Social Action Research Center, San Rafael, California

DAVID F. GREENBERG, Professor of Sociology, New York University

DENNIS HOFFMAN, Portland State University, Oregon

WAYNE JENNINGS, Director, The Open School, St. Paul, Minnesota

JAMES MASON, Portland State University, Oregon

JOE NATHAN, Vice Principal, Murray High School, St. Paul, Minnesota

ARTURO PACHECO, Assistant Professor of Education, Stanford University, Stanford, California

ARTHUR PEARL, Professor of Education, University of California, Santa Cruz

LEE PENN, Portland State University, Oregon

DAVID TYACK, Professor of Education and History, Stanford University, Stanford, California

ELIOT WIGGINTON, Foxfire Fund, Rabun Gap, Georgia

ERNST WENK, President, Responsible Action, Davis, California

EDWARD A. WYNNE, Associate Professor of Education in Policy Studies, University of Illinois at Chicago Circle

ACKNOWLEDGEMENTS

Reprinted in part or in toto with permission from the Publishers and the authors:

James S. Coleman, "Changing the Environment for Youth," PHI DELTA KAPPAN, January, 1978.

Lee Conway, "Classroom in the Sky: A Power Trip for Disadvantaged Youth," PHI DELTA KAPPAN, May, 1976.

Amitai Etzioni, "The Crisis of Modernity: Deviation or Demise?" JOURNAL OF HUMAN RELATIONS, Vol. 21, No. 4, 1973, pp. 370-394.

David F. Greenberg, "Delinquency and the Age Structure of Society," CONTEMPORARY CRISES, Vol. 1, 1977, pp. 189-223.

Wayne Jennings and Joe Nathan, "Startling/Disturbing Research on School Program Effectiveness," PHI DELTA KAPPAN, March, 1977.

Arturo Pacheco, "Alienation: A Closer Look," PHI DELTA KAPPAN, January, 1978.

Arthur Pearl, "Youth in Lower Class Settings," in THE PROBLEM OF YOUTH, Sherif & Sherif (eds.), Aldine, 1964.

David Tyack, "Socialization to What?" PHI DELTA KAPPAN, January, 1978.

Eliot Wigginton, "The Foxfire Concept," reprinted with permission from TEACHING MOUNTAIN CHILDREN: TOWARDS A FOUNDATION OF UNDERSTANDING, edited by David N. Mielke, published by the Appalachian Consortium Press.

Ernst Wenk, "Tomorrow's Education: Models for Participation," in Wenk and Harlow, (eds.), SCHOOL CRIME AND DISRUPTION: PREVENTION MODELS, National Institute of Education, 1978.

Edward A. Wynne, "Behind the Discipline Problem: Youth Suicide as a Measure of Alienation," PHI DELTA KAPPAN, January, 1978.

FOREWORD

As a potentially vital national resource, America's young people are tragically underutilized. Yet, with appropriate national review and revision of youth policies and programs, youth could contribute importantly to our society and our economy. *The Value of Youth,* an important and timely book, directs attention to questions that are critical to the internal defense of our social system. Increasing numbers of alienated and disaffected youth represent a "danger within" which, it is suggested, should be taken as seriously as external international threats.

With the exception of the public schools, government policymakers seldom focus attention on youth unless their behavior or status is defined as a "problem" (e.g., delinquency, running away, pregnancy out of wedlock, substance abuse, emotional disturbance, unemployment, etc.). Eligibility for public services or program participation generally requires a prior label of deviance. As a result, every youth who participates in public programs tends to acquire a stigma which adds to his or her problems or generates new ones.

The problem orientation of our youth programs is curious in light of the almost universal agreement that adolescence is a difficult, stressful, and uniquely important period of life. There seems to be wide recognition that all youth experience some stress in making the transition to adulthood, but this recognition has not been translated into a general policy of *developmental support* which does not require for eligibility overt acts of undesirable behavior. Evidence of growing numbers of alienated, disaffected youth, discussed in these pages, should encourage attention to this serious gap in public policy.

As will be noted, contemporary problems among youth are coming to be viewed not as individual maladjustments to a basically well-ordered society, but rather as understandable adaptations to social arrangements that impede a healthy transition to adulthood. This view demands that we move beyond training more counselors for the maladjusted or providing treatment-oriented services to "problem" youth. Instead we must change those basic institutional and social arrangements that appear to be producing an increasing number of troubled young people.

Widely recognized changes in the nature of work, the proximity of the work-place to the home, and the need for more specialized skills to gain meaningful employment have profoundly affected family life, public education, and the access of youth to work experience. For years, the key to eligibility for "successful adulthood" has been to remain in school longer and longer. Unfortunately, the positive impact of schools on youth has declined at precisely the same time that family supports have weakened, resulting in a "double failure" on the part of the two principal institutions affecting their present and future development. Neither the school nor the family currently is equipped to retain the interest of youth or to assist them in moving toward full adult status and productive employment. Without these vital supports many young people flounder, getting into serious trouble at worst or, at best, falling short of their full potential.

Improved youth development policy depends on a clear recognition that: (1) Government's stake in the successful transition of youth to adult status is enormous. (2) All youth experience stress in this developmental period and policies focused exclusively on "problem" youth are self-defeating in the long run. And (3) institutional barriers to constructive participation by young people must be overcome.

The writings included in this volume are intended to assist the development and implementation of new youth policies and programs based on these premises.

T.M. Jim Parham
Deputy Assistant Secretary
for Human Development Services
U.S. Department of Health, Education and Welfare

PREFACE

This volume speaks for the *value* of youth and suggests policies that are consistent with such an understanding. To value youth we must encourage young people to participate in all of society's functions. They must be active both in their own education and in activities that meet the real needs of society. They must, in short, become an important component of our political, social, and economic processes.

America needs a cohesive national youth policy. Current policies and programs affecting youth are fragmented and often work at cross-purposes. Schools are places where youth are segregated from the rest of society and isolated from meaningful participation. Employment for youth, where it exists, offers little in the way of preparation for a career or any real source of experience or learning.

This volume, focusing on the value of youth, both presents new theory and describes some of the social or structural factors that necessitate its development and application. Examples of programs that are based on valuing youth also are offered. Finally, key elements of a new national policy for dealing with youth are specified.

We need a national youth policy. The costs of youth unemployment, delinquency, and school failure are enormous both in dollars and in wasted lives. Our society has many unmet needs that can be fulfilled without significant increases in energy consumption. We need individuals to work in human services — to aid the elderly, the handicapped, and the infirm. We need to develop recreational pursuits that preserve, rather than destroy, the natural environment. We need help in upgrading public transportation systems. We need greater involvement in the creative arts. Young people have much to offer in these and many other areas.

A policy that values youth will enable our young people to learn to cope with a changing world, while enlisting them as agents in the change process. A policy that values youth need not be inflationary. New funds are not needed to begin to put youth to work. Much can be accomplished by redirecting funds that currently support programs which de-value youth. New programs could provide for more positive roles for youth in education, the community, the justice system, the economy, and other areas of vital interest to the local, national, and world communities.

Arthur Pearl
Douglas Grant
Ernst Wenk

CONTENTS

ILLUSTRATIONS   4
EDITORS   6
CONTRIBUTORS   6
ACKNOWLEDGEMENTS   8
FOREWORD   9
PREFACE   11
CONTENTS   12

**PART I: TOWARD A GENERAL THEORY OF
              VALUING YOUTH**   15

Arthur Pearl
    TOWARD A GENERAL THEORY OF VALUING YOUTH   17

PART II: ALIENATION AS A WAY OF LIFE   31

Arthur Pearl
    EMPLOYMENT DILEMMAS OF YOUTH   37
David F. Greenberg
    DELINQUENCY AND THE AGE STRUCTURE
    OF SOCIETY   51
Amitai Etzioni
    THE CRISIS OF MODERNITY: DEVIATION
    OR DEMISE?   81
Edward A. Wynne
    BEHIND THE DISCIPLINE PROBLEM:
    YOUTH SUICIDE AS A MEASURE OF ALIENATION   103
David Tyack
    SOCIALIZATION TO WHAT?   125
Arturo Pacheco
    ALIENATION: A CLOSER LOOK   129
James S. Coleman
    CHANGING THE ENVIRONMENT FOR YOUTH   133

**PART III: A POSITIVE ALTERNATIVE:
             YOUTH AS COMPETENT PARTICIPANTS**   135

Gerald Blake, et.al.,
    RECRUITING UNEMPLOYED YOUTH AS PLANNERS
    OF YOUTH EMPLOYMENT   141

Joe Berney
    A STUDENT BILL OF RIGHTS   159

Richard Carey
    STUDENT RESEARCH AS A SOURCE OF
    PROGRAM DEVELOPMENT: A CASE STUDY   169

Ronald Bucknam
    EXPERIENCE-BASED CAREER EDUCATION   177

Stephania Arness
    EXPERIENCE-BASED CAREER EDUCATION,
    FAR WEST HIGH SCHOOL, OAKLAND, CALIFORNIA   197

Wayne Jennings and Joe Nathan
    SOME DISTURBING RESEARCH ON SCHOOL
    PROGRAM EFFECTIVENESS   203

Students of St. Paul Open School
    CONSUMER ACTION SERVICE: HOW YOU CAN DO
    IT!   219

Lee Conway
    CLASSROOM IN THE SKY: A POWER TRIP FOR
    DISADVANTAGED YOUTH   235

Arthur Pearl
    YOUTH IN LOWER CLASS SETTINGS   249

Eliot Wigginton
    THE FOXFIRE CONCEPT   273

Ernst Wenk
    TOMORROW'S EDUCATION: MODELS FOR
    PARTICIPATION   291

PART IV: DIMENSIONS OF A NATIONAL YOUTH POLICY   307

Dennie Briggs and Douglas Grant
    DEVELOPING A POSITIVE NATIONAL YOUTH
    POLICY   309

PART I

TOWARD A GENERAL THEORY
OF VALUING YOUTH

TOWARD A GENERAL THEORY
OF VALUING YOUTH

Arthur Pearl

Americans believe in slogans. One often heard is that "youth are our most valuable asset." This theme is used to justify educational costs, recreational projects, and even the juvenile justice system. Unfortunately, as with many slogans, there is little truth to it. We operate on an assumption much closer to George Bernard Shaw's dictum: "Youth is such a wonderful thing; what a shame to waste it on children."

The fact is that young people in America are *de-valued*. They do not have the legal protection accorded adults. They have no political power. For all but a privileged few, schools are like warehouses rather than places for useful learning. In the work place, too, youth are restricted, by law and by discriminatory practices, from earning their own way. It is rare, therefore, that a young person can gain a sense of usefulness and meaningful participation in any contemporary social arena.

What makes all of this even more disturbing is that the problems of youth in today's highly industrialized society are treated the same as those of young people in the predominantly rural America of decades ago. Society today is fragmented and compartmentalized. Communities are no longer self-contained; they no longer meet all the essential needs of their residents. Food, shelter, and clothing needs, and work and leisure experiences typically are provided for by distant, impersonal bureaucracies. Schools are isolated from community organizations; the workplace often is many miles from home. Crime is dealt with by one agency, welfare by another, schooling by yet another and there are few connections and little continuity among them. Many people never participate in community events or local government.

Youth problems today derive from their changed position in society — there are few acceptable social roles for young people and not enough important work for them to do. They find it difficult to procure employment. Schooling is not as neat a solution to the work problem as implied by the slogan "stay in school and get a job." Youth are increasingly involved in crime (1). Black youth commit proportionately more crimes than whites; they also have poorer job prospects, do less well in school, drop out more frequently, and score lower on achievement tests. Young women also fare poorly in the job market. Compared to young males, they do not go as far in school (far fewer have doctorate degrees), and they score lower on SAT's (particularly in math) (2).

Yet the most notable aspect of the current situation of youth is the magnitude of their crime and employment problems and the inappropriateness of schooling to the solution of either. Schools, in fact, have become accessories to the former and are encumbrances to the latter. What also is different today is the morass of technology that affects all aspects of life — the data banks that maintain life-and-death records, locking people into their past, and the credentials that are visas to different work worlds. A diploma may not be an indication of knowledge gained, but without it more avenues are closed today than was ever the case in history.

Current attempts to explain youth problems and anti-social behavior do not reflect these changes. Youth crime, alienation, and unemployment are attributed, not to reasonable estimations of the situation, but to alleged deficiencies in individuals. The juvenile offender is believed to suffer from character defects or behavior problems; the unemployed youth has "bad work habits;" the school misfit is "culturally deprived," intellectually inferior, or a victim of accumulated environmental deficits.

The criminal justice system reflects this theoretical point of view. The underlying theme of the justice system is that criminally prone persons can be deterred from antisocial behavior by severe and certain punishment. As crime increases, those who see punishment as a deterrent push their ideas to the extreme. One such theorist, Edward C. Banfield, a distinguished Harvard professor, argues that some people have a great "proneness" to commit crimes, mostly young lower-class males because they have both "propensity" and "incentive." People who are very "present-oriented and have little ego strength and a preconventional conception of morality," according to Banfield, have criminal propensities. Thus, he argues, they should be dealt with *before* they commit crimes (3)!

Such theories dominate social science research today. In effect, they argue that the system is just and that it is the individual who is inadequate. Applied to youth, such a theoretical stance *de-values* the young person by negating the possibility that his or her behavior, however nonconforming, is meaningful and even rational in the context in which it occurs. Social policy based on deficit theory does not reflect the substantial economic and cultural changes that have taken place over the past several decades. It does not recognize the current position of young people in American society. To continue to rely on short-term crisis-reduction measures, hoping that youth will somehow "outgrow" their problems, is simply illogical, for these problems are unique and require new theory. We must begin to take young people seriously, to treat their needs seriously, and to acknowledge that even those behaviors that appear outlandish may be reasonable responses to their social and economic situation.

The analysis presented below details the ways in which contemporary work and school environments de-value the young and then turns to a discussion of a new theory of *valuing* youth. Involvement of youth in meaningful work is regarded as necessary not only for reducing youthful antisocial behavior, but also for ameliorating long-term social problems for which adults have neither the time nor the energy. Instead of assuming that young people are incapable of acting on their own or contributing to the problem-solving process, we must acknowledge their abilities, value their inputs, and encourage their active participation in all aspects of American society.

DEVALUATION OF YOUTH IN THE LABOR MARKET

A major way in which our society de-values youth is by denying them the opportunity to work or by offering them only those jobs that have neither long-term career potential nor immediate personal gratification. The grim employment picture for young people is not improving: 11 percent of youth aged 16 to 19 were unemployed in 1956; by 1976 that figure had climbed to 19 percent. (The situation is worse, as might be expected, for non-white youth: in 1976, compared to 17 percent for whites, 37 percent of non-white youths were out of a job.) (4)

It is often argued that young people, especially crime-prone or "troublesome" ones, do not *want* to work because they will not sacrifice for future gains. Banfield reports that a Harlem youth refused to push trucks in the garment district for $50 a week when he could make that much in a day selling marijuana, suggesting that this shows that young people are unwilling to accept the wages that their work is worth (5). Clearly, there are other interpretations. The jobs available to young people generally are not only low-paid, they are inherently unrewarding. There is evidence that many are willing to work at jobs that do not pay well if the work is meaningful and their contribution is valued. In the Howard project (6), for example, in which poor and delinquent youth worked as recreational leaders and researchers in child-care, many young people stayed in their jobs (despite the minimum wage) because they gained a feeling of usefulness, competence, and belonging. They stayed because others — their co-workers, employers, and, most important, the people they served — valued them and what they did.

19

Despite varied (although isolated) efforts to provide meaningful work for youth, most employment opportunities for persons of youthful age are in marginal employment sectors: low-paid, part-time, work in positions of little or no career potential. Fast-food chains, for example, are a major employer of young persons. While such jobs do provide spending money for a large number of youth, they generally are not available to inner-city or other low-income groups and they rarely represent a launching pad to a career. The private sector, it seems, is incapable or unwilling to absorb the youthful population in the labor market, much less deal constructively with those who are given no reasons to be motivated.

Youth employment is perceived, by employers and by the rest of the American public, as temporary, part-time, and marginal in its economic contribution. Most employment opportunities are viewed as a "learning experience," not intended to be as productive — or as remunerative — as similar work by adults. The language of the 1977 Youth Employment Act (7) reveals this bias. The purpose of the Act is "to provide youth, and particularly economically disadvantaged youth, with opportunities to learn and earn that will lead to meaningful employment opportunities *after they have completed the program"(8)*.The aim of this legislation, it seems, is to change young people — to make them employable at some later date — in the private sector of the economy.

One problem, of course, is that the private sector is not expanding at a rate that will permit absorption of this population of persons-in-training at any time in the foreseeable future. Government also is neither expanding its own employment capability nor encouraging, by any practical means, the necessary expansion in private sector employment. The Humphrey-Hawkins (1978) Full Employment and Balanced Growth Act, including its many revisions, reflects the same orientation as the Youth Employment Act. The explicit purpose of the Humphrey-Hawkins bill is "that the major expansion of employment occur in the private sector, that a very much smaller portion of it occur in state and local government in accord with long-term trends in the past, and that Federal employment increase only slightly" (9). According to the projections of the bill, by 1983 private employers will have absorbed 83 percent of civilly employed persons.

Unfortunately, the corporations that dominate the private sector economy do not generate a significant number of new jobs. Over the past two decades, the five hundred largest corporations have increased their hold on the economy without appreciably increasing the number of persons they employ. From 1960 to 1970, the proportion of the Gross National Product produced by these corporations rose by over 6 percent, while the proportion of labor they employed increased by about 4.5 percent (10). Since 1970 it appears that the larger these corporations get, the less likely they are to employ more workers. Between 1970 and 1977, the five hundred largest corporations increased by over 10 percent their contribution to the GNP, while employing almost 2 percent *less* of the work force (11).

There are other problems with reliance on the private sector for youth employment. Emphasis on private sector employment is likely to increase consumption of fossil fuels and will not create quality goods and services that are desperately needed by impoverished populations simply because production of these goods and services will not be profitable. Also, the orientation toward providing jobs for youth that will "pay off" only in the future (if at all) does little to motivate young people to accept legitimate employment and contributes to their alienation from society. In sum, expecting the private sector to generate enough jobs for meaningful youth involvement, while looking at work as a separate life function, will create, not reduce, the problems that young people face.

DEVALUATION OF YOUTH BY SCHOOLS

Schools are a crucial "mediator" for young people. They can, if properly structured, serve to prepare youth for full participation in social life. Or, as currently constituted, they may perpetuate inequality, confuse youth about social and economic realities, and contribute to the delinquency problem. The evidence that exists supports the notion that schools today do more harm than good.

If the heart of the youth "problem" lies in the employment situation, schooling, at least as it now exists, is the single most important obstacle to resolution of that problem. Public schools do not enhance "employability" because students are (1) misinformed about work and economics; (2) oriented to inequality by ability tracking, achievement testing, counseling, and a lack of first-hand life experiences; and (3) rendered passive and powerless even in the most trivial aspects of the educational experience.

Some years ago, after completing a review of high-school textbooks, anthropologist Jules Henry commented that students were educated to be "stupid" about blacks, labor, economics, poverty, communism, the Soviet Union and war (12). Henry complained that students were left ignorant about economics and made to believe that depressions come and go mysteriously.

In fact, the situation is much more insidious than that. Students are taught economics as if the policies that have guided the economic destiny of this country never existed. For the past fifty years the economy has been heavily regulated by government, which has attempted to steer a course between excessive unemployment and runaway inflation. The logic of those policies is not presented, nor is the particular influence of special interest groups analyzed. The inability of policies to attain desired results in recent years is made to appear to be due to corruption or incompetence. Students are neither encouraged to consider economic policies that might work nor informed that, like it or not, they will be responsible for the economics of the future. It may be too much to ask that, in a capitalist society, students be instructed in ''enemy ideologies'' such as socialism, but it should not be to explain modern capitalism to them. Without a knowledge of economics, youth are in no position to share in suggesting remedies for the problem of insufficient work which affects them so profoundly.

When it comes to explaining work, schools again are derelict. Not only is organized labor distorted, but the requirements of work — the simple activities of ordinary people — are not presented realistically, or in context. Doctors and scientists are made to appear as beyond the competencies of the ordinary person. Businessmen are presented as tough-minded pragmatists who have earned their way through self-sacrifice and enormous expenditures of energy. Many of the newly emerging technical activities are scarcely mentioned at all. Moreover, many occupations are presented as unattractive for middle-income youth and therefore, by implication, as appropriate only for blacks or the poor.

Career education, heralded by many educators as an advancement over the old vocational education, often contributes to the perpetuation of such stereotypes and attitudes. Some career education programs span a large number of the years a child is in school, beginning with ''career awareness'' in the elementary grades and continuing with ''career exploration'' in junior high through tenth grade. Such programs present to all students an alluring image of adult professional occupations to which only some high-school graduates can realistically aspire. They do not prepare students for the realities of limited job opportunities and an economy in which a great many jobs are non-professional or require unskilled labor. In addition, many career education programs gloss over the fact that socioeconomic status, race, or sex often have more to do with future job possibilities than individual capacities and potentials.

The truth is that, regardless of career exploration and knowledge, a student will not become a doctor unless admitted to an accredited medical school. This brings us to the second obstacle to youth employability mentioned earlier, that schools organize and reinforce inequality through ability grouping, achievement testing, counseling and denial of first-hand field experiences. Any student who wants to become a doctor must first negotiate elementary, junior high, and high school and emerge with both the academic record and the predilection to attempt college. At each step, some students are encouraged to continue, others are discouraged. One means by which students are differentially encouraged is by ability grouping in the early grades. As early as the first grade, some students are placed in high, middle, and low reading and math groups. In recent years, this has been even further stratified by designing individualized programs on the basis of alleged ability. The designation of high and low ability is not a self-assessment; it is a technical decision made by an "expert." The experts, of course, have "science" on their side. Tests have "validity" and "reliability" and determine precisely what and how much children know. Thus, one child is determined to be reading two years below grade level, another is above. The University of California recently decided to rely far more heavily in the future on such tests in deciding who will be admitted as students.

If students insist on aspiring to situations that experts "know" are unrealistic, then counselors step in to convince them of the folly of their ways. The "able" are encouraged to get back on track and those with "limited abilities" are encouraged to scale back their aspirations. Failure to heed such advice can lead to serious complications for the student, e.g., referrals to psychologists and painful encounters with parents. For some it is the first step in a process that could lead to entanglements with the juvenile justice system. Because such evaluations and counseling are done in isolation, the student never has the opportunity to gain the sort of independent self-assessment of ability which he or she could gain in an actual work situation. A career education program which emphasizes freely chosen student employment and individual responsibility for conduct on the job, such as in the Experience-Based Career Education program described in this book, is one way to begin a process of student self-evaluation.

As schools currently are structured, however, ability grouping, testing, and tracking all serve to perpetuate inequalities in youths' life patterns. Contrary to some educators' conclusions (13), it is the character of schooling that reinforces inequality. A different school could have fundamentally different results. Such a school would not encourage student passivity. A passive student is a de-valued student and schools de-value youth by not involving them in any important decision-making. The more schooling is dominated by tests, the less control youth have over their own experiences. The more youth are told that they are not yet ready for adult responsibility, the more alienated (and irresponsible) they become. It is not only in work that youth find themselves with no important responsibility. All other aspects of their lives are similarly affected. Youth have no real "say" regarding school rules, budgets, curriculum, and extra-curricular activities.

If we are to value youth, we must provide them with knowledge and experiences that allow them both to negotiate and to change the system in which they live.

TOWARD A GENERAL THEORY OF VALUING YOUTH

If youth are to be valued, they must be *of* the society — participants, not recipients. That is the crux of any theory of valuing youth. We must give up the romantic notion that adolescence is a "psycho-social moratorium" — a period in which youth are allowed to freely explore many roles before having to finalize on an adult identity (14). While it is true that adolescents must experiment, this experimentation must occur in activities or pursuits which fulfill genuine needs of their community or of the nation. Young people must be allowed and encouraged to produce things, perform services, and create art forms that all segments of the society can appreciate. Perhaps of equal importance, these activities must have a logical continuation; that is, there must be "career" possibilities in youth commitments and activities. A theory of valuing youth must also be redemptive. A youth who engages in a foolish act must be allowed to escape negative consequences and must not be encouraged to make such actions his or her career.

The valuing of youth has both an external and an internal component. In addition to being valued by others, youth also must value themselves. Attempts to treat youth problems have in many instances created a distance between established authority and those being helped. The more a youth is estranged from the dominant society, the wider the gulf between that society and the peer group. A theory that values youth, then, must integrate self and societal appreciation. It must apply across all aspects of adolescent life: it must explain youth behavior at work, in school, on the streets, in the home, and with friends.

A theory that values youth must bring together individual needs and societal needs. The important needs of adolescence can be clearly identified:

(1) Young people need *security*. As society finds fewer roles for youth, youth problems will increase. Youth cannot be financially secure if they cannot find work. This condition explains both low-income and affluent youth behavior because any family's interactions will become strained if employed teens continue to be supported by their parents.

(2) Young people need *relief from pain*. For many, youth is a painful experience. In 1974, 17 out of every 100,000 persons between the ages of 15 and 24 committed suicide and 99 more were killed in accidents (15). Unhappiness and death are preoccupations of the youth culture. The pain of youth is most often isolation and emptiness, for a society that has little need for young people leaves them to their own devices.

(3) Young people need a *sense of understanding about their world*. Meaninglessness devastates youth. The failure to "demystify" political, economic, social, and cultural life leaves youth without ownership of any part of their existence. It also requires the fabrication of mythology. These mythologies in turn tend to become boundaries of thought and action. Youth ascribe attributes to drugs, to social relationships, to institutions that are perfectly plausible given the lack of information available to them (16). Here lies the greatest deficiency of modern education. Even the "basics" become mystified in the increasing reliance on technologies of which teachers understand little and parents and students even less. Vital and important aspects of life, world relations, deterioration of the cities, the logic of monetary and fiscal policies, energy, transportation, and food are fragmented to defy any true understanding of the nature of the problems and the plausibility of any solutions.

(4) Young people need *friends and other social supports*. If adults, through the institutions they command, cannot generate activities in which young people can find a sense of belonging, they will create their own. The social systems young people create will provide for many activities that are at best disrespectful of adults and at worst dangerous to society. The lack of legitimate constraints in this system leads to drug abuse, sexual behaviors that often cause venereal disease, unwanted pregnancies and abortions, and various criminal acts.

(5) Young people need *a sense of usefulness*. If young people cannot be useful to society as workers and artists, they invent ways to be useful to each other. Drug use is one such invention. Drugs create occupations (manufacturers, salespersons, importers, truckers, health counselors, etc.) which provide opportunities to be useful and competent and to develop relationships. These factors may be as important to the continued use of drugs as are their physical or psychological effects.

(6) Young people need *a sense of competence*. It is difficult to be competent if there is little for one to do. Adult society offers the opportunity for a limited number of young people to be competent in school, but in the process at least as many are designated incompetent. This classification is

highly correlated with social background and, although school authorities insist that the system is just, there is no evidence to support that conclusion. A great many young people feel that they are not given a chance to demonstrate competence because teachers' evaluations are not negotiable since they often are based more on technical data than on personal judgments (17).

(7) Young people need *hope and excitement*. Hope is characteristic of youth and youth is often a culture's primary source of hope. Yet in our society there is clear evidence of loss of elasticity and optimism. Due to the poor employment situation, young people have little cause to be hopeful and great cause to feel trapped. Finally, a non-participatory society creates no legitimate opportunities for excitement. If youth cannot create their own excitement, they are likely to be apathetic; if they *create* excitement, they are likely to be delinquent.

These needs are precisely those that a modern technical society does not meet.

In order for valuing theory to become operative, work must be made available which can, first, meet the needs of youth as outlined above, and, second meet society's needs. It has been mentioned that currently there is little societal need for youth, and yet society has many unmet needs. The elderly are neglected, young children are neglected and abused. Public transportation is inconvenient and often unsafe. Parks are unattended. The environment is polluted. Too few people participate in various art forms because there are too few teachers, organizers, materials, etc. A great many people have health problems that are not treated.

The task in developing youth employment is to employ people in those activities that best satisfy these important unmet societal needs. No public youth work projects should be funded unless there is a clearly identified set of persons to be served. Evaluations of that project should include a measure of how well those persons were served. To the extent that young people recognize that they have aided this target population, they will be able to gain a sense of usefulness and this too should be measured and its effect on total youth behavior assessed.

If private employers are to generate sufficient employment, such exemplary public programs will provide the basis for future developments and will be justified less on what they give to youth (although this must be an important consideration) than on what they offer to society. Such an approach generates a constituency much larger than the persons employed. If, for example, services to the aged becomes one of the youth projects, and 20 youth provide 200 old people with a variety of services (home care, hot lunches, supervised recreation, escorts to and from home for shopping and cultural events), then public understanding and appreciation of that activity is much more likely to be won than if the program merely provides jobs for poor, out-of-work youth.

Many economists argue that attempting to employ youth is a cause of inflation. Application of a theory that values youth, however, could have a deflationary effect on the economy if (1) youth were employed in the expansion of mass transit systems, in the installation of passive solar devices, and in the insulation of homes, all of which help reduce energy consumption; and (2) if youth were employed in specific areas, such as health care, where employment configurations in the past have been highly inflationary.

The major obstacle to widespread reliance on public transit in America is public fear — of bodily harm, discomfort, being stranded, lack of help with cumbersome packages, unsupervised children, dangers between home and the transit system, etc. These concerns could be alleviated by the judicious employment of youth as escorts, stewards, child supervisors, and security guards. Young people could redistribute vehicles that carry individuals to outlying areas, or provide personal services as required. In addition, youth could provide diversions — musical groups in one subway car, food and drinks in another, perhaps a library in another. All of these activities are potential jobs and, for many, potential careers.

Involving youth in health care (which is not necessarily "medicine") has a long tradition in the U.S. Young people were the primary deliverers of service in the Army Medical Corps and they were able to generate high-quality service without first going to medical school or undergoing other long-term training. Similar accomplishments have been recorded by para-medical teams attached to fire departments and these, too, often employ young people. Youth could be involved in home care for the aged at a fraction of the cost of institutional care.

In order to meet adolescent *and* societal needs, schooling must be integrated with and connected to work. A school that values youth involves youth in every aspect of learning. A theory of valuing youth can be implemented through youth participation in planning, projects, program development and evaluation. Active student participation also can provide meaning and direction to education, bringing a coherence to a now fragmented system.

Youth can function as planners at every age level. The planning can take place at the district office, as a total activity, or within a single classroom. The planning can be complex and long-range, or simple and almost immediate. It can be as comprehensive as overhauling the entire curriculum or as homespun as organizing a carwash to raise funds for a class dance. The planning can be formal — students may be elected or otherwise officially designated to be members on advisory or policy boards — or their involvement can be unstructured and informal. What is important is that youth be actively and importantly involved in the planning of activities that affect their lives. No school function should exclude youth in the planning processes.

In summary, a theory that values youth offers to youth opportunities to meaningfully participate in life. Such a theory places youth participation in work and schooling as the critical variables and argues that delinquency is best treated when youth can gain fulfillment as participating citizens in all of life's socially desirable arenas. Such a theory can never be completely implemented without true full employment but, if utilized within current appropriations for school and work, could appreciably reduce the magnitude of the problems that youth face and the problems that they cause.

When he was inaugurated in 1961, President Kennedy, in a now famous slogan, challenged young people to devote their energies to America's needs instead of their own. Today we ask, what *can* youth do for our country? If we continue to regard them as inadequate or irresponsible, we will never know the answer. If we value them, however, we may see this great challenge met.

FOOTNOTES AND REFERENCES

1. Between 1960 and 1974, persons under the age of 18 arrested for violent crimes (in areas inhabited by 69 million residents) increased from 11,698 to 41,425. This is an increase of 254 percent. Fourteen percent of *all* arrests in 1969 were youth, whereas in 1974 25 percent of all arrests were youth. U.S. Department of Justice, FBI UNIFORM CRIME REPORTS. Washington, D.C., 1975.
2. U.S. Department of Commerce, U.S. STATISTICAL ABSTRACT, 1977. Washington, D.C.: U.S. Government Printing Office, 1977, pp. 127, 146-7. And, U.S. Department of Commerce, Bureau of Census

CURRENT POPULATION REPORTS. Series P-23, No. 46, Series P-20, No. 272.

3. Edward C. Banfield, THE UNHEAVENLY CITY. Boston, Mass.: Little, Brown & Co., 1968, pp. 158-184.

4. EMPLOYMENT AND TRAINING REPORT TO THE PRESIDENT, Washington, D.C., 1977.

5. Edward C. Banfield, op. cit., p. 101.

6. See Arthur Pearl, "Youth in Lower Class Settings" in this book.

7. Public Law 95-93, 95th Congress. H.R. 6138, August 5. See 321.

8. Ibid., Italics added.

9. Muriel Humphrey and Augustus F. Hawkins, GOALS FOR FULL EMPLOYMENT AND HOW TO ACHIEVE THEM UNDER THE "FULL EMPLOYMENT AND BALANCED GROWTH ACT OF 1978" (S.50 and H.R. 50). Leon H. Keyserling, 2610 Upton Street, N.W., Washington, D.C. 20008. February, 1978, p. 22, 30.

10. U.S. Department of Commerce. STATISTICAL ABSTRACT. Washington, D.C. FORTUNE MAGAZINE, June 1961, May 1965. May 1970, May 1975, May 1976, April 1977.

11. Ibid.

12. Jules Henry, "Education for Stupidity," in REASON AND CHANGE IN ELEMENTARY EDUCATION, 2nd National Conference, U.S. Office of Education, Tri-University Project in Elementary Education, Feb. 13, 1968, pp. 117-134.

13. The unwillingness to look at schools as they actually function has led to some mischievous pronouncements, such as the influential book by Christopher Jencks, INEQUALITY: A REASSESSMENT OF FAMILY AND SCHOOLING IN AMERICA (New York: Basic Books, 1972). Concluding that schooling does not have much effect on reducing income inequality in the United States, Jencks proposes a re-distribution of wealth — a solution which would further de-value poor youth by taking away any chance they already have to be useful.

14. Erik Ericson, IDENTITY AND THE LIFE CYCLE. New York: W.W. Norton & Co., 1968. Erickson allows that if an adolescent is unable to establish a positive sense of self after all that experiencing, s/he is in deep trouble. "Many a late adolescent, if faced with continuing diffusion would rather be nobody or somebody bad, or indeed dead ...than not be quite somebody" (p. 132).

15. U.S. Department of Commerce, U.S. STATISTICAL ABSTRACT, 1977, p. 62.

16. For the importance of meaning to human existence, see Viktor E. Frankel, MAN'S SEARCH FOR MEANING. New York: Washington Square Press, 1959.

17. The University of California faculty did not want high school teachers to determine student competence because they feared "grade inflation."

PART II

ALIENATION AS A
WAY OF LIFE

Youth is a time of life; but it is also a context. To understand young people, one must understand the forces that influence and are influenced by them. This book is based on the premise that our society has alienated its young people and their alienation, in turn, has created severe social problems.

It is easy to make too much of the problem of "alienation" in modern life. Themes of alienation dominate the arts and the social sciences, coming to represent more a lament than the object of serious analysis. In this section an attempt is made to sharpen the focus. Particular aspects of alienation are emphasized because these are activities and processes that can be altered. Schools, employment, and juvenile justice are examined together with the quality and nature of youth participation in various areas of social life. Alienation, in the essays that follow, is understood as a sense of exclusion from decision-making on issues that are perceived as vital to the individual.

The major employment dilemma of youth is that the economy cannot create jobs as fast as people demand them. Over the years a buffering system has been established that places the greatest burden of economic downswings on youth, particularly minority youth (along with women and minority adults). There can be no real solution to youth problems without creation of meaningful jobs for youth. As Pearl points out, social policy today is concerned with generating caretakers for youth rather than with opening up opportunities for youth to learn to take care of themselves by full participation in the work force.

The relationship between delinquency and economics is one that defies consensus. In this section, David Greenberg reviews the research data, concluding that theories that posit delinquency as an attribute of the individual simply do not hold up. Rather, he argues, delinquency is one of many responses to a highly developed, technically dominated capitalist economy that is stratified into social classes. The particular dimensions of society that contribute most heavily to the delinquency problem are employment and schooling. A lack of employment opportunities sufficient to maintain an acceptable socioeconomic standing often leads to crimes of acquisition. Denial of personal autonomy and public degradation in school may give rise to other delinquent acts. Although Greenberg offers no specific solutions, he does present excellent reasons for discontinuing those policies and practices that clearly have not worked.

Modernity, as seen by Amitai Etzioni, represents a state of worsening crisis that may not be resolved. Because only a small elite are allowed to participate fully in contemporary decision-making processes, the social structure no longer is perceived as legitimate and widespread alienation is one result. Although Etzioni does not single out delinquency, youth employment, or schooling for special emphasis, his arguments are germane to each of these areas. He argues, for instance, that alienation is universal and results in a sense of "being left out." Authentic participation, he concludes, could largely overcome alienation by fostering a "sense of belonging, public attention and competence" while revitalizing our political processes.

Edward Wynne examines alienation as it applies specifically to adolescents and their schooling. With Greenberg and Etzioni, he concludes that youthful alienation is a growing phenomenon, citing as symptoms the increases in rates of suicide, homicide, drug use, and venereal disease among the young. Drawing upon Durkheim's 19th century analysis of suicide as a measure of anomie, Wynne sees contemporary developments as evidence of our society's inability to be "integrative." The rise in suicide, he suggests, is caused by a growing "self-centeredness" and a breakdown in institutional integration. Schools contribute importantly to this phenomenon because they segregate by age, class, and race. They also deprive young people of longterm intimate associations and isolate them from meaningful social, political, and economic activities.

Neither Wynne's analysis nor his solutions escape criticism, and critiques by Tyack, Pacheco, and Coleman also help set the stage for better understanding of both the problems and the potentialities of youth. David Tyack accuses Wynne of "psychologizing" the issues and of minimizing the institutional factors that produce social problems. According to Tyack, youth problems occur most often when the economy is incapable of absorbing young people. Tyack recommends attention to the social structures rather than to one set of its victims — alienated youth.

Arturo Pacheco also criticizes Wynne's analysis, focusing on his "lack of precision" and his "misinterpretation" of Durkheim. To Pacheco, alienation derives from the early works of Karl Marx and refers specifically to alienation from economic production. Pacheco also faults Wynne for placing too much blame on the schools and chastises him for neglecting Durkheim's later conclusion that schools are incapable of producing real social change.

James Coleman's criticism is less strident. He is not convinced that small decentralized schools would benefit students, but he sees a need for schools to provide social supports that families no longer can provide. Despite their differences, Wynne and his critics agree that young people face increasingly difficult circumstances. What Tyack and Pacheco play down is the misery that many youth experience in school. Improvements, particularly in participatory projects such as those described in Part III, can reduce their pain. The manner in which broader social changes are likely to occur can only be surmised. However, it is proposed that linking education to work will provide currently unavailable information about the potential value of schooling.

EMPLOYMENT DILEMMAS OF YOUTH

Arthur Pearl

It is becoming increasingly difficult for young people to enter the working world. As our society changes its modes of production, its credentialling and licensing systems, and the nature of its sponsorships, job opportunities for youth rapidly decline. The jobs young people do find tend to be short-term, less than full-time, and limited in career potential. The labor market appears to them as a bewildering hodgepodge — in part because there exists no logical mechanism for entry to the world of work and in part because youth are bombarded with confusing messages about work.

Youth employment is a large and growing problem, but misconceptions about its nature could make it even more tragic. As the economy offers fewer job opportunities for youth the call goes out for removal of restrictions on the "private sector" so that it may expand and create new jobs. This proposal is reminiscent of one that was commonly heard in the late 1950s. At that time we were asked to "unleash" General Chiang Kai-shek; now it is General Motors. Unfortunately, there is no evidence that an unleashed private sector could produce any more jobs, but much to suggest that such a move would be highly inflationary and probably would precipitate severe energy crises.

In an essay entitled "The Job Problem," Eli Ginzberg (1) offers a succinct yet thorough review of the recent history of employment in the U.S. and an analysis of its implications. Using the available statistics, he demonstrates that from 1950 through 1976 the economy was sufficiently robust to create almost 30 million jobs. This remarkable achievement (an increase of 48 percent) slightly exceeded the growth of the working age population (47 percent), but the growth in the number of jobs did not keep pace with the growth in job demand. The average number of persons designated as unemployed in 1950 was 3.3 million; by 1976 this number had increased to over 7 million. The unemployment rate in 1950 — not a prosperous year — was 5.3 percent. In 1976, with an economy still reeling from the energy crisis, the unemployment rate was 7.7 percent. Only in 1975, when unemployment rose to 8.5 percent, was the unemployment rate higher in that 27-year period.

The period of time that Ginzberg selected for analysis begins and ends with high unemployment, but he argues that the entire period was characterized by excessive unemployment. Until recently economists generally have agreed that when unemployment rises to about 4 percent the economy is in trouble. Today some view 5 percent as the upper limit of "tolerable" unemployment. By either criterion, however, the economy has not functioned well. If the upper limit is used, 14 of the 27 years Ginzberg analyzes were high unemployment years; using the 4 percent figure, 20 of those years appear as high unemployment years. The only time unemployment averaged less than 4 percent a year was in 1951-53 and 1966-69 (these were the years of the Korean and Vietnam wars).

Ginzberg attributes this persistently high unemployment rate to the increase in the number of women who entered the job market. In 1976 there were 33 million more people in the labor market (both employed and unemployed) than there were in 1950; more than 20 million of these were women. In 1950 only one-third of all women over age 16 were in the labor force; by 1976 nearly half were working or seeking work.

One of Ginzberg's observations is especially significant in light of the growing resentment toward government employment. Ginzberg concludes that government has created many more "good" jobs than has private enterprise. Since 1950, he argues, only three of every ten jobs created by private employers paid well, were secure and offered opportunity for advancement, whereas two-thirds of government-created jobs were "good" by these criteria. The good jobs are not randomly distributed. According to Ginzberg, a dual labor market has been developed in which white males are granted "preferred access to the good jobs while women and members of minority groups . . . get trapped in the poor jobs."

The statistics reflect a situation that is disturbing enough, but Ginzberg insists that they minimize the true unemployment picture. As many as 17 million more persons, he says, would be working if the economy could generate jobs for them. In 1976, for example, five million people who were not in the labor force reported that they "wanted a job now." Others who might be working if opportunities were available include housewives, the partially disabled, the elderly, and young people who remain in school simply because they cannot find jobs.

Ginzberg believes that one is not necessarily "anti-business" if one concludes that the private sector cannot expand sufficiently to absorb a significant number of potential job seekers. The figures do indicate quite convincingly that the private sector cannot produce that many jobs — whether "good" or "bad." To illustrate, the 500 corporations with the largest annual dollar sales have enormously increased their domination of

38

the economy over the past 17 years, but they have created relatively few new jobs. These firms — Fortune's 500 — now account for well over half of the nation's business while they employ only one-sixth of the working population.

Table 1 shows that while the work force grew by 12 million jobs from 1970 to 1977, the largest corporations (which increased their contribution to the Gross National Product during that period from 47% to over 57%) generated fewer than one million additional jobs. Over the 17-year period from 1960 to 1977 Fortune's 500 increased their domination of the economy by 17 percent, while increasing the number of people they employ by less than 3 percent. It is no wonder that the jobs created in the private sector tend to be "poor," since those that are created are increasingly marginal industries and firms that often pay lower wages and may offer less than full-time employment.

TABLE 1
The Private Sector and Employment
— Fortune's "500" and the Work World —
1960 to 1977

Year	U.S. GNP (billions)	U.S. Emp. (millions)	Fortune's "500" Sales (billions)	Fortune's "500" Emp. (millions)	% Sales/ GNP	% Fortune 500 U.S. Employ.
1960	$ 506	65.8	$ 205	9.2	40.5%	14.0%
1965	688	71.1	298	11.3	43.3	15.9
1970	982	78.6	464	14.6	47.2	18.6
1975	1528	84.8	865	14.4	56.6	17.0
1976	1706	87.5	971	14.8	56.9	16.9
1977	1890	90.5	1087	15.3	57.5	16.9
change '60-'77						
No.	$1384	24.7	$ 882	6.1		
%	274%	27%	430%	40%	17.0%	2.9%

Source: STATISTICAL ABSTRACT. U.S. Dept. of Commerce, Wash., D.C.
FORTUNE MAGAZINE, June 1961, May 1965, May 1970, May 1975, May 1976, April 1977.

Unemployment does constitute a general social problem. The economy cannot create sufficient jobs and it is particularly incapable of creating good jobs. Under such conditions, however, it is to be expected that those just entering the job market will be more adversely affected than the general population. And, as the following observations indicate, this is exactly what has happened to youth:

(a) Regardless of the state of the economy, youth unemployment is higher than the national average.

(b) Minority youth unemployment is much higher than white youth unemployment.

(c) During recessions youth unemployment jumps much higher than the national average and minorities are much more adversely affected than whites.

(d) During economic recoveries youth do not gain as much as the national average and minority youth are barely helped at all.

Figure 1 depicts national unemployment trends for white and minority youth during the period 1950-1976. Three different trends can be detected. For white males age 20 and older the situation has been amazingly stable. Unemployment among white youth clearly is getting worse and the situation for blacks and other minorities is increasingly desperate.

To illustrate how little a general upswing in the economy helps minority youth, let us look at what happened during the most recent period when unemployment dropped below 4 percent. This was 1966-69, the heyday of the "war on poverty" and a time of constant escalation of the Vietnam War. During this period unemployment among minority youth averaged more than 25 percent — 6 percent higher than during the 1954 recession and only 2 percent less than 1958 and 1961 when general unemployment averages rose to 6.8 and 6.7 percent, respectively. Each recession establishes a new plateau of unemployment for minority youth which then becomes the standard. Subsequent improvements in the economy bring very little return to this particular segment of the population.

The fact that the economy works to the disadvantage of minority youth is reflected in Table 2. In 1954, a recession year, minority youth unemployment stood at 16.5 percent. When general unemployment rose again in 1960 to 5.5 percent, minority youth unemployment jumped to 24 percent. A drop of 4.5 percent in general unemployment in 1965 was not shared by minority youth who found themselves with 26 percent unemployment. When general unemployment dropped below 4 percent from 1966 through 1969, minority

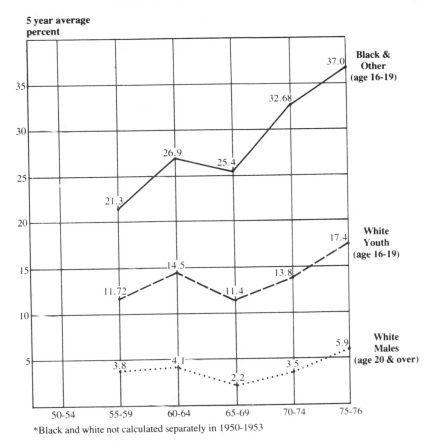

5 year average percent

*Black and white not calculated separately in 1950-1953

Sources: Manpower Report of the President, 1975
Employment & Training Report of the President, 1977

FIGURE 1
Unemployment Trends
National Rates, White & Minority Youth*

youth averaged 25 percent unemployment (this, remember, was during the war on poverty and the war in Vietnam).

The situation has worsened for white as well as black youth, but not so dramatically. During the period 1955-59 white teenage unemployment averaged 9 percent more than white male adults. From 1970 to 1974 the difference increased to over 10 percent. In 1975-76 the unemployment rate of white youth was 11.5 percent higher than the unemployment rate of white male adults (see Figure 1).

41

TABLE 2
Unemployment Rates
Selected Years 1954 to 1977
National Rates, White & Minority Youth Age 16-19

Year	National Rate	White	YOUTH AGE 16-19 Black & Other
1954	5.5	12.1	16.5
1957	4.3	10.6	19.1
1958	6.8	14.4	27.4
1960	5.5	13.4	24.4
1961	6.7	15.3	27.6
1963	5.7	15.5	30.4
1965	4.5	13.4	26.2
1966	3.8	11.2	25.4
1967	3.8	11.0	26.5
1968	3.6	11.0	25.0
1969	3.5	10.7	24.0
1970	4.9	13.5	29.1
1973	4.9	12.6	36.2
1974	5.6	14.0	32.9
1975	8.5	17.9	36.9
1976	7.7	26.9	37.1

Source:
Manpower Report of the President, 1975
Employment and Training Report of the President, 1977

Over the years, youth, women, and minority adult males have had to absorb more and more of the shock of sharp rises in unemployment. In 1954 white male adult unemployment was 1.1 percent less than the general average. With the recession of 1958, this figure increased to 1.3 percent.

In 1961, when general unemployment again rose to over 6 percent, the adult white male rate was 5.1 percent — a difference of 1.6 percent. In 1976 unemployment was 7.7 percent but the adult white male rate was 5.4 percent — 2.3 percent less than the national average (see Table 3). When only white males 20 years of age or older are considered, there were very few "bad" years by either a 4 percent or 5 percent standard.

TABLE 3
General Unemployment Rate
Employment Rate of White Males Age 20 and Over
Selected Years 1954 to 1976

Year	General Rate	White Males Age 20 & Over	Difference
1954	5.5	4.4	1.1
1957	4.3	3.2	1.1
1958	6.8	5.5	1.3
1960	5.5	4.2	1.3
1961	6.7	5.1	1.6
1963	5.7	3.9	1.8
1965	4.5	2.9	1.6
1966	3.8	2.2	1.6
1967	3.8	2.1	1.7
1968	3.6	2.0	1.6
1969	3.5	1.9	1.6
1970	4.9	3.2	1.7
1972	5.6	3.6	2.0
1973	4.9	2.9	2.0
1974	5.6	3.6	2.0
1975	8.5	6.4	2.1
1976	7.7	5.4	2.3

Source:.
Manpower Report of the President, 1975
Employment and Training Report of the President, 1977

The various procedures by which the most severe effects of recessions are passed on to youth, women, and minority male adults may help to explain the lack of public enthusiasm for "full-employment" legislation. Another explanation is the widespread belief, reinforced by the pronouncements of some prominent economists, that full employment would be negated by runaway inflation. The net result has been a lack of organized support for full-employment policies by organizations and institutions dominated by white males (e.g., the large corporations, many labor unions, the media, and, perhaps most insidiously, the major universities).

Youth, women, and minority adult males, the most direct casualties of recession, are not necessarily in direct competition with each other. There are instances of competition, but on the whole the economy has developed systems that define and separate youth work, women's work, and minority adult work. Rather than direct competition there is lack of mutual understanding which effectively prevents youth, women, and minorities from combining their efforts to influence social policy to an extent proportionate to their numbers.

An analysis of youthful unemployment by areas of residence sheds additional light on the nature of the problem. In the highest of all post-World War II unemployment years, youth unemployment rose to nearly 20 percent. But some youth found getting a job much more difficult than others. In 1975, central-city youth had a larger unemployment rate than did suburban youth, who in turn were more likely to be unemployed than were non-metropolitan youth. This relationship held up for both black and white male youth. Black female teenagers, on the other hand, had bleak employment prospects wherever they lived. Also, in every type of geographical area, the employment situation was much worse for blacks than whites. The unemployment figures were even more ominous when those not in the labor force (neither working nor looking for work) are added to the unemployed. Table 4 summarizes the employment situation for different categories of youth aged 16 to 19 by areas of residence.

Everything about the employment picture is different for suburban whites as compared to urban blacks. Even the pattern of non-participation in work differs. When white youth are not in the labor force the most likely reason is that they are in school. Young black women not working or looking for work are likely to be at home taking care of children. The kind of work blacks and whites perform in central cities, suburbs, and non-metropolitan areas also tends to be dissimilar. Blacks, far more than whites, work in government. More than one-quarter of black teenagers in central cities in 1975 worked for government, compared to only 7.2 percent of their white counterparts. In suburbs, these rates were 17.7 percent and 7.0 percent, and in nonmetropolitan areas 19.3 percent and 9.5 percent, respectively (see Table 4). Considering the importance of government work to black teenagers, the current trend toward taxpayer "revolt" may further jeopardize their employment possibilities.

There are those who anticipate some let-up in the youth employment problem. By 1980, the number of young people reaching working age will begin to decline. It cannot be disputed that the enormous increase in the number of persons in the labor force has created problems for the economy. (From 1950 through 1976 the civilian labor force grew by 52 percent; the number of adult women participants increased 106 percent, while youth ages

TABLE 4
Percent Unemployed and Not Employed*
by Sex-Race and Type of Residential Area
1975 (annual average)

	Males		Females	
Area	White	Black	White	Black
Central City				
Unemployment Rate	21.4	44.9	19.0	40.4
Not Employed Rate	53.0	78.4	57.5	80.1
Suburbs				
Unemployment Rate	18.9	35.1	16.6	41.9
Not Employed Rate	49.2	72.6	54.3	78.8
Non-Metropolitan Areas				
Unemployment Rate	15.6	28.7	17.4	40.8
Not Employed Rate	47.3	65.4	61.5	79.7

*Not Employed = unemployed and not in labor force

Source:
Youth in the Labor Force: An Area Study. Diane N. Westcott. MONTHLY LABOR REVIEW, July, 1976.

16-19 in the labor market rose by 113 percent.) Nonetheless, the optimistic prediction that a reduction in the youth population will reduce pressures for the creation of new jobs must be tempered by the projected ability of the private sector to create jobs. Even with a decline in the youth population and an increase in the number of persons reaching retirement age, for at least in the next 25 years one million more persons will enter the labor market each year than will leave it. Based on recent trends, it is doubtful that the largest corporations can generate more than 200,000 jobs a year even though by 1987 these corporations are likely to have grown to a point where they collectively produce two-thirds of the Gross National Product. Who, then, will generate the million or more new jobs a year required to keep youth unemployment from constantly rising?

The job dilemma for youth, in sum, is represented by the decline in the rate of job creation at the same time that youth entry into the labor market is rapidly rising. The dilemma may be insoluble; but it may not have to be resolved. There are those who argue that no solution is necessary. Youth, it is noted, eventually will grow up and the economy appears to have the resiliency to absorb at least the white adult male population. That conclusion, however, is acceptable only if it can be established that neither youth nor society as a whole suffers from their prolonged preparation for and separation from the working world. If, for example, youth unemployment does not lead to youth crime, drug abuse, etc., and if it does not deprive the society of needed goods or services, is there any reason for concern about its incidence?

It is important, in this context, to determine the precise relationship between youth unemployment and delinquency. Barry Stern, in an official HEW publication on education and work (2), declares that there is little solid evidence to suggest that not being able to find suitable work is related to higher rates of delinquency, drug abuse and alcoholism, or suicide. There are, however, some striking correlations. In recent years there has been a sharp rise in both youth crime and youth unemployment (see Table 5). From 1963 to 1975, arrests of persons under age 18 increased on the average 6.7 percent a year while unemployment grew at a rate of 7.7 percent a year.

But years of greatest increase in unemployment were not necessarily those in which youthful arrests grew the most. A year of large increases in unemployment, 1975, was virtually no different from 1974 in terms of youth arrests. Even if the statistics were to follow an identical pattern, they would not be wholly convincing. Both crime and employment indices have dubious validity. It is possible that both crime and unemployment are caused by other factors and there is no consensus on what constitutes "suitable" employment. A low-paying part-time job that is suitable for an affluent youth might be totally inadequate for an impoverished youth. One problem of our society is that while jobs are differentially available, advertising appeals to youthful consumers make no distinctions. A job that pays little and offers no other gratifications may provide both opportunities and incentives for crime. Indeed, much crime today is committed by employees.

A powerful argument in support of the value of work to youth is derived from various experiments that offer delinquents opportunity to work. Such experiments not only have been able to show that work can serve as an acceptable alternative to youth crime; they also have begun to develop some criteria for assessing job "suitability." In a project involving adults with long histories of criminal behavior, Doug and Joan Grant have demonstrated that sponsorship in jobs that offer social status, opportunities to develop competencies and interact with people not involved in crime, plus strong and consistent social supports can deter even confirmed felons from relapsing

TABLE 5
Change in Youth Arrest and Unemployment
1963 to 1975

Year	Percent Change over Previous Year	
	Arrest **Person under 18**	**Unemployment** **Person 16-19**
1975	+ 1.7%	+ 24.3%
1974	8.7%	15.1%
1973	4.9%	− 5.9%
1972	.8%	3.6%
1971	5.4%	13.8%
1970	3.9%	29.5%
1969	3.7%	1.7%
1968	9.7%	.1%
1967	10.5%	.2%
1966	6.6%	− 4.3%
1965	3.4%	.2%
1964	17.4%	− 1.2%
1963	11.0%	22.6%
Average change per year	6.7%	7.7%

Sources:
Federal Bureau of Investigation UNIFORM CRIME REPORTS, U.S. Department of Justice, Washington, D.C., 1963-1976.
Employment and Training Report of the President, 1977.

into criminal careers (3). A number of other projects in which meaningful work (paid or unpaid) has changed youthful attitudes and behavior are described in the third section of this volume. In a situation that is unclear, and where expert opinion is so sharply divided, replication and extension of such successful experiments are sorely needed.

Youth are capable of performing many useful tasks and, in the process, they may turn away from socially destructive behaviors. This would not be important for social policy if our society had reached such a stage of productivity that there was nothing useful for young people to do. It is obvious that this stage has not been reached. Articulated social needs are increasing rather than decreasing. Urban transit systems are decaying, as is inter-community rail transit. Large numbers of persons — e.g., the old, the young, the mentally ill, and the handicapped — are offered inadequate services and in some important areas are totally neglected. There is a paucity of services in national parks and in inner-city recreational facilities. The environment is deteriorating. Too few persons are given instruction in the arts or encouraged to be participants rather than recipients of our culture. The list of unmet needs, physical as well as social, is virtually endless — housing, preservation of resources, development and installation of alternative energy systems, reclamation of wastes, beautification of cities — to name but a few. We lack not socially useful things to do but the vision and sense of mission to get them done.

Dilemmas for youth are inherent in our current social policies. Although the relationship between work and delinquency is poorly delineated, social policy operates as if we are dealing with known phenomena. High rates of youthful unemployment, delinquency, and alienation are treated as symptoms of deficiencies in youth. Genetic, cultural, and environmental deficits are posited as the causes of youth problems. We have spent billions of dollars in remedial education, delinquency rehabilitation, and vocational training — with little or no effect.

Ironically, the greater the evidence that such policies have failed, the more they are intensified. Our youth policies are based on the assumption that if youth were to learn vocational skills and could manage their impulses better, they would be employable. Ignored completely is the inability of the economy to generate jobs to employ them. The dilemma is aggravated by government efforts to increase youth employment: publicly-funded jobs offered youth are short-term, they have no career possibilities, and they cannot compete with private enterprise. The results inevitably are wasteful. Youth never do become skilled in or committed to their work. The only permanent positions in government work programs for youth are occupied by the adults who administer them. The youth employment bureaucracy has become increasingly entrenched and accountable only to adult political structures. Yet when these programs fail it is accepted as further evidence of the deficiencies of young people.

Such approaches must be inflationary since they are designed to spend public monies while producing few or no goods or services. That more real employment is generated for adults than for youth may help to explain why, in the days of the "war on poverty" — when so many job training and employment programs for youth were launched — adult male unemployment dropped to 2 percent a year while minority teenage unemployment remained at 25 percent.

The misdirection of youth policy is one important reason that youth job dilemmas are growing. Another is the retreat from social commitment that is a response to the growing threat of inflation. Youth (and particularly minority youth) are most affected when the economy takes a downturn. Thus they receive the brunt of the effects of "anti-inflationary" measures — e.g., tightening the money supply by increasing interest rates (which is supposed to "cool down" the economy by reducing aggregate demand but which also increases unemployment); or reducing government spending and attempting to "balance the budget" (which results in a cutback in government jobs, often those occupied by inner-city minority youth).

Interestingly, the primary cause of inflation is not to be found in government spending, nor is it a function of the rate of employment. A cursory examination of the data indicates that these common assumptions simply do not hold up. For example, during the last period when unemployment dropped below 4 percent (1965-69) the consumer price index increased less than 4 percent (4). From 1972 through 1976, unemployment averaged over 6 percent and inflation increased over 7 percent. It appears that growing unemployment accompanies a rise in inflation.

The increases in both unemployment and inflation in recent years have been related to greater dependency on foreign imports and to social policies that control the licensing and credentialling of practitioners. From 1970 to 1975 imports of foreign oil increased by 75 percent. When prices were suddenly increased in 1974 a crisis of major proportions occurred. The result was a marked rise in energy costs, a decline in consumption, a setback to the economy, double-digit inflation, and almost double-digit unemployment. This plus the passage of social services legislation that serves the needs of special interest groups, largely explain the "stagflation" that still remains with us. Solutions, at least for the immediate future, involve limiting the power of professional monopolies and reducing energy consumption. This can happen only if we devise new ways to employ people.

Fortunately, the most promising solution to the job dilemma of youth is also the most promising solution to the problem of inflation: we must cut back on commitments to energy-consuming activities (such as private auto travel and the production of many unneeded trinkets) and increase our investment in energy-conserving activities (e.g., mass transportation, energy-efficient housing, education and other helping services). If this shift can be accomplished by private enterprise alone — so much the better. But many are traditionally public responsibilities; and, at the very least, there should be experiments to determine how society can best produce such goods and provide such services. We may not have the will to solve the problems of youth, but we should look at the "youth problem" realistically and not continue to attempt to rehabilitate youth when it is the job structure of society that needs reform.

Unless we alter our social and economic policies to allow young people a variety of productive roles, youth unemployment will continue to grow. Accompanying that growth in youth unemployment is likely to be an increase in all forms of youth crime and misbehavior, as well as an increase in the resort to expensive official actions against youth. The monies we now devote to the punishment, control, and rehabilitation of youth could be used to generate opportunities for youth to be employed in socially useful projects. We have only to decide which is the most desirable alternative.

FOOTNOTES AND REFERENCES

1. Eli Ginzberg, "The Job Problem," SCIENTIFIC AMERICAN, November, 1977.

2. U.S. Department of Health, Education and Welfare, TOWARDS A FEDERAL POLICY ON EDUCATION AND WORK, by Barry Stern. Washington, D.C.: U.S. Government Printing Office, 1977.

3. J. Douglas Grant and Joan Grant, FINAL REPORT, NEW CAREERS PROJECT. Unpublished manuscript. Sacramento, Calif.: Institute of Crime and Delinquency, 1970.

4. U.S. STATISTICAL ABSTRACT, 1977.

DELINQUENCY AND THE
AGE STRUCTURE OF SOCIETY

David F. Greenberg

Adolescent peer groups and orientation to the expectations of peers are found in many societies (1). In American society, the natural tendency of those who share common experiences and problems to prefer one another's company is accentuated by the importance parents and schools attach to popularity and to the development of the special skills they believe will be necessary for later occupational success (2). In addition, the exclusion of young people from adult work and leisure activity forces adolescents into virtually exclusive association with one another, cutting them off from alternative sources of validation for the self (as well as reducing the degree of adult supervision). A long run trend toward increased age segregation created by changing patterns of work and education has increased the vulnerability of teenagers to the expectations and evaluations of their peers (3).

This dependence on peers for approval is not itself criminogenic. In many tribal societies, age-homogeneous bands of youths are functionally integrated into the economic and social life of the tribe and are not considered deviant (4). In America, too, many teenage clubs and cliques are not delinquent. Participation in teenage social life, however, requires resources. In addition to personal assets and skills (having an attractive appearance and "good personality," being a skilled conversationalist, being able to memorize song lyrics and learn dance steps, and in some circles, being able to fight), money is needed to purchase clothing, cosmetics, cigarettes, alcoholic beverages, narcotics, phonograph records, transistor radios, gasoline for cars and motorcycles, tickets to films and concerts, meals in restaurants (5), and for gambling. The progressive detachment of teenage social life from that of the family and the emergence of advertising directed toward a teenage market (this being a creation of postwar affluence for major sections of the population and the "baby boom") have increased the importance of these goods to teenagers and hence have inflated the costs of their social activities.

When parents are unable or unwilling to subsidize their children's social life at the level required by local convention, when children want to prevent their parents from learning of their expenditures, or when they are reluctant to incur the obligations created by taking money from their parents,

51

TABLE 1

1970 Arrests Per 100,000 Population by Age*

OFFENSE / AGE	13-14	15	16	17	18	19	20	21	22	23	24	25-29	30-34	% under 18	% under 21
Murder and non-negligent manslaughter	3.5	13.2	20.1	25.2	35.8	35.5	35.2	*40.2*	35.3	36.6	37.8	30.7	24.4	10.2	24.5
Forcible rape	12.5	32.5	43.2	54.3	61.8	*64.7*	60.6	60.4	54.3	52.6	50.6	36.1	22.9	20.6	41.6
Robbery	164	274	340	373	393	*394*	358	346	293	250	250	154	82.5	32.2	55.3
Aggravated assault	109	189	243	272	309	317	320	347	328	316	*355*	284	240	17.6	30.5
Burglary	979	979	*1463*	1302	1176	968	788	697	585	527	505	320	191	50.9	69.8
Larceny over $50	2178	*2741*	2740	2408	2183	1788	1460	1309	1100	953	936	631	463	50.4	66.4
Auto Theft	397	898	*965*	759	556	436	344	295	236	197	193	119	69.1	52.9	71.6
Vandalism	570	*613*	514	375	238	191	141	134	111	76.4	97.1	69	50.6	71.6	80.8
Narcotic drug laws	215	665	1169	1585	1971	*2073*	1187	1763	1447	1199	1039	587	312	22.0	52.2

*Arrests are based on F.B.I. statistics for 1970, population is number of males recorded in the 1970 census. The peak age in each offense category is set in italic type.

alternative sources of funds must be sought. Full or part-time employment once constituted such an alternative.

The long-run, persistent decline in teenage employment and labor force participation has progressively eliminated this alternative. During the period from 1870 to 1920, many states passed laws restricting child labor and establishing compulsory education. Despite a quadrupling of the "gainfully employed" population from 1870 to 1930, the number of gainfully employed workers in the 10 - 15 year-old age bracket *declined*. The Great Depression resulted in a further contraction of the teenage labor force and increased the school-leaving age (6). Only in 1940 did the U.S. government stop counting all persons over the age of 10 as part of the labor force (7). In recent years, teenage labor market deterioration has been experienced mainly by black teenagers. From 1950 to 1973, black teenage labor force participation declined from 67.8% to 34.7%, while white teenage labor force participation remained stable at about 63%. The current recession has increased teenage unemployment in the 16-19 year-old age bracket to about 20%, with the rate for black teenagers being twice as high (8).

This process has left teenagers less and less capable of financing an increasingly costly social life whose importance is enhanced as the age segregation of society grows. Adolescent theft then occurs as a response to the disjunction between the desire to participate in social activities with peers and the absence of legitimate sources of funds needed to finance this participation.

Qualitative evidence supporting this explanation of adolescent theft is found in those delinquency studies that describe the social life of delinquent groups. Sherif and Sherif noted in their study of adolescent groups that theft was often instrumentally related to the group's leisure time social activities.

In several groups . . . stealing was not the incidental activity that it was in others. It was regarded as an acceptable and necessary means of getting needed possessions, or, more usually, cash. Members of the aforementioned groups frequently engaged in theft when they were broke, usually selling articles other than clothing, and often using the money for group entertainment and treats (9).

Carl Werthman reports that among San Francisco delinquents:

Shoplifting . . . was viewed as a more instrumental activity, as was the practice of stealing coin changers from temporarily evacuated buses parked in a nearby public depot. In the case of shoplifting, most of the

53

boys wanted and wore the various items of clothes they stole; and when buses were robbed, either the money was divided among the boys, or it was used to buy supplies for a party being given by the club (10).

Studies of urban delinquent gangs or individuals in England, Israel, Sweden, Taiwan, Holland and Argentina present a uniform picture: unemployed or employed but poorly-paid male youths steal to support their leisure-time, group-centered social activities.

Joseph Weis' study of middle class delinquency using self-reports (11) is also consistent with the interpretation of adolescent theft presented here. Using key cluster analysis, Weis extracted three distinct factors from the correlation matrix for involvement in different forms of delinquency for the males in the sample. These oblique factors could be characterized as social, property, and aggression. The analysis for girls produced two factors: there was no aggression factor, while the other two factors were very similar to the social and property factors among the boys. For both boys and girls, the correlation between the oblique factor domains for social offenses (drinking, marijuana use, curfew violations, gambling, use of false I.D. cards, drag racing, and similar offenses) and for property offenses (theft, burglary, shoplifting, etc.) was positive and moderately strong, as would be predicted if thefts are undertaken to finance peer-related social activities.

On the reasoning presented here, strain should be experienced most acutely by teenagers who are unable to achieve popularity on the basis of personal attributes and who lack alternative sources of self-esteem (e.g. school success or warm relationships with parents). Indeed, teenagers in this position may attempt to win friends by spending money on them (12). Evidence that unpopular boys are more likely to become delinquent (13) and that delinquents tend to have unsatisfactory relations with peers (14) and parents (15) is consistent with my argument.

Where parents subsidize their children adequately, the incentive to steal is obviously reduced. Because the cost of social life can increase with class position, a strong correlation between social class membership and involvement in theft is not necessarily predicted. Insofar as self-reporting studies suggest that the correlation between participation in nonviolent forms of property acquisition and parental socio-economic status is not very high (16), this may be a strong point for my theory. By contrast the theories of Cohen, Miller, and Cloward and Ohlin all clash with the self-reporting studies.

In view of recent suggestions that increases in female crime and delinquency are linked with changing gender roles (of which the women's liberation movement is taken either as a cause or a manifestation), it is of interest to note that the explanation of adolescent theft presented here is applicable to boys and girls, and in particular, allows for female delinquency in support of *traditional* gender roles related to peer involvement.

Weis' work is consistent with this interpretation, as are differences in the forms of theft boys and girls undertake. Boys, who traditionally have paid girls' expenses on dates and therefore have a greater need for cash, are more likely to rob or to burglarize homes and stores, taking items for resale, while girls more often steal items (such as clothing and cosmetics) for personal use.

Increases in female crime which have occurred largely in those forms of theft in which female involvement has traditionally been high (17) are thus more plausibly attributed to the same deteriorating economic position in the face of escalating costs of social life that males confront, than to changes in gender role.

As teenagers get older, their vulnerability to the expectations of peers is reduced by institutional involvements that provide alternative sources of self-esteem; moreover, opportunities for acquiring money legitimately expand. Both processes reduce the motivation to engage in acquisitive forms of delinquent behavior. Consequently, involvement in theft should fall off rapidly with age, and it does.

DELINQUENCY AND THE SCHOOL

My explanation of juvenile theft in terms of structural obstacles to legitimate sources of funds at a time when peer-oriented leisure activities require access to financial resources implicitly characterizes this form of delinquency as instrumentally rational: the theory assumes that money and goods are stolen because they are useful. Acts of vandalism, thefts in which stolen objects are abandoned or destroyed, and interpersonal violence not necessary to accomplish a theft cannot be explained in this way. These are the activities that led Albert Cohen to maintain that much delinquency is "malicious" and "non-utilitarian" (18) and to argue that the content of the delinquent subculture arose in the lower class male's reaction to failure in schools run according to middle class standards.

Although Cohen can be criticized for not indicating the criteria used for assessing rationality — indeed, for failure to find out from delinquents themselves what they perceived the goals of their destructive acts to be — and though details of Cohen's theory (to be noted below) appear to be inaccurate, his observation that delinquency may be a response to school problems need not be abandoned. Indeed, the literature proposing a connection between one or another aspect of school and delinquency is voluminous (19). I will concentrate on two features of the school experience, its denial of student autonomy and its subjection of some students to the embarrassment of public degradation ceremonies.

In all spheres of life outside the school, and particularly within the family, children more or less steadily acquire larger measures of personal autonomy as they mature. Over time, the "democratization" of the family has reduced the age at which given levels of autonomy are acquired. The gradual extension of freedom that normally takes place in the family (not without struggle!) is not accompanied by parallel deregulation at school. Authoritarian styles of teaching, and rules concerning such matters as smoking, hair styles, manner of dress, going to the bathroom, and attendance, come into conflict with expectations students derive from the relaxation of controls in the family (20). The delegitimation of hierarchical authority structures accomplished by the radical movements of the 1960s has sharpened student awareness of this condition.

This symbolic significance attached to autonomy exacerbates the inherently onerous burden of school restrictions. Parents and other adults invest age-specific rights and expectations with moral significance by disapproving "childish" behavior and using privileges to reward behavior they label "mature." Because of this association, the deprivation of autonomy is experienced as "being treated like a baby," that is, as a member of a disvalued age-status.

All students are exposed to these restrictions, and to some degree, all probably resent them. For students who are at least moderately successful at their schoolwork, who excel at sports, participate in extra-curricular school activities, or who are members of popular cliques, this resentment is likely to be more than compensated by rewards associated with school attendance. These students tend to conform to school regulations most of the time, rarely collide with school officials, and are unlikely to feel overtly hostile to school or teachers. Students who are unpopular, and whose academic record, whether from inability or disinterest, is poor, receive no comparable compensation. For them, school can only be a frustrating experience: it brings no current gratification and no promise of future pay-off. Why then should they put up with these restrictions? These students often get into trouble, and feel intense hostility to the school.

Social class differences must of course be taken into account. Preadolescent and early adolescent middle and upper class children are supervised more closely than their working class counterparts, and thus come to expect and accept adult authority, while working class youths, who enter an unsupervised street life among peers at an early age have more autonomy to protect, and guard their prerogatives jealously (21). To the extent that they see in the school's denial of their autonomy preparation for a future in occupations that also deny autonomy, and see in their parents' lives the psychic costs of that denial, they may be more prone to rebel than middle-class students, who can generally anticipate entering jobs that allow more discretion and autonomy.

Middle class youths also have more to gain by accepting adult authority than their working class counterparts. Comparatively affluent parents can control their children better because they have more resources they can withhold, and are in a better position to secure advantages for their children. Likewise, children who believe that their future chances depend on school success may conform regardless of whether they reject close regulation intellectually. Where returns on school success are reduced by class or racial discrimination, the school loses this source of social control. It similarly loses control over upper class children, whose inherited class position frees them from the necessity of doing well in school to guarantee their future economic status.

Only a few decades ago, few working class youths — or school failures with middle class family backgrounds — would have been exposed to a contradiction between their expectations of autonomy and the school's attempts to control them because a high proportion of students, especially working class students, left school at an early age. However, compulsory school attendance, low wages and high unemployment rates for teenagers, and increased educational requirements for entry-level jobs have greatly reduced dropout rates. Thus in 1920, 16.8% of the 17 year-old population were high school graduates; and in 1956, 62.3% (22). In consequence, a greater proportion of students, especially those who benefit least from school, is exposed to this contradiction.

Common psychological responses to the irritation of the school's denial of autonomy range from affective disengagement to the school ("tuning out" the teacher) to smouldering resentment and at the behavioral level from truancy to self-assertion through the flouting of rules. Such activities as getting drunk, using drugs, joy-riding, truanting, and adopting eccentric styles of dress, apart from any intrinsic gratification these activities may provide, can be seen as forms of what Gouldner has called "conflictual validation of the self'' (23). By helping students establish independence from authority (school, parental, etc.), these activities contribute to self-regard. Their attraction lies in their being forbidden.

As a status system, the school makes further contributions to the causation of delinquency. Almost by definition, status systems embody invidious distinctions. Where standards of evaluation are shared and position is believed to reflect personal merit, occupants of lower statuses are likely to encounter problems in maintaining self-esteem (24). The problem is somewhat alleviated by a strong tendency to restrict intimate association to persons of similar status. If one's associates are at roughly the same level as oneself, they provide the standards for self-evaluation (25). In addition, ''democratic'' norms of modesty discourage the flaunting of success and boasting of personal merit, thereby insulating the less successful from an implied attribution of their failures to their own deficiencies.

These norms are not, however, universal in applicability. In our society, certification as a full-fledged social member is provided those whose commitment to the value of work and family is documented by spouse, home, car and job (for women, children have traditionally substituted for job). Institutional affiliations are thus taken as a mark of virtue, or positive stigma. Those who meet these moral tests are accorded standards of respect in face-to-face interaction not similarly accorded members of unworthy or suspect categories — e.g. prison and psychiatric hospital inmates, skid row bums, the mentally retarded, and unaccompanied women on the streets of New York. In particular, members are permitted to sustain self-presentations as dignified, worthy persons, regardless of what may be thought or said of them in private (26). Students, however, especially failing students and those with lower class or minority origins, are accorded no comparable degree of respect. As they lack the appropriate institutional affiliations, their moral commitment to dominant institutions of society is suspect. In this sense, they are social strangers; we don't quite know what we can expect from them. They are, moreover, relatively powerless. In consequence, they are exposed to evaluations from which adults are ordinarily shielded.

This is especially true at school, where school personnel continuously communicate their evaluations of students through grades, honor rolls, track positions, privileges, and praise for academic achievement and proper deportment. On occasion, the negative evaluation of students conveyed by the school's ranking systems is supplemented by explicit criticism and denunciation on the part of teachers who act as if the academic performance of failing students could be elevated by telling them they are stupid, or lazy, or both. Only the most extreme failures in the adult world are subjected to degradation ceremonies of this kind.

The feelings of students subjected to this form of status derogation are well captured by a high school student describing a conversation with his school principal.

> *I told him that the teacher was always trying to "put me down" in front of the class. I told him that the teacher knew I didn't like math so why did he keep calling on me, just to "put me down," to make me look bad. I'm not as dumb as he thinks, so I "turn it around" on him and got the class to laugh at him. See how he likes being the fool. The principal said I was a wise guy, thought I was a "smart alec." He said that what I needed was a good old fashioned talk behind the wood shed. I told him "Who're you going to get to do it; better not try or somebody is going to get hurt, bad!" Man he turned white and started to shake. "You're suspended for threatening a school official." That's good, I said, this school, this school ain't worth a shit anyway (27).*

Cohen has argued that working class youths faced with this situation protect their self-esteem by rejecting conventional norms and values. Seeking out one another for mutual support, they create a delinquent subculture of opposition to middle-class norms in which they can achieve status. This subculture is seen as supporting the non-utilitarian acts of destructiveness that alleviate frustration (28).

There is little difficulty in finding evidence of adolescent destructiveness. However the choice of target may be more rational than Cohen allows. The large and growing volume of school vandalism and assaults on teachers indicate that delinquents often see the school in antagonistic terms. Other targets, too may be chosen for clear reasons. In his study of gang violence, Miller found that,

> *Little of the deliberately inflicted property damage represented diffuse outpouring of the accumulated hostility against arbitrary objects; in most cases the gang members injured the possession of properties of particular persons who had angered them, as a concrete expression of that anger (defacing automobile of mother responsible for having gang member committed to correctional institution; breaking windows of settlement house after eviction therefrom). There was little evidence of 'senseless' destruction; most property damage was directed and repressive (29).*

Other targets may be chosen because of their symbolic value, e.g. membership in a despised racial group or class stratum, or in the adult world, which represents repressive authority. It is not unlikely that an unanticipated consequence of recent black nationalist movements has been an increase in crimes by minority group members that victimize whites.

Empirical research suggests the need for revision of other components of Cohen's theory as well. Delinquents do not necessarily reject conventional values or career goals except when in the presence of their peers (30). A modern society contains numerous status systems that are not in competition with one another; acceptance of one need not require repudiation of others. In particular, students who do not reject the value system endorsed by parents and school officials but who do not succeed in its terms can nevertheless accept the value system of a subculture of delinquency (in the sense of Matza [31]) as a "second best" alternative on pragmatic grounds.

Self-reporting studies of delinquency indicate the association between class and most forms of delinquency to be weaker than Cohen supposed. School failure, though class-linked, is not the monopoly of any class, and the self-esteem problems of middle class youths who fail are not necessarily any less than those of working class schoolmates. Since parental expectations for academic achievement may be higher in middle class families, and since school failure may auger downward mobility, these problems could conceivably be worse. If delinquency restores self esteem lost through school failure, it may serve this function for students of all class backgrounds.

The impact of school degradation ceremonies is not limited to their effect on students' self-esteem. When a student is humiliated by a teacher the student's attempt to present a favorable self to schoolmates is undercut. Even students whose prior psychological disengagement from the value system of the school leaves their self-esteem untouched by a teacher's disparagement may react with anger at being embarrassed before peers. The high school student quoted earlier complained of being ridiculed *in front of his class*. It is the situation of being in the company of others whose approval is needed for self-esteem that makes it difficult for teenagers to ignore humiliation that older individuals, with alternative sources of self-esteem, could readily ignore .

Visible displays of independence from, or rejection of authority can be understood as attempts to re-establish moral character in the face of affronts. This can be accomplished by direct attacks on teachers or school, or through daring illegal performances elsewhere. These responses may or may not

reflect anger at treatment perceived to be unjust, may or may not defend the student against threats to self-esteem, may or may not reflect a repudiation of conventional conduct norms. What is crucial is that these activities *demonstrate* retaliation for injury and the rejection of official values to an audience whose own resentment of constituted authority causes it to be appreciative of rebels whom it would not necessarily dare to imitate. Secret delinquency and acts that entailed no risk would not serve this function.

Field research on the interaction between teachers and delinquent students (32) and responses of delinquent gangs and individuals to challenges to honor (33) support this dramaturgical interpretation of delinquency. Most gang violence seems not to erupt spontaneously out of anger, but is chosen and manipulated for its ability to impress others. Nonutilitarian forms of theft, property destruction and violence may well be understood as quite utilitarian if their purpose is the establishment or preservation of the claim to be a certain sort of person, rather than the acquisition of property.

Goffman (34) has called attention to the common features of activities in which participants establish moral character through risk-taking. Such activities as dueling, bull fighting, sky diving, mountain climbing, big game hunting, and gambling for high stakes are undertaken for the opportunity they provide to carve out a valued social identity by exhibiting courage, daring, pluck and composure.

These qualities are those the industrial system (factory and school) tend to disvalue or ignore: the concept of seeking out risks and ''showing off'' is antithetical to the traditional ethos of capitalism, where the emphasis has been placed on minimizing risk, using time productively, and suppressing the self to demonstrate moral character. Consequently, participants in action systems based on displays of risk-taking have traditionally been drawn primarily from classes not subject to the discipline and self-denial of industrial production, e.g. the European nobility, bohemian populations, and the unemployed poor.

More recently, as production has come to require less sacrifice and self-denial from large sectors of the work force, and to require the steady expansion of stimulated consumption for its growth, the more affluent sectors of the labor force are increasingly encouraged to seek an escape from the routinicity of daily life through mild forms of risk-taking (e.g. gambling and skiing) as well as through the leisure uses of drugs and sex.

The similarity between the subculture of delinquency and that of the leisurely affluent (35) makes sense in view of the position of the delinquent *vis-*

à vis the school. Like the factory, the school frequently requires monotonous and meaningless work. Regimentation is the rule. Expressions of originality and spontaneity are not only discouraged, but may be punished (36). Students who reap no present rewards in return for subordinating themselves to the discipline of the school are free to cultivate the self-expressive traits which the school fails to reward. As Downes (37) has pointed out, they may come to regard adults who work as defeated and lifeless because of their submission to a routine that necessitates self-suppression, and hence try to avoid work because of the cost in self-alienation.

Traditionally this has been especially true of students with lower class backgrounds: Finestone (38) has described their adaptation and Rainwater (39) has interpreted the expressive features of lower class black male urban culture in these terms. However, when the political and occupational sectors of society lose their legitimacy, students of other classes may find the prospect of entering conventional careers in those sectors so repugnant that they lose the motivation to achieve in school, and also cultivate life styles based on self-expression and politically motivated risk-taking. The bright hippies and radicals from white middle-class backgrounds in the late 1960s are a case in point.

The similarity between delinquent and non-criminal recreational risk-taking warns us that the pursuit of status through risk-taking need not *necessarily* arise from problems in self-esteem. Once a status sytem rewarding delinquent activity exists, students may act with reference to it in order to *increase* prestige in the group, not only to prevent prestige from falling. Thus teachers may be provoked (40), gang rivals taunted, and daring thefts and assaults perpetrated, even in the absence of humiliation.

When students drop out or graduate from high school, they enter a world that, while sometimes inhospitable, does not restrict their autonomy and assault their dignity in the same way that school does. The need to engage in crime to establish a sense of an autonomous self, and to preserve moral character through risk-taking is thus reduced. In addition, the sympathetic audience of other students of the same age is taken away: Thus school-leaving eliminates major sources of motivation toward delinquency.

In this respect, it is especially ironic that delinquency prevention programs have involved campaigns to extend the duration of schooling. American panel studies indicate that the self-esteem of dropouts rises after leaving school (41) and that dropping out produces an immediate decline in delinquency (42). In England, when the school-leaving age was raised by one year, the peak age for delinquency also rose simultaneously by one year.

Despite this evidence that the school contributes to delinquency, it is hardly necessary. In Cordoba, Argentina, patterns of delinquency are fairly similar to those in the United States even though the school-leaving age for working-class children is 10, and delinquents report generally favorable attitudes toward school. Unsatisfactory school experiences simply add to the economic motivations created by the exclusion of juveniles from the labor market.

MASCULINE STATUS ANXIETY
AND DELINQUENCY

Many observers have remarked on the disproportionate involvement of males in delinquent activity and the exaggerated masculine posturing that characterizes much male delinquency. Though sex differences in delinquency are not as pronounced in self-report studies as in arrest reports, and seem to be gradually narrowing, they nevertheless remain considerable, especially in the violence offense categories. Theoretical explanations for these differences not based on innate sex differences have alternatively emphasized differences in the socialization of boys and girls, which lead to differences in gender role (43), and "masculine protest" against maternal domination and identification (44), especially in the female-based households of the lower class (45). In such households, the argument goes, boys will tend to identify with the mother, and hence will experience uncertainty and anxiety in later years in connection with their identification as a male. To allay this anxiety, they reject the "good" values of the mother and engage in "masculine" forms of delinquency.

Application of the theory to delinquency in the United States has not been entirely successful. Male delinquency does appear to be associated with what has been interpreted as anxiety over masculinity, but is independent of whether the household in which the child is raised lacked an adult male (46).

This finding points to the need for a revision in the argument. Hannerz (47) has pointed out that children raised in homes without fathers may still have alternative male role models. Indeed, children raised in a community where adult male unemployment rates are high may spend more of their time in the company of adult males who could serve as role models than their middle class peers. I would argue, in addition, that Miller's adherence to the psycho-analytic framework blinds him to important sources of anxiety connected with masculinity that are unrelated to the family configuration in early childhood. Males who are not in doubt about their identity as males may nevertheless feel anxiety in connection with anticipated or actual inability to fulfill traditional sex role expectations concerning work and support of family. This masculine *status* anxiety can be generated by a father who is present but ineffectual, and by living in a neighborhood where, for social-structural reasons, many men are unemployed — regardless of whether one's own father is present in the household.

Men who experience such anxiety because they are prevented from fulfilling conventional male role expectations may attempt to alleviate their anxiety by exaggerating those traditionally male traits that *can* be expressed. Attempts to dominate women (including rape) and patterns of interpersonal violence can be seen in these terms. In other words, crime can be a response to masculine status anxiety no less than to anxiety over male identification; it can provide a sense of potency that is expected and desired but not achieved in other spheres of life.

In this interpretation, a compulsive concern with toughness and masculinity arises not from a hermetically sealed lower-class subculture "with an integrity of its own" nor from the psychodynamics of a female-headed household (48) but as a response to a contradiction between structural constraints on male status attainment imposed by the larger economic and political order and the cultural expectations for men that permeate American society. The role of the subculture Miller describes is to make available the behavioral adaptations that previous generations have developed in response to this contradiction, and thus to shape those responses. We should therefore expect persons suffering from masculine status anxiety who were members of groups in which the structural sources of masculine status anxiety have been common and long-standing to develop more coherent and stereotyped adaptations than individuals who were not members of such groups, e.g. in lower class blacks as compared with recently unemployed white collar employees (49). We should also expect those adaptations to attenuate in groups that ceased to encounter such contradictions, either because structural constraints to the fulfillment of traditional role expectations had been eliminated, or because expectations for men in the larger society had changed.

If I am correct in assuming that delinquents in the last years of elementary school and early years of high school are not excessively preoccupied with their occupational prospects, but become more concerned with their futures toward the end of high school — and there is some qualitative evidence to support this assumption (50) — then masculine anxiety during these early years must stem from other sources. One plausible source lies in the contradiction between the school's expectations of docility and submission to authority, and more widely communicated social expectations of masculinity. While the school represses both boys and girls, the message that girls get is consistent: the message boys receive is contradictory. This difference would help to explain sex differences in delinquency in early adolescence.

Most of the behavior that can be explained plausibly in this way — smoking, sexual conquests, joy-riding, vandalism, fighting between boys — is fairly trivial, and either becomes legal in mid to late adolescence, or abates rapidly. Anxiety over ability to fulfill traditional male occupational roles would show up late in adolescence. If I am correct in holding that such anxiety is an important source of criminal violations, the ratio of male to female participation should increase with age during adolescence, and there is evidence from self-reports that it does, at least among middle class youths (51).

One would expect masculine status anxiety to appear with greatest intensity and to decline most slowly in those segments of the population in which adult male unemployment is exceptionally high. This conforms to the general pattern of arrests for violence offenses such as homicide, forcible rape and assaults — offenses often unconnected with the pursuit of material gain, and hence most plausibly interpreted as a response to masculine status anxiety. Rates of arrest for those offenses peak in the immediate post-high school age brackets (several years later than for the property offenses) and the decline is slower than for property offenses. Moreover, blacks are over-represented in violence offense arrests to a much greater degree than in arrests for property offenses. Thus in 1973, the ratio of black to white arrests for burglary, larceny and auto theft was 0.45; for non-negligent homicide, forcible rape and aggravated assault, 0.85; for robbery, 1.79 (52). This relative over-representation of blacks is confirmed in victimization studies (53) and in self-reporting studies of delinquency (54) and thus cannot be explained as a manifestation of racial differences in risk of apprehension.

COSTS OF DELINQUENCY

So far some possible sources of variation with age in motivation to participate in common forms of criminal activity have been identified, but this is only half the story, for one may wish to engage in some form of behavior but nevertheless decide not to do so because the potential costs of participation are deemed unacceptably high. Costs can be a consequence of delinquency, and must be taken into account. Control theorists have begun to do so (55).

Costs can originate with internal or external sources of control. Superego restraints and favorable self-concepts and ideals exemplify internal

66

sources of control (56). They threaten the potential delinquent with guilt and shame. External costs can include parental disapproval and loss of privileges, school-imposed sanctions (ranging from teacher's disapproval to suspension or expulsion), loss of job and reduced prospects for future employment, acquisition of a police or juvenile court record, and deprivation of freedom through a reformatory sentence. Although external costs are actually imposed only on those who are caught, fear of incurring costs can inhibit potential delinquents and lead actual delinquents to desist.

To what extent can internal or external costs contribute to the age distribution of criminality? With the exception of those forms of minor delinquency considered far more discrediting to adults than to juveniles (57), it is unlikely that *internal* controls play a major role in generating age *differences* in criminal involvement, for it seems unlikely that moral inhibitions substantially increase from mid to late adolescence. Indeed, we generally expect people to take a more pragmatic view of morality as they get older.

External costs, however, are likely to vary with age. In early adolescence the potential costs of all but the most serious forms of delinquency are relatively slight. Parents and teachers are generally willing to write off a certain amount of misbehavior as "childish mischief," while enormous caseloads have forced juvenile courts in large cities to adopt a policy that comes very close to what Schur (58) has called "radical nonintervention" for all but the most serious cases. Moreover, the confidentiality of juvenile court records reduces the extent to which prospects are jeopardized by arrest.

Given the slight risk of apprehension for any single delinquent act, the prevalence of motivations to violate the law, and the low costs of lesser violations, we should expect minor infractions to be common among juveniles, and the self-reporting studies generally suggest that they are. Where the risk of incurring costs does procure abstention, we should suppose fear of parental disapproval would be the most salient. Teenagers who have good relationships with parents would presumably be the most concerned with incurring their disapproval, and they do have lower rates of involvement in delinquency (59).

As teenagers get older, the potential costs of apprehension increase, victims may be more prone to file a complaint, and police to make an arrest.

Juvenile Court Judges are more likely to take a serious view of an older offender, especially one with a prior record. Older offenders risk prosecution in criminal court, where penalties tend to be harsher, and where an official record will have more serious consequences for later job opportunities.

Delinquents are acutely sensitive to these considerations. According to several youthful offenders testifying before the New York State Select Committee at a hearing on assault and robbery against the elderly:

> *If you're 15 and under you won't go to jail . . . That's why when we do a "Rush and Crib" — which means you rush the victim and push him or her into their apartment, you let the youngest member do any beatings. See, we know if they arrest him, he'll be back on the street in no time* (60).

In interviews, former delinquents often attribute their own desistance to their unwillingness to risk the stiffer penalties they would receive if arrested and tried as adults (61). Thus the leniency of the juvenile court contributes to high levels of juvenile crime.

Just as the costs of crime are escalating, new opportunities in the form of jobs, marriage, or enlistment in the armed forces create stakes in conformity and, as Matza points out (62), may also relieve problems of masculine status anxiety. Toward the end of high school, when student concern about the future increases, the anticipation of new opportunities is manifested in desistance from delinquency and avoidance of those who do not similarly desist. Consistent with this interpretation is the fact that in both England and the United States, the peak year for delinquent involvement is the year *before* school-leaving.

Labeling theorists have tended to emphasize the role that apprehension and official processing of delinquents may play in increasing their subsequent delinquent involvement, either through the effect of labeling on self-concept and attitudes (63) or because prospects for legitimate employment are jeopardized through stigmatization (64). The evidence available does not suggest that this happens to any great extent (65). This is not necessarily surprising. As Schur (66) has pointed out, children may develop psychological defenses that serve to neutralize the discrediting imputations of others. When the negative label is applied by adults who are perceived as antagonists (police, judges, jailers) it should not be difficult to avoid being deeply influenced by their evaluations. Moreover, the confidentiality of juvenile court records helps to shield delinquents from later stigma.

Those whose opportunities for lucrative employment are limited by obstacles associated with racial and/or class membership will have far less reason to desist from illegal activity than those whose careers are not similarly blocked. The kinds of jobs available to young members of the lower strata of the working class tend to be tedious and financially unrewarding (when they are available at all). Marriage may appear less appealing to young men whose limited prospects promise inability to fulfill traditional male expectations as breadwinner. Even an army career may be precluded by an arrest record, low intelligence scores, physical disability, or illiteracy. Thus the legitimate opportunity structure, even if relatively useless for understanding entrance into delinquency, may still be helpful in understanding patterns of desistance.

The same may be said of the illegal opportunity structure. Those few delinquents who are recruited into organized crime or professional theft face larger rewards and less risk of serious penalty than those not so recruited, and their personal relationships with partners may be more satisfying. They should be less likely to desist from crime, but their offense patterns can be expected to change.

This reasoning suggests that the association between criminal involvement on the one hand and race and class on the other should be stronger for adults than for juveniles. If this is so, arrest rates in a given offense category should decline more rapidly for whites and youths with middle class backgrounds than for blacks and youths with working class and lower class backgrounds. In the male birth cohort studied by Wolfgang, Figlio and Sellin, whites were more likely to desist after an offense (67). F.B.I. crime career data also suggest higher rearrest rates for blacks than for whites (68) and a number of studies of recidivism of released prisoners have found somewhat higher recidivism among black ex-prisoners than among white ex-prisoners. Though based on small samples, Chambliss' field study of delinquency (69) does indicate a much higher desistance rate for middle class delinquents.

If, as is often suggested, crimes of violence involve less reflection and deliberation than crimes of acquisition, violence offenses should respond less elastically to increased external costs than property offenses. For this reason, we should expect violence crime rates to decline less rapidly with age than property crime rates, and this prediction is verified (see Table 1).

DELINQUENCY AND THE SOCIAL CONSTRUCTION OF THE JUVENILE

Among the structural sources of adolescent crime identified here, the exclusion of juveniles from the world of adult work plays a crucial role. It is this exclusion that simultaneously exaggerates teenagers' dependence on peers for approval and eliminates the possibility of their obtaining funds to support their intensive, leisure-time social activities. The disrespectful treatment students receive in school depends on their low social status, which in turn reflects their lack of employment. In late adolescence and early adulthood, their fear that this lack of employment will persist into adulthood evokes anxiety over achievement of traditional male gender role expectations, especially among males in the lower levels of the working class, thus contributing to a high level of violence.

Institutionalized leniency to juvenile offenders, which reduces the potential costs of delinquency, stems from the belief that teenagers are not as responsible for their actions as adults (70). The conception of juveniles as impulsive and irresponsible gained currency around the turn of the century (see for example, Hall [71]) when organized labor and Progressive reformers campaigned for child labor laws to save jobs for adults, a goal given high priority after the Depression of 1893. This conception was, in a sense, self-fulfilling. Freed from ties to conventional institutions, teenagers *have* become more impulsive and irresponsible.

The exclusion of teenagers from serious work is not characteristic of all societies. Peasant and tribal societies could not afford to keep their young idle as long as we do. In such societies, juvenile crime rates were low. Under feudalism, too, children participated in farming and handicraft production as part of the family unit beginning at a very early age.

In depriving masses of serfs and tenant farmers of access to the means of production (land), European capitalism in its early stages of development generated a great deal of crime, but in a manner that cut across age boundaries. Little of the literature on crime in Elizabethan and Tudor England singles out juveniles as a special category.

The industrial revolution in the first half of the nineteenth century similarly brought with it a great deal of misery, but its effect on crime was not restricted to juveniles. Children of the working class in that period held jobs at an early age and in some sectors of the economy were given preference. Only middle and upper class children were exempt from the need to work, and they were supervised much more closely than they are nowadays. As far as can be judged, juvenile crime in that period was a much smaller fraction of the total than at present, and was more confined to the lower classes than it is now (72).

In modern capitalist societies, children of all classes share, for a limited period, a common relationship to the means of production (namely exclusion) which is distinct from that of most adults, and they respond to their common structural position in fairly similar ways. Although there are class differences in the extent and nature of delinquency, especially violent delinquency, these are less pronounced than for adults, for whom occupational differentiation is much sharper.

The deteriorating position of juveniles in the labor market in recent years has been ascribed to a variety of causes, among them the inclusion of juveniles under minimum wage laws, changes in the structure of the economy (less farm employment), teenage preference for part-time work (to permit longer periods of education) which makes teenage labor less attractive to employers, and the explosion in the teenage labor supply created by the baby boom at a time when women were entering the labor market in substantial numbers (73). Whatever contribution these circumstances may have made to shifting teenage employment patterns in the short-run, the exclusion of juveniles from the labor market has been going on for more than a century, and may more plausibly be explained in terms of the failure of the oligopoly-capitalist economy to generate sufficient demand for labor, than to these recent developments (74).

In both the United States and England, the prolongation of education has historically been associated with the contraction of the labor market (75), casting doubt on the view that more education is something that the general population has wanted for its own sake. Had this been true, the school leaving age would have jumped upward in periods of prosperity, when a larger proportion of the population could afford more education, not during depressions. Moreover, the functionalist argument that increased education is necessary as technology becomes more complex would apply at best to a small minority of students, and rests on the dubious assumption that full-time schooling is pedagogically superior to alternative modes of organizing the education of adolescents.

The present social organization of education, which I have argued contributes to delinquency, has also been plausibly attributed to the functional requirement of a capitalist economy for a docile, disciplined and stratified labor force (76), as well as to the need to keep juveniles out of the labor market.

Thus the high and increasing level of juvenile crime we are seeing in present-day United States and in other Western countries originates in the structural position of juveniles in an advanced capitalist economy.

Delinquency is not, however, a problem of capitalism alone. Although there are many differences between crime patterns in the United States and the Soviet Union, the limited information available indicates that delinquency in the Soviet Union is often associated with leisure-time consumption activities on the part of youths who are academic failures, and who are either not working or studying, or are working at or preparing for unrewarding jobs (77). This suggests that some of the processes described here may be at work in the Soviet Union. Since Soviet society is based on hierarchical domination and requires a docile, disciplined and stratified labor force, this parallel is not surprising.

One might, in fact, generalize from this analysis, to conclude that any society that excluded juveniles from the world of adult work for long periods and imposed mandatory attendance at schools organized like ours would have a substantial amount of delinquency.

FOOTNOTES AND REFERENCES

1. S.N. Eisenstadt, FROM GENERATION TO GENERATION: AGE GROUPS AND SOCIAL STRUCTURE. New York: Free Press, 1956; H.A. Bloch and A. Niederhoffer, THE GANG. New York: Philosophical Library, 1958, pp. 29-30.

2. P.H. Mussen, J.J. Conger and J. Kagan, CHILD DEVELOPMENT AND PERSONALITY. New York: Harper & Row, 1969.

3. Panel on Youth of the President's Science Advisory Committee, YOUTH: TRANSITION TO ADULTHOOD. Chicago: University of Chicago, 1974.

4. M. Mead, FROM THE SOUTH SEAS: PART III, SEX AND TEMPERAMENT IN THREE PRIMITIVE SOCIETIES. New York: Morrow, 1939; S.N. Eisenstadt, op. cit., 1956, pp. 56-92; I. Minturn and W.W. Lambert, MOTHERS IN SIX CULTURES: ANTECEDENTS OF CHILD REARING. New York: Wiley, 1964.

5. Insofar as meals are not served regularly in some lower class families, biological and social needs here converge. Mertonian theory implicitly but erroneously assumes that the welfare state functions well enough to meet basic biological needs.

6. Panel on Youth, op. cit., 1974, pp. 36-38.

7. B. Tomson and E.R. Fiedler, "Gangs: A Response to the Urban World (Part II)," in Desmond S. Cartwright, Barbara Tomson and Herschey Schwartz (eds.), GANG DELINQUENCY. Monterey, Cal.: Brooks/ Cole, 1975.

8. A.H. Raskin, "The Teenage Worker is Hardest Hit," NEW YORK TIMES, May 4, 1975, p. F3.

9. M. Sherif and C.W. Sherif, REFERENCE GROUPS: EXPLORA-TION INTO CONFORMITY AND DEVIATION OF ADOLES-CENTS. New York: Harper & Row, 1964, p. 174.

10. C. Werthman, "The Function of Social Definitions in the Development of Delinquent Careers," In TASK FORCE REPORT: JUVENILE DE-LINQUENCY. Washington, D.C.: Government Printing Office, 1967, p: 157.

11. J. Weis, "Liberation and Crime: The Invention of the New Female Criminal," CRIME AND SOCIAL JUSTICE, Vol. 6, 1976, pp. 17-27.

12. J. Toby, "Affluence and Adolescent Crime," in The President's Com-mission on Law Enforcement and Administration of Justice, TASK FORCE REPORT: JUVENILE DELINQUENCY AND YOUTH CRIME. Washington, D.C.: Government Printing Office, 1967, pp. 136-137.

13. M. Rolf and S.B. Seils, "Juvenile Delinquency in Relation to Peer Ac-ceptance-Rejection and Socioeconomic Status," PSYCHOLOGY IN THE SCHOOLS, Vol. 5, 1968, pp. 3-18; D. West, "Are Delinquents Different?" NEW SOCIETY, Vol. 26, November 22, 1973, p. 456.

14. E. Rothstein, "Attributes Related to High School Status: A Compari-son of the Perceptions of Delinquents and Non-Delinquent Boys," SOCIAL PROBLEMS, Vol. 10, 1962, pp. 75-83; J.F. Short, Jr. and F.L. Strodtbeck, GROUP PROCESS AND GANG DELINQUENCY. Chicago: University of Chicago Press, 1965, pp. 243-244; T. Hirschi, THE CAUSES OF DELINQUENCY. Berkeley: University of Califor-nia Press, 1969, pp. 145-161.

15. F.I. Nye, FAMILY RELATIONSHIPS AND DELINQUENT BE-HAVIOR. New York: Wiley, 1958, ch. 8; T. Hirschi, op.cit., 1969, pp. 83-109.

16. J.F. Short, Jr. and F.I. Nye, "Extent of Unrecorded Delinquency: Tentative Conclusions," JOURNAL OF CRIMINAL LAW, CRIMINOLOGY AND POLICE SCIENCE, Vol. 49, 1958, pp. 296-302; A.J. Reiss, Jr. and A.L. Rhodes, "The Distribution of Juvenile Delinquency in the Social Class Structure," AMERICAN SOCIOLOGICAL REVIEW, Vol. 26, 1961, pp. 730-732; R. Dentler and L.J. Monroe, "Early Adolescent Theft," AMERICAN SOCIOLOGICAL REVIEW, Vol. 26, 1961, pp. 733-743; J.P. Clark and E.P. Wenninger, "Socio-Economic Class and Area as correlates of Illegal Behavior Among Juveniles," AMERICAN SOCIOLOGICAL REVIEW, Vol. 27, 1962, pp. 826-834; R.L. Akers, "Socio-Economic Status and Delinquent Behavior: A Re-test," JOURNAL OF RESEARCH IN CRIME AND DELINQUENCY, Vol. 1, 1964, pp. 38-46; T. Hirschi, op. cit., 1969, pp. 66-82.

17. R.J. Simon, WOMEN AND CRIME. Lexington, Mass.: Lexington Books, 1975.

18. A.K. Cohen, DELINQUENT BOYS. New York: Free Press, 1955, p. 25.

19. W.E. Schafer, K. Polk, "Delinquency and the Schools," in TASK FORCE REPORT: JUVENILE DELINQUENCY AND YOUTH CRIME. Washington, D.C.: Government Printing Office, 1967; K. Polk and W.E. Schafer, SCHOOLS AND DELINQUENCY. Englewood Cliffs, N.J.: Prentice-Hall, 1972.

20. These expectations are derived from young people's knowledge of family arrangements in our society generally, not only from their own family circumstances. When controls in their own family are not relaxed, this can provide an additional source of conflict.

21. G. Psathas, "Ethnicity, Social Class, and Adolescent Independence from Parental Control," AMERICAN SOCIOLOGICAL REVIEW, Vol. 22, 1957, p. 415-421; S. Kobrin, "The Impact of Cultural Factors in Selected Problems of Adolescent Development in the Middle and Lower Class," AMERICAN JOURNAL OF ORTHOPSYCHIATRY, Vol. 33, 1962, pp. 387-390; C. Werthman, op. cit., 1967; L. Rainwater, BEHIND GHETTO WALLS. Chicago: Aldine, 1970, pp. 211-234; J. Ladner, TOMORROW'S TOMORROW: THE BLACK WOMAN. Garden City: Doubleday, 1971, pp. 61-63; G. Elder, CHILDREN OF THE GREAT DEPRESSION: SOCIAL CHANGE IN

LIFE EXPERIENCE. Chicago: University of Chicago Press, 1974.

22. J. Toby, op. cit., 1976, p. 141.

23. A. Gouldner, THE COMING CRISIS IN WESTERN SOCIOLOGY. New York: Basic Books, 1970, pp. 221-222.

24. A. Cohen, op. cit., 1955, pp. 112-133; R. Sennet and J. Cobb, THE HIDDEN INJURIES OF CLASS. New York: Alfred A. Knopf, 1972.

25. H.H. Hyman, "The Psychology of Status," in H.H. Hyman and L. Singer (eds.), READINGS IN REFERENCE GROUP THEORY AND RESEARCH. New York: Free Press, 1968, pp. 147-168.

26. E. Goffman, "On Face-Work: An Analysis of Ritual Elements in Social Interaction," PSYCHIATRY, Vol. 18, 1955, pp. 213-231.

27. H.G. Ellis and S.M. Newman, "The Greaser is a 'Bad Ass': The Gowster is a 'Muthah': An Analysis of Two Urban Youth Roles," in Thomas Kochman (ed.), RAPPIN' AND STYLIN' OUT: COMMUNICATION IN BLACK AMERICA. Urbana: University of Illinois Press, 1972, pp. 375-376.

28. A. Cohen, op. cit., 1955, pp. 121-137.

29. W.B. Miller, "Violent Crime in City Gangs," ANNALS OF THE AMERICAN ACADEMY OF POLITICAL AND SOCIAL SCIENCE, Vol. 364, 1966, pp. 96-112.

30. D. Matza, DELINQUENCY AND DRIFT. New York: Wiley, 1964, pp. 33-68; J.F. Short, Jr. and F.I. Strodtbeck, op. cit., 1964, pp. 47-75.

31. D. Matza, op. cit., 1964, p. 33.

32. C. Werthman, op. cit., 1967.

33. J.F. Short, Jr. and F.L. Strodtbeck, op. cit., 1965, pp. 185-216; R. Horowitz and G. Schwartz, "Honor, Normative Ambiguity and Gang Violence," AMERICAN SOCIOLOGICAL REVIEW, Vol. 39, 1974, pp. 238-251.

34. E. Goffman, "Where the Action Is," in INTERACTION RITUAL. Garden City: Anchor Books, 1974, pp. 149-270.

35. D. Matza and G.M. Sykes, "Juvenile Delinquency and Subterranean Values," AMERICAN SOCIOLOGICAL REVIEW, Vol. 26, 1961, pp. 712-719.

36. G. Dennison, THE LIVES OF CHILDREN: THE STORY OF THE FIRST STREET SCHOOL. New York: Random House, 1969; E.Z. Friedenberg, THE VANISHING ADOLESCENT. Boston: Beacon Press, 1964; COMING OF AGE IN AMERICA: GROWTH AND ACQUIESCENCE. New York: Random House, 1965; P. Goodman, COMPULSORY MISEDUCATION. New York: Horizon Press, 1964; M.F. Greene and O. Ryan, THE SCHOOL CHILDREN: GROWING UP IN THE SLUMS. New York: Pantheon, 1965; D.H. Hargreaves, INTERPERSONAL RELATIONS AND EDUCATION. London: Routledge and Kegan Paul, 1972; N. Hentoff, OUR CHILDREN ARE DYING. New York: Viking Press, 1966; J. Herndon, THE WAY IT SPOZED TO BE. New York: Simon and Schuster, 1968; P.W. Jackson, LIFE IN CLASSROOMS. New York: Holt Rinehart and Winston, 1968; H. Kohl, 36 CHILDREN. New York: New American Library, 1967; C. Nordstrom, E.Z. Friedenberg and H.A. Gold, SOCIETY'S CHILDREN: A STUDY OF RESENTMENT IN THE SECONDARY SCHOOL. New York: Random House, 1967; J.I. Roberts, SCENE OF THE BATTLE: GROUP BEHAVIOR IN URBAN CLASSROOMS. Garden City: Doubleday, 1970; J. Webb, "The Sociology of a School," BRITISH JOURNAL OF SOCIOLOGY, Vol. 13, 1962, pp. 264-272.

37. D.M. Downes, THE DELINQUENT SITUATION: A STUDY IN SUBCULTURAL THEORY. New York: Free Press, 1966.

38. H. Finestone, "Cats, Kicks and Color," SOCIAL PROBLEMS, Vol. 5, 1957, pp. 3-13.

39. L. Rainwater, op. cit., 1970.

40. C. Werthman, op. cit., 1967.

41. J.G. Bachman, S. Green and I. Wirtanen, DROPPING OUT: PROBLEM OR SYMPTOM. Ann Arbor: Institute for Social Research, 1972.

42. D.S. Elliot and H.L. Voss, DELINQUENCY AND DROPOUT. Lexington, Mass.: Lexington Books, 1974, pp. 115-122; S.K. Mukherjee, A TYPOLOGICAL STUDY OF SCHOOL STATUS AND DELINQUENCY. Ann Arbor: University Microfilms, 1971.

43. C. Grosser, JUVENILE DELINQUENCY AND CONTEMPORARY AMERICAN SEX ROLES. Unpublished Ph.D. Dissertation. Harvard University, 1952.

44. T. Parsons, "Certain Primary Sources and Patterns of Aggression in the Social Structure of the Western World," PSYCHIATRY, Vol. 10, 1947, pp. 167-181; A. Cohen, op. cit., 1955, pp. 162-169.

45. W.B. Miller, "Lower Class Subculture as a Generating Milieu of Gang Delinquency," JOURNAL OF SOCIAL ISSUES, Vol. 14, 1958, pp. 5-19.

46. R.A. Tennyson, "Family Structure and Delinquent Behavior," in M.W. Kienin (ed.), JUVENILE GANGS IN CONTEST. Englewood Cliffs, N.J.: Prentice-Hall, 1967; T.P. Monahan, "Family Status and the Delinquent Child: A Reappraisal and Some New Findings," SOCIAL FORCES, Vol. 35, 1957, pp. 251-258; L. Rosen, "Matriarchy and Lower Class Negro Male Delinquency," SOCIAL PROBLEMS, Vol. 17, 1969, pp. 175-189.

47. U. Hannerz, SOULSIDE: INQUIRIES INTO GHETTO CULTURE. New York: Columbia University Press, 1969.

48. W.B. Miller, op. cit., 1958.

49. A similar perspective on subcultures of violence and their relationship to masculinity has been developed by L. Curtis, VIOLENCE, RACE AND CULTURE. Lexington, Mass.: Lexington Books, 1975.

50. C. Werthman, op. cit., 1967.

51. J. Weis, op. cit., 1976.

52. Federal Bureau of Investigation, CRIME IN THE UNITED STATES. UNIFORM CRIME REPORTS — 1973. Washington, D.C.; Government Printing Office, 1974, p. 133.

53. Task Force Report, THE ASSESSMENT OF CRIME. Washington, D.C.: Government Printing Office, 1967.

54. J.E. Puntil, "Youth Survey Marginals." Chicago: Institute for Juvenile Research, (n.d.).

55. S. Briar and I. Piliavin, "Delinquency Situation Inducements, and Commitment to Conformity," SOCIAL PROBLEMS, Vol. 13, 1965, pp. 35-45; J.M. Piliavin, A.C. Vadum and J.A.Hardyck, "Delinquency, Personal Costs and Parental Treatment: A Test of a Reward-Cost Model in Juvenile Criminality," JOURNAL OF CRIMINAL LAW, CRIMINOLOGY AND POLICE SCIENCE, Vol. 60, 1969, pp. 165-172; T. Hirschi, op. cit., 1969; I, Ehrlich, "Participation in Illegitimate Activities: A Theoretical and Empirical Investigation," JOURNAL OF POLITICAL ECONOMY, Vol. 81, 1973, pp. 521-565.

56. W.C. Reckless, S. Dinitz and E. Murray, "Self Concept as an Insulator against Delinquency," AMERICAN SOCIOLOGICAL REVIEW, Vol. 21, 1956, pp. 744-746.

57. J.P. Clark and E.W. Havrek, "Age and Sex Roles of Adolescents and their Involvement in Misconduct: A Reappraisal," SOCIOLOGY AND SOCIAL RESEARCH, Vol. 50, 1966.

58. E.M. Schur, RADICAL NONINTERVENTION: RETHINKING THE DELINQUENCY PROBLEM. Englewood Cliffs, N.J.: Prentice-Hall, 1973.

59. T. Hirschi, op. cit., 1969, pp. 81-109.

60. L. Williams, "Three Youths Call Mugging the Elderly Profitable and Safe," NEW YORK TIMES, December 8, 1976, p. B2.

61. I have discussed the question of desistance with male juveniles on probation in Manhattan for theft offenses, and with a number of my students who have been involved in various forms of theft. The latter group includes both apprehended and unapprehended former thieves. No claim is made for the representativeness of this small sample.

62. D. Matza, op. cit., 1964, p. 55.

63. F. Tannenbaum, CRIME IN THE COMMUNITY. New York: Columbia University Press, 1938, pp. 19-20.

64. R.D. Schwartz and J.H. Skolnick, "Two Studies of Legal Stigma," SOCIAL PROBLEMS, Vol. 10, 1962, pp. 133-142.

65. T. Hirschi, "Labelling Theory and Juvenile Delinquency: An Assessment of the Evidence," in Walter R. Gove (ed.), LABELING OF DE-

VIANCE: EVALUATING A PERSPECTIVE. New York: Halsted Press, 1975; C.R. Tittle, "Labelling and Crime: An Empirical Evaluation," in Walter R. Gove (ed.), THE LABELLING OF DEVIANCE: EVALUATING A PERSPECTIVE. New York: Halsted Press, 1975; A.R. Mahoney, "The Effect of Labeling upon Youths in the Juvenile Justice System: A Review of the Evidence," LAW AND SOCIETY REVIEW, Vol. 8, 1974, pp. 583-614.

66. E.M. Schur, op. cit., 1973, p. 125.

67. M.E. Wolfgang, R.M. Figlio and T. Sellin, DELINQUENCY IN A BIRTH COHORT. Chicago: University of Chicago Press, 1972, p. 201.

68. Federal Bureau of Investigation, CRIME IN THE UNITED STATES. UNIFORM CRIME REPORTS — 1972. Washington, D.C.: Government Printing Office, 1972, p. 138.

69. W.J. Chambliss, "The Saints and the Roughnecks," SOCIETY, Vol. 11, 1973, pp. 24-31.

70. This leniency has increased over the past decade, partly in response to the arguments of labeling theorists such as E.M. Schur, op. cit., 1973, that punishment of delinquents would be counter-rehabilitative, and because of the state's growing fiscal inability to cope with the social problems engendered by a deteriorating capitalist economy and policy, described by J. O'Connor, THE FISCAL CRISIS OF THE STATE. New York: St. Martin's Press, 1973. A. Scull, DECARCERATION: COMMUNITY TREATMENT AND THE DEVIANT — A RADICAL VIEW. Englewood Cliffs, N.J.: Prentice-Hall, 1977, explicitly discusses the community corrections movement in these terms.

71. G.S. Hall, ADOLESCENCE, ITS PSYCHOLOGY AND ITS RELATIONS TO PHYSIOLOGY, ANTHROPOLOGY, SOCIOLOGY, SEX, CRIME, RELIGION AND EDUCATION. New York: Appleton, 1904.

72. In nineteenth century England, juveniles were over-represented in crime statistics by comparison with the continent not because the social position of juveniles was very different, but because the age distribution of the English population was skewed toward the younger age brackets by the rapid growth in the English population during the nineteenth century. In the latter half of the century, juveniles were again under-

represented by comparison with their numbers in the English population, despite the high percentages of offenders who were juveniles, see C. Lombroso, CRIME: ITS CAUSES AND REMEDIES. Montclair, N.J.: Patterson Smith, 1968, p. 176; J.J. Tobias, URBAN CRIME IN VICTORIAN ENGLAND. New York: Schocken Books, 1972, pp. 78, 167.

73. E. Kalacheck, "The Changing Economic Status of the Young," JOURNAL OF YOUTH AND ADOLESCENCE, Vol. 2, 1973, pp. 125-132.

74. R.B. Carson, "Youthful Labor Surplus in Disaccumulationist Capitalism," SOCIALIST REVOLUTION, Vol. 9, 1972, pp. 15-44; N. Bowers, "Youth and the Crisis of Monopoly Capitalism," in RADICAL PERSPECTIVES ON THE ECONOMIC CRISIS OF MONOPOLY CAPITALISM. New York: Union of Radical Political Economy, 1975.

75. F. Musgrove, YOUTH AND THE SOCIAL ORDER. Bloomington: Indiana University Press, 1965.

76. D.K. Cohen and M. Lazerson, "Education and the Corporate Order," SOCIALIST REVOLUTION, Vol. 8, 1972, pp. 47-72; A. Gorz, "Technologie, Techniker und Klassenkampf," in A. Gorz, SCHULE AND FABRIK, 1972. Quoted in Gero Lenhardt, "On the Relationship between the Education System and Capitalist Work Organization," KAPITALISTATE, Vol. 3, pp. 128-146; S. Bowles and H. Gintis, SCHOOLING IN CAPITALIST AMERICA: EDUCATIONAL REFORM AND THE CONTRADICTIONS OF ECONOMIC LIFE. New York: Basic Books 1975.

77. W. Connor, DEVIANCE IN SOVIET SOCIETY. New York: Columbia University Press, 1970; K. Polk, "Social Class and the Bureaucratic Response to Youthful Deviance." 1972. Paper presented to the American Sociological Association.

THE CRISIS OF MODERNITY:
DEVIATION OR DEMISE?

Amitai Etzioni

There are those who believe that the contemporary crisis of our society is a temporary one, a limited setback as our civilization rises to higher plateaus of organization, knowledge, planning, and competence, onward and forward into the ultra-modern (or "technetronic") age. The swelling symptoms of disaffection, especially the youth's counter-culture, are viewed as limited in scope and significance, and only delaying progress (1). Even among the young, it is argued, only a minority rebels and those who do are mainly from among the students, largely in the humanities and some of the social sciences, who react to the growing obsolescence of their generalistic, abstract perspective. These rebelling few, these reactionary neo-Luddites, are said to correctly perceive that they will be even more out of place in the 1980's than they were in the late 1960's, as society will be increasingly run by a technological elite, applied scientists, and administrators. The rebellion is thus written off as a small, albeit troublesome, price which progress exacts.

But obviously, we point out, not only students rebel. Several racial minorities, senior citizens, and significant segments of women are also increasingly disenchanted with "the good life" the contemporary society is supposedly offering, and act out their alienation. Yet the significance of this broadening front is discounted because the goals of the various member groups vary significantly. The blacks (and other ethnic minorities), it is said, are basically fighting for their share in the system, their cut of the affluent pie; while the young radicals wish to slay the modern goose which lays the consumer eggs and return to the culture (and economics and ecology) of poverty. And, it is added with some *schadenfreude,* even the rebelling youth are not in agreement. Some seek a traditional revolution in the old left sense of the term, daydreaming of storming a bastille or a palace, mounting the barricades, followed by soviets of students, workers, and peasants taking over, ushering in the sunshine society. Others expect the same result to be achieved by personal acts of faith (by raising consciousness) and change of life style ("What could General Motors do if we all chose to ride bicycles or, better yet, walk?").

The friends of modernity point to the rapid rise and fall of various rebellion fads to further document their complacent thesis. In 1968 there were major outbreaks of riots in black ghettoes in scores of American cities; it was widely argued that unless major reforms were made to favor the blacks, the subsequent summers would grow hotter until the whole country would go up in the flames of civil war. Actually, while the reforms that followed were small tokens, there were fewer fires in 1969, still fewer in subsequent years. The student uprising, which gained momentum in the mid- and late 60's, was said then to endanger academia and polity alike. Louis J. Halle, writing in the *New Republic*, saw a "student drive to destruction" which threatened "the breakdown of the discipline of civilization," and it was no longer impossible that "Mr. George Wallace or someone like him will become President of the United States in 1973" (2). Dire consequences were predicted if the rebelling youth who gave the political system its "last chance" in the 1968 elections, by campaigning for Eugene McCarthy, were to find it unresponsive. The editor of *The Nation* opined that a "sizable number of voters will turn to a third party or a fourth . . . which if it cannot prevail in 1968 will pave the way for national, radical change in 1972," adding ominously, "providing the fat has not gone into the fire by then" (3). But 1968 came and went; not just Gene but even Humphrey lost, and Nixon — anathema of anathemas — took over; yet in the following years the young were heard less of, not more. Soon, it is said, few will recall what the initials SDS stand for and even the extremist, violence-prone Weathermen, who finally decided to talk down dynamiting, have just about blown themselves away. By 1971, not only had the campuses ceased to boil over, but even their internal turmoil had subsided.

Still, it is my thesis that the crisis remains a real enough one (albeit much less dramatic and less visible than the headline-writers first had it, then lost sight of). I shall try to show that America is being transformed and, more globally, that modernity is coming to an end. That America is not falling apart, or returning to pastoral primitiveness, is hardly to the point; there are other, much more historical, much more frequently encountered ways for a particular form of society to be superseded. The thesis I shall try to advance is that the modern world is step-by-step being replaced by a new pattern which will make more room for individual self-actualization along with enhanced community values, and which will gear the instrumental process more closely to the advancement of humanist and social values. The present counter-culture movement — as inept, fad-ridden, apolitical, splintered as it is — is not the last hurrah of obsolete humanist ideas, but a hothouse of new personal, cultural, and societal experimentation. The future America, we shall see in some detail, is not about to look like a Hippie commune, a Woodstock festival, an Aspen Marathon, or an Earth Day teach-in. However, I shall attempt to show that these all contain the seeds of possible future developments of societal significance, among which we must choose (or elect to combine) and, above all, adapt to apply on a society-wide scale. But let me proceed one step at a time.

SOME DATA ON THE SCOPE AND NATURE OF THE CRISIS

How can one sustain, in the face of the observations of the technetronic prophets cited above, the thesis that a grand transformation toward a new society has begun? There can be no gain-saying the fact that various forms, organizations, and ideological factions of the rebellion have come and gone with a faddish speed hitherto known only in the world of clothing and cosmetics. However, what the friends of ultra-modernity — the technetronicrats — seem to fail to perceive is that as one rebellious form is replaced by another, the rebellion itself is swelling in scope and growing in depth. The expressions of protest do shift about rapidly among civil disobedience, peaceful marches, confrontation demonstrations, dynamiting, political campaigning, and other forms. The mass media, which quickly tires of any one form of protest, rewards with prime-time or front-page coverage the finding of a new format. Moreover, time and again, one segment or another of the highly unorganized movement lapses into restless and alienated apathy, seemingly disappearing, only to be available again (or at least many of its members) for protest against the system; it has remained hostile even in its latency. Expressive politics and apathetic alienation, both of which require no more than a short fuse, are more akin to each other than either is to sustained involvement in routine politics.

Thus, for instance, the blacks, while recently disinclined to sit-in or burn out — and although the mode of expression of their disenchantment has swiftly shifted from one form to another and from various kinds of activism to alienated passivity and then again back to the streets — are highly disenchanted with the system. They are systematically and significantly and increasingly less satisfied with their personal fortunes and futures than are whites (4). And a sizable group believes only violence will gain them equality — 21% of a national sample, 36% of Northern young blacks. But what about the others? Four out of ten endorse militant organizations (41%) and are willing to take to the street in protest (42%); six out of ten feel "people who have power are out to take advantage of you" (61%); nearly seven out of ten favor organizing boycotts where whites discriminate against blacks (68%), while over three quarters of the blacks approve keeping up the heat on the federal government (77%) (5). It is true that large-scale riots are less common; however, the number of small-scale civil disorders, arson, shooting of policemen and firemen, bombing, prison riots (wardens speak of a new breed of militant inmates), has significantly increased (6). John Herseky, author of the *New York Times* article just cited, referred to "shifting battlegrounds" of group violence.

Similarly, much has been made of the finding that only one out of five students believe "that some degree of violence is necessary to produce needed social change in this country" (7). However, a third of the respondents in a student sample back extreme left politics; 44% believe in the need for radical pressure to bring about social change, and 75% see a need for fundamental changes. 90% of the seniors of one class (1968—9) said they are "very critical of our basic institutions." Thus, the "hard-core" radical activists and the prospective militants have all the sea they possibly could wish to fish in, and the potential scope of the rebellion is not narrow, but — compared to other periods — seems uncommonly encompassing. That only small minorities of the social groupings involved are themselves militants, and that they hardly all march in the same direction and to the same tune, should not lead one to underestimate the rebellion. A study of *any* previous successful uprising, from the French revolution to the Russian, from the Boston Tea Party to the wars of national liberation in Asia and Africa, show beyond any doubt that rebellions are all carried out by small minorities, backed by much larger groups of occasional participants and sympathizers. Thus, there were no more than 10,000 full-timers in the Israeli underground which caused the British to pack up and leave. The French Revolution was largely a Parisian matter, involving about 80,000; and the number of those who stormed the Bastille was only in the hundreds.

Splintering, intra- and inter-sectarian feuding, fanatical ideological hairsplitting, are the noises emitted by all rebellious movements, from Protestants rising against Rome to European socialists battling capitalism, from pre-Independence Indian nationalists to the Cuban underground against Battista. The noise is hardly raised for the purpose of lulling the powers that be; the infighting is real enough. Nor is the suggestion that it shows a weakness of the movement without foundation. But we should also not ignore the fact that divergent as the directions the various dissenting groups march in may be, they all lead away from the existing system. And the day the system is seriously challenged, the conflicting factions often suddenly find a common tune, a "united front," and those groups which do not actually join in will still stick to the sidelines rather than uphold the system. Thus, the goals of some blacks who feel excluded from the affluent society may well not coincide with those of student anarchists who seek to abolish affluence, but these blacks were not seen rushing to defend Columbia University the day students took over its building, or trying to stop CORE from blocking New York City's bridges, or blocking the march on the Pentagon.

84

Most important, this line of reasoning — led by Lipset — as to what proportion of a social group (generation, students, blacks, etc.) is willing to use force to overthrow the system is chiefly relevant to those who expect a traditional revolutionary movement. For those who expect a transformation, the scope of alienation from the old values — whether mobilized or apolitical — and the spread of commitments to new values, is more to the point. As we have seen, for every student, black, and other rebelling person who is willing to use force (or says so to a pollster or writes it on a questionnaire), there are three or four others who are turned off by the system. How many of those are already turned on to a new set of values and active work in reshaping a new personal and collective life is harder to assess. An attempt at such estimates will be made later when the most important of the new systems are discussed.

The lineup of groups that are alienated in various forms and degrees from contemporary America is by now much longer than one ethnic minority yet to be cut in, or students laboring under humanistic hangups. The list of minorities which are unsettled encompasses not only a rising portion of the blacks (12% of the U.S. population), but a large number of Spanish Americans (especially Puerto Ricans and Chicanos), Red or Indian Americans, Americans of oriental descent, and others. The growing population of older people has been for decades a major source of alienation politics. That a significant proportion of women have been caught up in the liberation movement is well known; 24% of American women sampled agreed with the most ideological statement of Women's Liberation, that "women are discriminated against and treated as second-class citizens" (8). Many more agreed with specific demands. Nearly 70% favored low cost child care centers for working mothers. More than 70% favored equal job opportunity for women; over 80%, equal pay (9). Rejected out of hand in the Roper poll were more esoteric notions such as that women should not be appraised on the basis of sex, beauty and appeal, or be drafted. In another poll, 42% of American women favored "most of the efforts to strengthen and change women's status in society" (10).

Not even nearly correct is the image of a majority in favor of modernity being challenged by a wild disarray of minorities, inasmuch as a large segment of the white working class and middle class population is deeply alienated, too. The reasons "Middle Americans" or the "ethnics" are resentful are many and varied; they need not be explored here (11). Whatever the reasons, it is evident that the new high standard of living, the main payoff of modernity, has not kept them jumping with joy. While a large majority tend to feel that tension is a constant element in modern life (73% in 1968, and 83% in 1972), and an even larger majority would like to rid life of constant tensions 86% and 93%), a decreasing minority believe that such a condition can be achieved (16% in 1968, 9% in 1972) (12). A poll of Middle Americans at the end of the sixties found that 40% thought that "the U.S. has changed for the worse over the past decade," (the figure in 1972 was 54%),(13) and 58% expected it was likely to change for the worse over the next decade (14). In the poll of the sixties half (48%) agreed that there was need to experiment with new ways of dealing with the nation's problems, and even more (54%) that "young people are not unduly critical of their country." In the sixties, a sizable proportion favored the government's spending more money on public needs (e.g., 56% cited de-pollution) and social justice (47%, medical care for the old and needy) (15). Now, more than ever, people want the focus of the nation's efforts to shift from foreign missions to reform at home (77% in 1971 as compared to 31% in 1965).

True, construction workers (hardhats), American Legionnaires, groups of Poles in Detroit, Chicago or Cleveland may be counted upon to show up (also, a small fraction of their total groupings) in support of the flag, the Fatherland, and the beating up of those "hippies" or "niggers." But study after study confirms that they are bewildered, frightened, and disappointed with the system. They are patriotic, loyal to the nation, but not to the values of modernity, rationalism and liberalism. On the contrary, they tend to be anti-science, against "big government," impulsive, and restive. They, too, seek more from a society than fleshpots or porkchops.

Institutions which used to be the citadels of conservatism and the mainstays of the society are hollowed out by internal erosion of authority and confidence. Two-thirds of the Roman Catholic priests in the U.S. disclosed in an NORC study conducted by the Reverend Andrew Greeley that in their judgment Pope Paul VI misused his authority in issuing his 1967 encyclical against artificial birth control. Only 40% of the priests agreed in 1971 with the official Church position on divorce. And 56% believed priests should be free to marry. Even the Army has been shaken by a crisis in morale and discipline as serious as any its oldest and toughest soldiers can remember (16). The rate of the absent-without-leave rose from 57 out of a thousand in 1966 to 177 in 1970, and deserters from 15 out of a thousand in 1966 to 74 in 1970. "According to an Army study, there may well exist such a profound crisis of discipline that the Army's ability to function is in doubt" (17). Police departments are becoming increasingly alienated. Nothing seems to be exempt from the crisis of legitimation and authority.

No wonder, then, when polls take random national samples rather than studying one group or another, the result is a combination of disaffected minorities — those who seek to outgrow modernity, those who have not

made it yet into the modern society, and those who do not wish to make it —
into a disaffected majority.

The kingpin of a system is its political structure, which rests on two pillars, legitimation and power. When this is absent, power is naked and tends to weaken because it has to be used so frequently; this increasingly alienates the subjects, and since its inherent weakness is exposed no elite had sufficient force to control all or most of the subjects, especially positively to induce them to fulfill their various roles. A measure of voluntarism, of consent, of legitimation by at least the majority of the citizens is vital. Underdeveloped societies, which conduct little business collectively, and whose citizens' awareness of the political processes is often limited, may do with a combination of voodoo and tyranny (as Haiti under Papa Doc and the Dominican Republic under Trujillo have demonstrated). However, modern societies, especially active societies, which require a high degree of collective activity and citizens' involvement, need legitimation as badly as they need electricity. It is widely agreed, even by the super-optimists of modernity, that a polity cannot draw forever on the stock of legitimacy provided by its founders. Without renewal of the investments — without the continuous investiture of power through legitimation — the depletions lead inevitably to loss of the inheritance.

While public feelings about the main branches of the polity — the Supreme Court, Congress and the President — rise and fall from year to year, even with daily events, there is a persistent pattern. The majority of Americans view all three as ineffectual, at best, grading them unenthusiastically as "fair." Thus, for instance, a 1968 national poll by Gallup found that little more than a quarter of Americans (28%) considered the Supreme Court to be doing a good job; a meager 8% graded it "excellent," while over half the nation (53%) rated its performance as "fair" or "poor." More generally, "Only 23% of the adult population think that the system of justice in America is working well today, compared with 46 percent who say they would have given it high marks five years ago" (18). The positive rating of Congress, given by two-thirds in 1965 (64%), declined year after year until it reached a low 26% in 1971 (19). By 1972, a majority (52%) of pre-election representative voters agreed that they "do not trust people in power" as much as they used to (20).

Distrust of the President is high. Two-thirds of the public believed LBJ was not telling them the truth about the Vietnam War (65%, Gallup, February, 1967). About the same level of distrust continued in the Nixon era: Asked if Nixon was "frank and straightforward" about Laos, Cambodia and

Vietnam, those who distrusted him have varied from 45% to 50% and those who trusted him from 33% to 43%, in several polls taken in 1971. At no point did the majority mark the President as creditable. In 1971, 51% agreed with a more general and stronger statement: "People are not told the real truth" (21). Even before publication of the Pentagon Papers, the term "credibility gap" was widely applied — at least since the Eisenhower era. Richard Harris, writing in the *New Yorker,* put it:

While the American political system is variously attacked and defended within the United States today, there seems to be increasing agreement on one point; those who run the nation are not to be trusted. That point is critical, for, in order to survive, democracy must have the trust of the governed; without trust there can be no consent, and without consent there can be no democracy (22).

Distrust of President Nixon increased during the course of investigation of the Watergate bugging affair. Asked to rate the President on "inspiring confidence personally" the public moved from 48% positive in February to 33% positive in April (23). His overall rating fell from 60 percent positive in February to 50 positive in April (24). Asked specifically whether the White House was frank and honest regarding the Watergate affair, 63% felt that the White House was not (25).

When a national sample of white middle class Americans, considered the nation's mainstay, was asked about the government in general, "only 24% of the sampling said the government was doing a 'good' or 'excellent' job of dealing with the nation's problems, two-thirds said 'fair' or 'poor'!" (26). Asked how the leadership in various nongovernmental areas now compares with the past, the public replied affirmatively as far as medicine, science, and business were concerned (all rated "better" by no less than 64 percent), but the federal government and politics scored, respectively, a very low 19 percent and 13 percent.

Americans show very little confidence in the capacity of their government to provide them with even the most basic personal security. The percentage of those worried about safety on the streets ("more than last year") has risen from 49% to 53% in five years (1966-1971), (64% of American women feel less safe in the streets than a year ago[27]), and those who personally fear racial violence, in the same period, from 43% to 52%. While 99% of the Americans felt that "a decline in violence in the U.S." would be desirable, only 33% felt that the decline would come in their lifetime, and 57% felt there would be no decline (28). By early 1973, big city residents said crime was the worst problem in their city, followed by traffic and drug abuse (29). If one takes into account that a proportion of the population still lives in small towns and areas without minorities, obviously the overwhelming majority in the relevant areas feel personally threatened.

Elections are the corrective American democracy offers the public to express its discontent. They are meant to grant legitimation to the course of the society ("this is what the people wanted") and to provide new alternatives, a ready-made, "institutionalized," nonviolent way to enter the system. However, the candidates among whom the public must choose are selected with little public participation. This is especially true in national elections with two major party candidates to choose between. The question, hence, is to what extent do the citizens feel that the people they would like to vote for are before them, to choose from. While it is impossible to run all those who are wanted by someone, the higher the proportion of the public whose preferences are excluded, the more alienating are the elections. In September, 1968, pollster Harris asked a national sample of Americans: "Suppose instead of voting in the election, you yourself could pick anyone who is living and has been active in politics, to be President of the United States. Who would you pick from this list?" Only 21 percent opted for Nixon, and only 9 percent wanted Humphrey. Many of the few who named LBJ (6 percent) or Romney (3 percent) may not have felt too cheated by being restricted to a choice between Nixon and Humphrey. However, those who asked for Nelson Rockefeller (12 percent), Eugene McCarthy (7 percent) or John Lindsay (4 percent) and those who named Edward Kennedy (18 percent) — all these no doubt felt that their kind of man never had a fair chance. This would hold even more for the 13 percent who named George Wallace, because of the obvious hurdles faced by third-party candidates.

The 1972 election results are interpreted by many as an indication of the stability of the American establishment and of the limited appeal of demands for radical change. And yet, as I see it, the election results do not reflect the feelings of the country. Why? First, many of the alienated did not vote at all. Actually, the count of those who did not vote in the 1972 election is bigger than that of those who voted for the Democratic candidate. It might hence be stated that McGovern came in, not second, but third. The reason public-opinion polls, which gained so much attention before the election, do not reflect this large segment of Americans, is that they cover only those they define as "likely voters."

While it is true that some of the nonvoters absented themselves for reasons other than resentment, it is also true that some of the resentfuls did vote, and, thus, these two "inaccuracies" in our generalization tend to cancel each other out. Moreover, even if people did not vote for other reasons, e.g., because they did not register, this often reflects at least a degree of apathy even if not active alienation.

In addition, McGovern failed not so much because there was no alienated majority but because he did not succeed in capturing the divergent alienated groups. Unlike the populism of Bobby Kennedy, who seems to have mobilized (for a while) the left-liberals, part of the Wallace potential from the middle classes, and many of the disaffected working class, the McGovern brand appealed mainly to the left-liberal wing.

Finally, and most significant, being even more opposed to McGovern's alleged radicalism than to the system, many of the center and conservative alienated who did vote, voted for Nixon as the lesser of the two evils. This group represented the majority of those who feel ignored, unrepresented, disaffected.

The two political parties constitute the main channel of political expression. Yet there has been a steady erosion in the proportion of Americans who are willing to classify themselves as belonging to either, and a steady increase in those who defined themselves as independent. In 1960 the parties still polled 77%; in 1971 the proportion had declined to 60%, with the percentage of independents rising from 23% to 31% (30).

At the same time, there has been a rise in reports of extra-institutional expressions of protest (see Table I).

The statement "campaigns are so expensive these days that only a rich man can afford to run for office," agreed with by 81% of the public(31), most of whom are not rich, is another indication of the sense of unrepresentation.

Nor does the American public show great confidence in the working of other civic or commercial institutions. Asked over the last 12 years to rate the "job" done by local government, schools, and newspapers, less than half the respondees thought they did a good or excellent job, and in all three categories the favorable responses declined substantially during this period (32). In another poll, a clear majority (59%) saw the quality of products as declining, probably more a sign of rising disaffection and critical orientation than of a change in the goods themselves, a mood also reflected in that about the same proportion (58%) considered that "business has become too big to take a real interest in its customers" (33). Moreover, confidence in the leaders of financial institutions has fallen from 67% in 1966 to 39% in 1972 (34). In late 1972, Harris noted a general public skepticism toward leaders of most public and private institutions. Thus while in 1966, 61% had "a great deal of confidence" in educators, this figure dropped to 37% in 1971 and 33% in 1972. As for medical personnel, only 48% felt full confidence in 1972 as opposed to more than half the public in 1971 (35).

TABLE I
Annual Totals of Indicators of U.S. Domestic Turmoil
January 1961 July 1968*

	1961	1962	1963	1964	1965	1966	1967	1968
Indicators of domestic turmoil:								
Antiwar protests					57	53	58	17
Participants in antiwar protest (000)					222	137	385	329
Urban riots/clashes				16	23	53	82	65
Participants in civil rights demonstrations (000)					117	51	37	42
Labor strikes (00)	34	36	34	37	39	44	45	26
Violent Crime (000)	1926	2048	2259	2604	2780	3243	3802	

*Raymond Tanter, "International War and Domestic Turmoil: Some Contemporary Evidence," in Hugh Davis Graham and Ted Robert Gurr (eds.), *Violence in America*. Historical and Comparative Perspective, A Report To The National Commission On The Causes And Prevention Of Violence, June 1969, Signet Books, New York, 1969. (This table is a modification of a fuller table appearing on p. 526 of the volume cited.)

More generally, Americans are pessimistic about the state of the nation. A general sense of where the public at large is at is revealed in that two-thirds of the American people were reported, in 1971, to believe that the country had lost its proper sense of direction(36). Less than one-fourth said "things in this country are generally going in the right direction today" (13% had no opinion). A similar finding was reported by Potomac Associates. They found that in 1971 about half the people (47%) were pessimistic about the nation's future and believed there could be "a real breakdown in this country" (37).

People are not just bitching; in unprecedented numbers, they are considering the ultimate out — to cut out and quit. In 1971, 12% (about the equivalent of 16 million adults) told Gallup they would like to move abroad (38), twice as many as were so inclined in 1959, and three times more than the number who were, psychologically speaking, ready to pack soon after World War II. An even grimmer statistic, which must be viewed with great caution because of the difficulties in gaining and interpreting reliable data, is that suicides among young Americans are reported on the rise, reaching the level of 4,000 verified suicides a year in age group 15-19 by 1971 (39).

Yet at the same time people seem highly satisfied as to their personal status. Thus, Gallup found in 1971 that four out of five Americans (81%) were satisfied with their jobs, 6 out of 10 with their incomes (62%) and with educational opportunities for their children (63%) (40). Fewer but still a clear majority (56%) were satisfied as to their personal and their family's future. While in all these matters Americans have grown less satisfied since 1963 (although more satisfied as compared to postwar scores), the striking point is that large majorities are quite satisfied in personal terms. David C. Anderson of the *Wall Street Journal* staff, commenting on feeling personal satisfaction along with a sense of social malaise, observed that while people find themselves "more opulent than they had ever expected," they also realize that personal well-being does not solve everything and can bring on new problems. "People are reexamining old ideas of progress and trying to formulate new ones." The same conclusion was reached by a group of survey researchers: ". . . the major concern of Americans is not with their own well-being or their personal financial prospects. It is rather with the environment in which they live" (41). This news has not reached the *U.S. News and World Report*, which published a typical gee-whiz book about the U.S.A., full of quantitative statistics on the flow of material goods into private hands (42).

Haynes Johnson, who traveled across the U.S.A. for six months for the *Washington Post*, deserves to be quoted at length because he seems to me to have captured best "qualitatively" what the statistics of polls reflect:

Everywhere there is evidence that America is in the midst of a kind of revolution it has not experienced before. Not over labor and capital, not over race, not over political theories or forms, not over ideologies, but over personal attitudes and values. Never, in nearly a decade of extensive travels throughout the nation, have I encountered so many people asking so many serious, intensely personal and searching questions — about their jobs, their wives or husbands, their children, their country, their aspirations, their future.

Americans have changed. They have re-examined some of their most deeply held values — about the worth of their material comforts, their desire for their children to "succeed" or even automatically go to college, their old vision of the good life in the city or suburbs, their supreme confidence in their country's inevitable rightness — and rejected many of them.

"I want a life that is whole rather than chopped up," said a teacher, explaining why she had left the city for a new life in a rural New England town. Out on the West Coast, a middle-aged professional man who was also starting over again put it differently: "I think people are missing the point because they confuse money with real wealth. They spend a lifetime working for a future that never comes (43).

Johnson adds:

Modern myth-making aside, it isn't only young Americans who are raising those kinds of questions about their society. In fact, the most noticeable change in attitudes is taking place among parents — and from whatever stereotyped group you might choose: hard-hats, Middle Americans, silent majority or what have you. They, too, are wrestling with new questions about American life (44).

The Potomac study, cited above, shows that Americans express less concern with material elements than they did five or ten years ago, as if they felt that this kernel of the American has been or is being taken care of. It is here that the rustic wing of the counter-culture has caught the essence and yet missed a vital point. True, beyond doubt, that the citizenry at large is increasingly concerned with quality and not just quantity, with the human and environmental cost of progress rather than merely the statistics of GNP, with public goods (education, health, safety) and not just personal materialism. There is a genuine and widespread yearning for a quality of life. However — and this is the point missed by the counter-culture — not at the cost of returning to the poverty, the short lifespan, the illness-infested life of pre-modernity. What the overwhelming majority yearns to achieve is a life of more freedom, less alienating work, more cultivation, beauty, "quality," sensitivity to others and openness to self, on top of and not instead of the material comforts (though not necessarily all the gadgets) and high standards of health that modernity acquired.

MORE AND BETTER OF THE SAME?

Does this not fall right in with the technetronic prophets? Would not the ultra-modern society, equipped with an ever-larger GNP, be able to pay for all the newly desired public goods, from depollution to preventive health care — on top of affluent consumption? Could it not — equipped with better planning, higher coordination, more knowledge — offer to the individual a greater variety of jobs, and after hours a greater flexibility and more leisure, as work of the routine kind is increasingly automated? No doubt more can and will be achieved by greater cybernation, by more and wider use of applied science, administration, computers. The sense of imbalance due to rampant consumerism (twenty-nine kinds of soft drinks, eighty-eight kinds of lipstick in every suburban supermarket) and meager public services — Galbraith's well-known lament — can be in fact corrected, and the sense of an *incompetent* government and hence nation possibly reduced.

But several key ingredients will be missed. Without a clear view of the priorities in ordering public goods, without a clear understanding of the constraints involved, and without an overriding perspective, the demand will be as ceilingless as it is in private consumption. There is absolutely no reason to believe that given more and more products — a summer house, three color TV sets, a 36-foot boat — the person becomes truly sated. He may grow jaded, even increase his interest in non-consumeristic goods (e.g., free time), but still not feel deeply satisfied. Similarly, America is now experiencing a revolution of rising aspirations in demand for public goods, which knows no acceptable definition of a ceiling. Thus, for instance, in health services the quest is to provide each citizen with the same services now provided by a few elite hospitals in major urban centers (Massachusetts General, Presbyterian) to their rich clientele. However, this kind of service is so demanding, not so much in cost as in numbers of talented physicians, that it is not possible to provide it to 200 million Americans. Even if we should assign to this field all of the resources it could use, there still would be significant differences in talent among the million or so physicians we would need, to offer every American top quality service. This is not an argument against social justice in medicine. We could, at least theoretically, share equally all we have or will have (although this would require forcing top professionals to move out of the preferred urban centers to the South, Southwest, and Midwest, and other less blessed parts of the country). But the share each would get would be substantially lower than the rich are now getting. More or less the same holds for the quality of other services, e.g., education, but it will not all be the same as that given by Bronx High School of Science or Harvard College, which is precisely what is called for now (45).

We must remember, too, that the leaders and members of the counter-culture come chiefly from those sons and daughters of the upper middle class who have grown up in the most affluent and thus educationally, medically,

etc. best served sector of the country. Their example hardly reassures us that the ultra-modern society — merely spitting out more goods and services — will be any more loved than its modern predecessor.

We need, then, both in private and in public goods consumption, a new world-view which puts ceilings on aspirations and redefines levels of satisfaction. Social justice provides one such definition. It says, in effect, "O.K., I'll settle for less as long as I get the same share as everybody else," or, "as long as everybody else gets the same share I have." Alternatively, increased interest in interpersonal, community, cultural, or spiritual matters could reduce the saliency of private and public goods consumerism, especially among those who materially are quite well off, releasing all or most of new resources to serve those lacking now. Otherwise, this act in itself would prove to be so alienating to the affluent majority that it would be politically impractical, or would require, to make it politically practicable, giving some to all; the latter would be intolerably expensive, especially in regard to scarce resources. To put it succinctly, if the affluent classes would go to Zen Buddhism, the rest would be easy. However, citizens' involvement in such a new "enough-is-enough" world-view cannot be engineered. To some degree it will grow out of the spreading and rising "counter-culture" as it gains in followership. (We do not expect millions to drop out and turn on, but to accept, in a moderated way, many of the core values of the counter-culture; aspire for less, accept their given world more, consume less, enjoy more the beauty of the mountains, the peace of the soul.) Overall, it can be achieved only through authentic participation of the citizen in the setting of goals.

Participation, both in various levels of government and in the management of work, housing, health clinics, schools, and other so-called "private governments," is the only way to drive home to the citizens, once the initial dogmatic belief and political passivity have been overcome, that one must set ceilings to goals, square them with each other, and face environmental constraints. All these are limitations which those in positions of decision-making face, and which typically uninvolved citizens — and the "irresponsible" utopian thinkers — tend to ignore. It is no wonder the citizens would ask for stable prices, full employment, rapid economic growth, lower taxes, more government services, rapid depollution, high public safety, elimination of poverty, and then some, here and now, inasmuch as they have never experienced the limitations posed by limited resources, insufficient knowledge, lack of consensus, and so on. They have not been sufficiently involved to understand that these are not fully compatible demands. The elites do not wish to involve the citizens, but not because they believe them incapable of absorbing the necessary information or reaching sensible judgments. The chief reason is that in the process the citizens would discover that the system is tilted against them and in favor of the elites. Hence, opening up to citizens participation in their government involves "de-elitization," another value which the ultra-modern society does not offer; yet society would be advanced by authentic participation of the citizens in the rearrangement of their lives.

The term *consensus* has acquired the status of a dirty word ever since President Johnson said, " 'Come, let us reason together' [but meant that] he was merely giving everyone a chance to agree with him" (46). Consensus is nevertheless a major prerequisite for effective public policy, especially so in a society that is highly coordinated and carries a large volume of public activities. It is not just that it is almost impossible to make stick a policy most citizens reject—*vide* Prohibition (and there are serious limitations to the extent consent can be manipulated)— but that policy is by definition unable to satisfy the citizens when there are serious differences among major groups of them as to what the desired direction is. Thus, for instance, if 50 million Americans favor spending $20 billion on space exploration and another 40 million favor spending the $20 billion on restoring the environment on earth, not only is neither policy likely to be enacted but it will not be pleasing if it is — or is not. One main reason desegregation proceeded so slowly is that major segments of the public in both North and South never consented to its implementation. Consensus is never unanimous, but measures which are endorsed by 3 out of 4 Americans have a much greater chance of being effected than do those endorsed by 5 out of 9. Measures put on the books to placate a vocal minority (or a weakly committed majority) are later not implemented by adequate legal teeth (e.g., automobile safety acts) or funding (most new domestic programs were initiated under the Kennedy and Johnson administrations; Nixon has not initiated any). The consensus of a large majority, strongly committed, kept alive and well, will expand such programs as social security (favored by about 90%) and government support for low-income housing (favored: 70% [*Fortune,* September, 1948]; 75% [1964]).

Will those 38% of Americans unhappy about their incomes and those 37% worried about the educational opportunities of their children be pacified if given a chance to "participate?" Or more generally, is participation not a luxury of the rich, whereas the rest need more income, education, etc.? As I see it, participation is the chief way they will get their just share of that which is to be had. The rich may be able to rely on their extra resources for gaining control of the state or the economy, but most people must draw on their political participation, first to transform the system toward equality, then to keep it responsive to their changing needs. Not participation as a substitute for resources, but the gaining of political resources via participation. Social justice will be achieved in no other way; it will not be handed down.

Agreement among the citizenry can be marshalled only in an open give-and-take between them, which only participation offers. True, increased and broadened participation may bring out — at least initially — even greater conflict; but out of this the citizens may come to see why their community or nation is not moving, at least understand their deadlock, and thus will be moved to draw closer together. In any case, the sense of incompetence and of being shut out will be reduced. A significant segment of our overdue business is, to begin with, largely a matter of public consensus — and little else needs to be done than for the public to have a deeper and more encompassing understanding. Computers, administrators, and applied scientists will not help in those problem areas where all that is required is for the public to be more tolerant, at least to the point of removing the state's power of intervention; e.g., as in proscription of certain sex acts between consenting adults or penalizing use of arbitrarily selected stimulants and drugs. Moreover, greater tolerance of each other's morality, sexual mores, and lifestyles, as well as ethnic differences may well be the major step needed to remove irrational (as distinct from "interest") opposition to the transforming forces. The conservative majority is not pleased by anything the transforming minorities do, nor does it grant any moral, specifically sexual, latitude. A sense of moral discomfort seems prevalent: 78% of Americans sampled stated that they felt life in the U.S. was getting worse in terms of morals; only 8% felt that it was getting better (47); 86% of middle-class Americans sampled said sexual permissiveness was undermining the nation's morals (48). This is accompanied by a sharp increase in the sense that religion is losing its influence on American life. In the fifties there was a sense of religious revival; in 1957, 69% reported increased influence, 14% a declining one (49). By 1970 the figures reversed themselves sharply: according to Gallup, 75% saw a waning influence, and only 14% an increase. An unusually large majority felt the country was coming apart due to the sexual amorality of the younger generation — especially the "hippies." One could argue that sexual freedom is just picked upon as a convenient symbol for resentment by the elders, who resent the have-fun, hell-why-work nowness of the young, as well as their radical political ideas. Nonetheless, nothing seems to raise as much heat as sex; in race relations the ultimate challenge seems not to lose your job/house/school to a "nigger" — else he'll marry your daughter or prove more potent to your wife. In the attitudes toward the radical, nothing seems as provocative as sexualism. One must hence also assume that if the harmlessness of sexual variety and freedom from taboos would only be understood, the heat of the opposition to the transforming message would be cooled down to a point such that at least most of the conservative citizens could bear, if not condone it.

A major source of the crisis is the sense of being shut out, governed by forces one neither understands nor controls, being assigned and manipulated, powerless and unheeded. Harris uses a set of various questions to measure the sense of alienation. More than six out of ten Americans sampled (62%) felt that the United States is a country in which "the rich get richer and the poor get poorer." Close to half (44%) felt that "what I think doesn't count very much," and about the same proportion (41%) felt that "people running the country don't care what happens to people like me." Fewer (33%) felt that "people with power are out to take advantage of you" (which may be more a sign of lack of paranoia than lack of alienation), and even fewer (20%) said, "I feel left out of things around me," which, since it refers to the immediate environment, may be more a sign of social participation than of lack of alienation (50).

No super computer, power of applied science, or efficient bureaucracy will eradicate this feeling; on the contrary, it is their frequent lapses that now allow for some humanization: the first offender finds his way back into society because his file is not forwarded and he gets the job; homosexuals are able to meet in a gay bar; lack of official planning allows for individual plans. The more efficient the controls, the greater probably will be the sense of alienation.

Participation will foster a sense of belonging, public attention and competence. It can be a major source of personal satisfaction, excitement, fulfillment, of precisely the kind that materialism is lacking and profit-making is losing. Participation provides the individual with an opportunity to feel relevant, socially effective, involved, and to integrate one's fragmented world. For the society, it provides a legitimate and constructive release for energies otherwise explosively bottled up and a source of the resources needed to fuel mass systems, which require a volunteer staff and "watchdogs" — from "Pals" for youngsters without effective parents to monitors at election time. None of this will be achieved by elites dealing with each other.

FOOTNOTES AND REFERENCES

1. Zbigniew Brzezinski, BETWEEN TWO AGES: AMERICA'S ROLE IN THE TECHNETRONIC ERA. New York: Viking Press, 1970.

2. THE NEW REPUBLIC. October 19, 1968.

3. THE NATION. July 22, 1968.

4. Gallup, SAN FRANCISCO CHRONICLE. September 29, 1971; Harris August 30, 1971, NEW YORK POST.

5. NEWSWEEK. June 30, 1969. A later poll shows higher proportions so inclined. TIME, April 6, 1970.

6. "Summer Urban Violence Strikes Fears of Terrorism," NEW YORK TIMES. September 31, 1971.

7. Questionnaire administered in 1969 by the University of Michigan's Institute for Social Research; reported in the NEW YORK TIMES, May 26, 1971. Sample equals 1,374 men between the ages of 16 and 54 who "represent all races, regions, economic and social classes."

8. Roper, SAN FRANCISCO CHRONICLE. September 28, 1971.

9. The fact that these statements can be favored also on the basis of other values, e.g., the traditional liberal, does not resolve alienation when one is aware that the demands are not realized.

10. Harris, NEW YORK POST. May 20, 1971.

11. See Andrew M. Greenley, WHY CAN'T THEY BE LIKE US? New York: Dutton, 1971.

12. Louis Harris, "Harris Poll: Unity on Goals," NEW YORK POST. December 26, 1972.

13. Louis Harris, "Nixon Changes Approved; Poll," NEW YORK POST. October 30, 1972.

14. NEWSWEEK. October 6, 1969.

15. Only 3% and 5% respectively would cut back.

16. NEW YORK TIMES. September 5, 1971.

17. TIME. August 9, 1971.

18. NEWSWEEK. March 8, 1971, p. 39.

19. Harris, March 1, 1971.

20. TIME. August 28, 1972, p. 15.

21. Harris, March 11, 1971.

22. "Annals of Politics: A Fundamental Hoax." Vol. 47, August 7, 1971, p. 37.

23. Louis Harris, "Harris: 63% Find Nixon Evasive on Watergate," NEW YORK POST. April 28, 1973.

24. Ibid.

25. Ibid.

26. Gallup in NEWSWEEK. October 6, 1969, p. 47.

27. Louis Harris, THE 1972 VIRGINIA SLIMS AMERICAN WOMEN'S OPINION POLL. N.Y. Ruder Finn Inc., 1972.

28. Louis Harris, "Harris Poll: Unity on Goals," NEW YORK POST. December 26, 1972.

29. "Poll Finds Crime Exceeds Reports," NEW YORK TIMES. January 14, 1973.

30. Gallup, October 10, 1971, NEW YORK TIMES.

31. Harris, November 5, 1970.

32. Roper Report, p. 11. Omitted is the response on TV, which remained unchanged.

33. Harris, February 14, 1970.

34. Robert Metz, "Market Place," NEW YORK TIMES. March 23, 1973.

35. "Public's Confidence in Education Drops," THE CHRONICLE OF HIGHER EDUCATION, Vol. 7, no. 11, December 4, 1972.

36. Roper, July 9, 1971.

37. The polling for Potomac Associates was carried out by Lloyd Free using Gallup Facilities.

38. Finding reported in the NEW YORK TIMES, September 26, 1971.

39. Dr. Matthew Ross, Harvard University Medical School, quoted in the WASHINGTON POST, August 15, 1971.

40. White Americans only. SAN FRANCISCO CHRONICLE, September 29, 1971. Data are not given for years between 1949 and 1963. Since 1963 there have been numerous annual variations.

41. George Katona, Burkhard Strumpel, Ernest Zahn, ASPIRATIONS AND DIFFERENCE. New York: McGraw-Hill, 1971, p. 142.

42. GOOD THINGS ABOUT THE U.S. TODAY. New York, Collier-Macmillan, 1970.

43. "The Revolution in American Values," WASHINGTON POST, July 4, 1971.

44. For additional reports see Haynes Johnson, WASHINGTON POST, May 30, 1971, and Bill Moyers' insightful book, LISTENING TO AMERICA.

45. One must note also that the services compete with each other for talented manpower and resources; while we might be able to jack up any one of them relatively quickly, education *and* health *and* depollution *and* anti-poverty measures cannot be so easily elevated. The U.S.S.R., for instance, still limits quality education to 2% of its students.

46. Roger Bediner, "Passionately Moderate," NEW YORK TIMES, October 11, 1971.

47. Gallup, September, 1968.

48. NEWSWEEK, October 6, 1969, p. 47.

49. Moore Indicators, p. 389.

50. Morris, July 1, 1971.

BEYOND THE DISCIPLINE PROBLEM: YOUTH SUICIDE AS A MEASURE OF ALIENATION

Edward A. Wynne

There is a widespread public perception that ''discipline'' is the major problem facing modern education. It has been so listed in eight of the nine annual Gallup Polls of public attitudes toward the schools taken between 1969 and 1977. However, the professional literature on education does not fairly reflect this fact. Discipline is not ignored as a topic, but it is apparently not a matter of high concern.

Ironically, there is a great deal of scientific data that amply support the public's view of the primacy of discipline — or lack of it — as a problem. True, these data do not deal directly with trends in school conduct while in school. They do, however, reveal a number of long-range trends toward increasing disorder, anger, and despair among American adolescents. Essentially, these data reveal certain adolescent conduct and attitudes that can be characterized as symptomatic of increasing youth alienation. While not all of this alienation is reflected in acts of ''indiscipline,'' it is understandable that laypersons should use the nontechnical term ''discipline'' to articulate their sense that something is profoundly wrong with many children and adolescents.

The data not only portray increased alienation, they also raise important questions about the continuing vitality of American society. After all, that vitality ultimately depends upon the ability of adult-operated institutions such as schools to rear children and adolescents to become effective and competent adults. The data suggest that the proportion of youths maturing into such competence may be steadily declining.

This article will present relevant data about contemporary youth alienation and offer an interpretation and prescription. Unfortunately, data showing trends cannot always be current. The basic facts are collected through elaborate counting systems, and there is necessarily a time lag in reporting and publication. Still, in view of the long-term, incremental patterns disclosed, one would have to be extremely optimistic to suppose that up-to-date data would reveal dramatic reversals. At the conclusion of my report, three prominent persons from different fields offer responses and proposals.

103

DATA ABOUT YOUTH CONDUCT

Between 1950 and 1975 the annual suicide rate of white youths between the ages of 15 and 19 increased 171%, from 2.8 deaths for each 100,000 to 7.6 (1). No other age group had so high a rate of increase. During these same years the overall white suicide rate increased by only 18%. (See Figure 1.) As the graph demonstrates, the increase in adolescent suicides was relatively steady and incremental. The gradualness of the increase suggests that it was not directly related to the major political and social upheavals of the period. For instance, the rate of climb during the allegedly quiescent late 1950s was about the same as the rate of climb during the turbulent late 1960s.

FIGURE 1

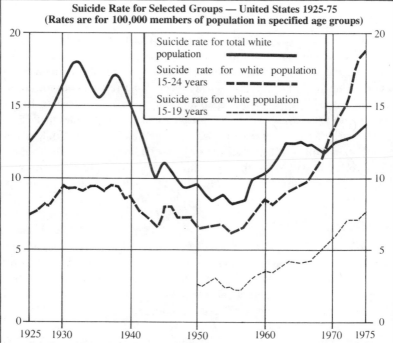

Suicide Rate for Selected Groups — United States 1925-75
(Rates are for 100,000 members of population in specified age groups)

Suicide rate for total white population

Suicide rate for white population 15-24 years

Suicide rate for white population 15-19 years

In order to portray long-range trends, the above chart displays national suicide rates for three age groups: 1) the total white population, 2) white males aged 15 to 24, and 3) white males aged 15 to 19. Suicide data are not conveniently available for the 15 to 19 age group before 1950, hence the rate for that group has only been graphed for 25 years. Note that increases in rates for the 15 to 19 age group have been an important element in the dramatic upward shift in the long-term pattern of suicide rates for the 15 to 24 age group.

Sources: Department of Health, Education, and Welfare, Public Health Service, National Center for Health Statistics

Suicide statistics are a reliable measure of comparative changes in the suicide rate. The tabulations reflect the judgments of thousands of local health officers and coroners as to cause of death. Sometimes these individual judgments are incorrect. However, there is no reason to believe that the basic random pattern of "incorrectness" that prevailed years ago is not still in operation today.

The absolute number of youths involved in the increase is, fortunately, comparatively small. We have perhaps 3,000 to 4,000 reported suicides a year among whites aged 15 to 19. This is a minute fraction of our youth population. But the "problem" has immense symbolic and indicative significance. For each identified adolescent suicide, we undoubtedly have other suicides not identified as such, attempted suicides that are not tabulated, and youths who suffer from serious anxiety or depression but do not attempt suicide. Hence the 171% increase represents a concurrent 171% increase in general depression among our young people. This increase has occurred at a time when naive observers would infer that American youth, especially those from white families, "never had it so good."

There have also been increases in the rate of death by homicide among white males aged 15 to 19. In 1959 the rate was 2.3 such deaths per 100,000 members of the group. That rate steadily increased, so that by 1969 it was 4.9; by 1975 it was 8.2 (2). This represents a greater than 200% increase over 26 years. During the same period no other age group had a comparable increase in its homicide rate. The highest previous homicide rate for white males aged 15 to 19 during the twentieth century was 5.2 in 1919. (Incidentally, the rate for black males in the same age group started from a much higher base, and it also has been rising; but between 1969 and 1975 the black rate began to decline. In 1975 it was 47.8. In general, the black suicide rate is lower than the white rate.)

Like the suicide rate, the homicide death rate probably measures other events, albeit indirectly — e.g., woundings, beatings, threats, and the stimulation of profound fear. There is every reason to believe that such increased crimes against the young have generally been committed by their peers, i.e., other white male adolescents.

There is evidence of increased drug use by the young. In 1971, 30% of all college students surveyed in a national sample reported having used marijuana within 30 days of the survey; in 1970, 28% of a similar sample reported such use. And this use and experimentation sometimes include other, more powerful drugs. Seven percent of the respondents in the 1971 sample reported having used cocaine (3). Again, two successive surveys of national samples of "youths" (no ages were given in the report) conducted in 1972 and 1974 asked respondents about their use of five illegal drugs. The 1974 respondents reported higher levels of usage for all five drugs than did the 1972 respondents (4). A 1975 report of the National Institute on Drug Abuse also concluded that "there is no indication of any recent decline in the annual prevalence of any drug, with the possible exception of psychedelics" (5).

We do not have statistics about the national level of youth drug use before the late 1960s. Thus the issue of long-term trends in drug use is complicated. However, we do have some trend statistics from the late 1960s onward. The most thorough statistics cover San Mateo County (California) students for every year from 1968 to 1976 (6). San Mateo is an affluent suburban county. It is recognized as having relatively intense drug use and is, therefore, not typical. Still, there is evidence that trends originating in California tend to spread. For example, the 1968 San Mateo levels represent current rates of adolescent marijuana use in many communities. The statistics thus provide a potential forecasting indicator. The San Mateo statistics on marijuana use among certain high school grades are set out in Figure 2.

These statistics reveal a stabilization of use at a comparatively high level of intensity. Other tabulated San Mateo data reveal steady increases in student use of a variety of drugs. Nationally, it is also significant to recall that arrests of males under age 18 for narcotics law violations increased 1,288% between 1960 and 1972 (7).

FIGURE 2

Percentage of Marijuana Use Among Male San Mateo County, California, High School Students for the Period 1968 to 1976.

Year	One or more uses in past year		Ten or more uses in past year		Fifty or more uses in past year	
	Grade 9	Grade 12	Grade 9	Grade 12	Grade 9	Grade 12
1968	27	45	14	26	na	na
1969	35	50	20	34	na	na
1970	34	51	20	34	11	22
1971	44	59	26	43	17	32
1972	44	61	27	45	16	32
1973	51	61	32	45	20	32
1974	49	62	30	47	20	34
1975	49	64	30	45	20	31
1976	48	61	27	42	17	30

Source: San Mateo County, Department of Public Health and Welfare, *Summary Report, 1976, Surveys of Student Drug Use* (San Mateo, Calif.: Department of Public Health, 1976).

There are also statistics on increased use of alcohol by youths. The San Mateo survey reported that the percentage of seventh-grade boys who had begun drinking during the previous year increased from 52% in 1969 to 72% in 1973. This increase is consistent with equivalent increases reported in other surveys in Duval County, Florida, and Toronto, Ontario. And this adolescent drinking is not simply tasting. In 1974, 23% of a national sample of youths between the ages of 13 and 18 reported being drunk four or more times during the past year (8).

The increase in drug and alcohol use is obvious evidence of the growing drive for speedy gratification among the young — and of an effort to avoid or escape the environment around them. Incidentally, since much of that environment consists of their peers, the statistics might also imply that some adolescents are finding each other's company less and less pleasant without the support of drugs or alcohol.

The use of cigarettes has also increased among the young. Typical data disclose that between 1969 and 1975, in a national sample of females aged 13 to 17, the proportion of respondents who smoked a pack or more of cigarettes a day rose from 10% to 39% (9).

Changes in the area of youth sexual relations have been significant. Between 1950 and 1975 the estimated number of illegitimate births for unmarried white females, aged 15 to 19 went from 5.1 per 1,000 to 12.1 (10). Technically, illegitimacy is measured by an entry on a birth certificate — either "married, and to whom" or "unmarried." For many years nearly all births in America have been registered, and the entry "married" goes on the certificate only if the particular married male is designated. Thus the "estimated" statistical shift is an accurate indication that increasing proportions of females are having babies without being married; the statistics represent a change in the conduct of successive groups of young males and females.

This increase in illegitimacy has occurred during a period characterized by increasing availability of contraceptives, abortion, and sexual information. Presumably, the increase means that young males are more willing to get females pregnant, that young females are more willing to risk (and accept) pregnancy, and that both females and males feel less responsible for burdening infants with the handicaps of being born into a one-parent family consisting of a young and vulnerable mother.

Another pertinent sex-related change has been the spread of venereal disease among the young. Between 1956 and 1974, reported cases of gonorrhea (per 100,000 members of the 15 to 19 age group) rose more than 200%, while syphilis increased 100% (11). These increases were associated with an increased availability of medicines, treatment centers, and appropriate preventive information. Obviously, the increases reflect a growth in casual (or promiscuous) sexual relations and in irresponsible attitudes among sex partners who feel little concern for "protecting" one another.

Some national trend statistics are available on delinquency. Between 1957 and 1974 the number of delinquency cases per 1,000 persons aged 10 to 17 disposed of by American juvenile courts rose from 19.1 to 37.5 (12). Throughout the period, the proportion of status offenses (e.g., running away and other noncriminal conduct) to criminal acts (e.g., shoplifting, robbery) added together to calculate total delinquency remained relatively constant. Drug cases were a significant but not central element in the increase. There are also statistics for increased antisocial conduct in schools. One survey reported that, in the national sample of schools studied, assaults on teachers increased 85% between 1970 and 1973. During the same period the number of weapons confiscated from students by authorities in the schools surveyed rose by 54% (13).

We should also consider the student unrest, building takeovers, and other youth disorders of the late 1960s and early 1970s. Occasional student disorder has always been a fact of American history, but the most recent wave involved a higher proportion of youth and took more destructive forms. For example, during 1969 and 1970 more than 8,000 bomb threats, attempted bombings, and bombings were attributed to student unrest (14). In 1970 nine of the top 16 FBI most-wanted persons were youth activists, their crimes including murder, bank robbery, and bombing (15). I shall discuss the significance of this particular form of disorder in more detail later.

I have presented data on a variety of self-destructive and other-destructive acts committed by adolescents from all races and social classes. In any particular year one measure may go up and another down. But if we were able to develop any system of accumulating and weighing these measures, such a system would, I believe, reveal a steady increase in these acts of alienation. And wherever comparable statistics are available, the data reveal that the rate of increase in youth alienation is greater than the rate for adults. Obviously, we must look at these acts cumulatively rather than discretely. We shouldn't make alcohol the issue one year, suicide the next, and so on. A segmented approach robs us of the chance to recognize the more general and shocking totality: Our children and adolescents are increasingly engaged in killing, hurting, and abusing themselves and others.

108

STATISTICS ON CHANGES IN ATTITUDES

Not surprisingly, changes in youth conduct have been accompanied by changes in adolescent attitudes. Some trend data are available. Between 1948 and 1968 successive freshman classes at Haverford College in Philadephia took the Minnesota Multiphasic Personality Inventory (MMPI), a short-answer test that measures attitudes. Figure 3 reports a sample of statistics derived from the student answers. The numbers listed for each item represent the proportion of students who answered "yes." Clearly, these data are not up to date, but they do help us to understand shifts in youth attitudes over a considerable part of the last quarter century and constitute the most complete longitudinal study available. When we consider more recent data later, a consistent relationship between the changes that occurred among the Haverford students and those revealed in current polls will become apparent. Finally, if we are concerned with interpreting the deeper meaning of the campus unrest of the Vietnam war period, the Haverford students represent a classic group of student militants — articulate, upper-middle-class, status-conscious. It is easy to recognize an overall attitudinal trend in their shifting answers. Essentially, the successive classes of students became less sympathetic to cooperative and group activities; more and more, they evinced attitudes consonant with withdrawal from contact or cooperation with others.

This increase in withdrawn attitudes among students was coupled with an apparent simultaneous increase in their self-centeredness. Between 1948 and 1968 the proportion of Haverford students who thought they could work great benefit to the world if given a chance rose from 40% to 66% while the proportion of these 17-year-olds who thought they knew more than experts rose from 20% to 38%. It is not clear how these increasingly withdrawn and introverted students could render such benefit without human interaction or acquire the experiences incident to becoming so knowledgeable (16).

Other statistics about youth attitudinal trends show that the Haverford patterns are representative of trends displayed by successive cohorts of late adolescents on other college campuses. Attitudinal tests were administered to students at Dartmouth College in 1952 and 1968 and at the University of Michigan in 1952 and 1969 (17). Several similar questions were asked of all students queried at both colleges. For example, they were asked whether "Human nature is fundamentally more cooperative." Agreement declined from 66% and 70%, at Dartmouth and Michigan respectively, to 51% and 55%. Another question asked whether "most of what I am learning at college is very worthwhile." Agreement declined from 67% and 74% respectively to 58% and 57%. Again, these students were asked to identify the private and public institutions (e.g., school, church, family) to which they felt related. The number and intensity of summed identifications declined from 296 and 259, respectively, to 269 and 206. In other words, successive groups of students have felt less and less relationship to the world. They have become increasingly *alienated*.

FIGURE 3

**Haverford College, Sample MMPI Items for the
Classes of 1948 through 1968**

Item	Percent "Yes"							
	48-49	52	56	60	61	65	67	68
When I was a child I didn't care to be a member of a crowd or gang	33	35	35	38	49	58	19	47
I could be happy living all alone in a cabin in the woods or mountains	23	28	34	38	33	35	42	45
I am a good mixer	77	49	48	63	60	58	38	43
I like to go to parties and other affairs where there is lots of loud fun	65	56	55	53	44	40	38	40
At parties I am more likely to sit by myself than to join in with the crowd	23	35	40	27	44	38	47	50
My worries seem to disappear when I get into a crowd of lively friends	71	69	73	68	58	65	56	55
If I were in trouble with several friends who were equally to blame, I would rather take the whole blame than to give them away	63	56	50	57	47	43	33	45
When a man is with a woman he is usually thinking about things related to her sex	29	37	15	27	35	28	36	43
I enjoy reading love stories	55	49	35	25	44	30	18	25
I like dramatics	80	74	73	75	60	73	67	65
I would like to be a singer	51	47	37	36	33	38	31	23

We also have the 1969 and 1973 Yankelovich youth surveys (18). Unfortunately, they do not replicate questions asked in the Haverford, Michigan, and Dartmouth studies, nor do they cover precisely equivalent groups of adolescents. Still, I contend that they show a continuation of the trends toward egotism and withdrawal. Among the college students surveyed in Yankelovich's national samples, the importance of "privacy" as a value increased from 61% in 1969 to 71% in 1973. At the same time, the respective importance of "religion" and "patriotism," two values that stress the individual's obligation to extrapersonal concerns, declined from 38% and 35% to 28% and 19%. The two surveys also showed a continuing pattern of gradual dissemination and acceptance of the views of college youths among non-college youths. In general, the views disclosed in the surveys demonstrate an enlargement of expectations about the rights of students and citizens and a lessening of expectations about the responsibilities of these same persons.

It is true that some of the period covered by the Yankelovich surveys encompassed the Watergate episode. Readers may deduce that this sorry national experience was an essential cause of the trend toward withdrawal. This interpretation is significant, because if Watergate was the "cause," and if Watergate was a transitory phenomenon, then we might expect youth attitudes to return to more healthy earlier patterns. However, the more long-range attitude trend statistics already presented suggest that the trend toward withdrawal long antedated Watergate. For example, between 1949 and 1952 the first shifts toward withdrawal were already appearing in the Haverford statistics. And over the next 20 years, as more and more Americans became prosperous, as poverty declined, as the status of blacks generally improved, and as large-scale international war was avoided, those students (plus those at Michigan and Dartmouth) became increasingly alienated.

The preceding data about trends toward increasingly individualistic and withdrawn youth attitudes are also supported by the diverse studies summarized by Dean Hogue in an analysis of the shifting values of college students over the past 50 years. Obviously, many of the measures used by Hogue to describe such trends are relatively imprecise. Still, the cumulative effect of the variety of data he has collected is highly persuasive (19).

Increasingly withdrawn attitudes have appeared among students during an era when the adult society has been dedicating increasing proportions of its economic resources to help the young. Thus, between 1950 and 1972 per-pupil daily expenditures in public schools increased by 170%, measured in constant dollars (to show for inflation), while the national average pupil/teacher ratio (combining both elementary and high schools) declined from 25:1 to 21:1. It would seem that students were given more than ever before but liked their status — and, implicitly, the givers — less.

There are also significant cross-cultural statistics about the attitudes of American children. The statistics were developed in a contemporary international study of youth interaction patterns in six cultures (20). Five of the cultures represented underdeveloped or primitive environments. The sixth group of students were children in a New England community. A common rating scale was used by observers in all locations to evaluate youth conduct on the dimension of altruism versus egotism. A total of 134 children between ages 3 and 6 and between ages 7 and 11 were observed in the entire study.

Approximately 9,500 interacts were identified. When the median level of altruistic conduct was treated as 50%, the American children, with a level of 8%, scored as the most egotistic. The next lowest group was a tribe in India, with a level of 25%. The number of children involved was small. Still, the dramatically high level of egotism among the American children, compared with that of children in non-Western cultures, suggests that the data may justify comparative generalizations about the overall level of egotistic conduct among American youths or youths from industrial societies.

WHAT THE CHANGES MEAN

The preceding statistics invite analysis. But the analysis must be put in an appropriate framework. The statistics do not tell how any particular youth will act, since the proportions of youths afflicted with dramatic forms of character deterioration — suicide, violent crimes, alcoholism — are fortunately small. In general, the statistics are not decomposed into socioeconomic classes, although some of the changes (e.g., student unrest, drug use, evidence of withdrawn attitudes) are clearly common among upper-middle-class youths. Despite the rather dramatic nature of some of the conduct trends disclosed, relatively little longitudinal research is available concerning the socioeconomic status of the youths involved in certain acts (e.g., suicide) 10 and 20 years ago in comparison with the status of the youths involved at present. Still, the statistics that are available provide an important albeit imperfect tool for forecasting general trends affecting youths and younger adults and for interpreting significant elements of youth conduct.

The rising suicide rate, in particular, while it directly involves a small number of youths, may provide a vital clue to the possible causes of the spread of alienation. During the late nineteenth century the French sociologist Emile Durkheim identified that rate as an important index of social cohesion and vitality (21). He discovered that in European societies suicide was more prevalent among Protestants than among Catholics, urbanites than rural persons, the affluent than the middle and lower-middle classes, unmarried adults and childless married adults than married adults with children, males than females, and persons in the liberal professions than laborers and tradesmen. In other words, people were shielded from suicidal impulses because of the communal intensity of their religion, the stability of their life patterns, the predictability of their aspirations, the intensity and complexity of their social commitments, the focus of their responsibilities, and the tangibility of their work products. All of these shields were forces that placed human beings in complex but predictable patterns of human relations that moved toward identifiable goals.

Suicide is not so much the outcome of "pressure," but *pressure without social support*. Suicide does not automatically mean that a person has not been loved or cared for. It probably does mean that he was not needed by others in an immediate, tangible fashion. "Needed" should be understood in the sense we imply when we say we need the first-string member of an athletic team, the paper delivery boy, the only secretary in a small office, or the only wage earner in a family. The person needed must be obviously relied upon by others, and his absence should create a disruptive and foreseeable gap. In this light, it is understandable that one of the highest suicide rates is that of middle-aged bachelors and one of the lowest is that of married women with children; yet which of these two groups is subject to the greater pressure? Indeed, the most "pressured" status is that of being left without apparent and immediate responsibilities to help others. It is nice to know we are loved, but essential to know we are needed.

In effect, suicide is a measure of the extent to which a given modern society has succeeded or failed in integrating its citizens and its institutions. If that level of integration is low, suicide will increase, because people will be self-centered and lonely, and they will crumple under the inevitable tensions that life generates. Less self-centered persons will withstand such pressures better, because they will be tied to social systems that provide them with demands as well as help. Thus suicide is a measure of both individual self-centeredness and the efficacy of a society's integrating institutions. Evidently, both our adolescents and the institutions around them are increasingly tending to fail that test.

The other statistics already cited provide additional evidence of the growth of patterns of extreme individualism and even selfishness among adolescents. Thus it is often selfishness that promotes delinquent acts: the injuring or threatening of others or stealing from them. It is selfish to destroy public property made by the money and sweat of others in order to make one's point or to release one's frustration. It is selfish to become pregnant — or to make someone else pregnant — and bring into the world a child who will not receive the emotional support of a stable family.

We should also recognize that much of this adolescent antisocial conduct does not float around in space; rather, it descends on tangible victims — most of them adolescents. For instance, adolescents have the highest rates of crime victimization (22). The victimization rate in 1974 (per 1,000 members for each age group) was 122 for 16- to 19-year-olds, 64 for the total U.S. population. In other words, adolescents were twice as likely to be victimized — usually by other adolescents. The most frequent crimes committed against the young were larceny and rape. And of course most of the despised drug pushers who sell drugs to young users are other adolescents, trying to earn money to buy motorcycles, maintain cars, or dress in expensive or flashy clothes.

The shifts in youth attitudes, as well as conduct, are also consonant with a growth of self-centeredness. For example, a common belief of mature adults is that it is right for a group member — one who is himself equally at fault — to take blame for his fellows. We call such an attitude loyalty or fidelity. In the Haverford questionnaire this measure of potential fidelity declined from 63% to 45%. It may also represent a selfish (or self-centered) attitude when students at public colleges, where 60% to 70% of the costs are borne by taxpayers, describe the world as largely uncooperative. Without the cooperation and sacrifices of others — not only their parents, but all citizens — the students would not be given most of the cost of their education.

But Durkheim was concerned with more than self-centered conduct. He also hypothesized that alienated persons would be excessively inclined toward loneliness, withdrawal, and self-destruction. The use of drugs, alcohol, and cigarettes is often associated with such attitudes. The same sense of inadequacy is implied by the responses to the attitudinal questions that suggest increasing drives toward isolation as reflected in the growing emphasis on privacy as a personal aspiration.

It is clear that the statistics demonstrate the increase of self-centeredness and loneliness among the young. Apparently, people expect more and more from society, but are simultaneously less and less willing to participate. Who, then, will be left to do the giving?

Durkheim's general analysis about dis-integrating social structures has obvious applicability to a variety of modern phenomena that increasingly surround our youths and young adults. These phenomena, while they also affect adults, have special significance for younger persons, since the younger a person is, the higher the proportion of his life has been spent in modern environments. Conversely, the older a person is, the less likely it is that his formative years were spent surrounded by modern phenomena. Figure 4 indicates a variety of modern phenomena that affect our young and suggests the specific effects they have on human interaction, the attitudes taught by such effects, and the supporting evidence that discloses the attitudes.

Schools are simply one of the modern phenomena affecting the young.

But schools are uniquely focused on the young and have been absorbing increasing proportions of the time of children and youths; and modern formal education at all levels, from preschool to higher education, is also highly disintegrating. These educational systems:

FIGURE 4

Modern Phenomena (A) That Affect Human Interaction (B), and
Thus Teach Attitudes (C), Plus Statistics That Demonstrate
Visible Patterns of Character Change (D)

A. Phenomena	B. Effects on Human Interaction	C. Attitudes Taught	D. Supporting Statistics
1. Technology	1. Lessening in frequency of intense human interaction	1. Less willingness to accept deferred gratification	1. Increase in youth suicide, illegitimacy, delinquency, drug and alcohol abuse, and self-centered attitudes
2. Urbanization and suburbanization			
3. Affluence	2. More frequent peripheral contacts	2. Loneliness (and latent anger and resentment)	
4. Decline of youth work roles			
5. Large institutions	3. Segregation among age groups	3. Ineptness in talking to strangers and adults	2. Public perception that discipline is number one education problem
6. Mass media	4. Healthy adult role models less available for the young	4. Instability and exploitiveness in personal relations	
7. Rationality and individualism			3. Statistics on declining public faith in important institutions, both public and private
8. Important and legitimate institutions and interest groups having a stake in the continuation of current "unhealthy" trends	5. Less pressure on the young to learn and display maturity	5. Low levels of loyalty and increased disaffection from society	
	6. Less willingness to demand cooperation or loyalty from the young, or to ask them to display respect for traditions and symbols of the society	6. Fear of serious commitment	
		7. Greater willingness to hurt others	

1. Segregate the young from adults except for their immediate family and teachers, a highly restricted class of adults.

2. Segregate the young from contact with youths not in their immediate age range.

3. Segregate the young from contact with youths of different ability levels or from different socioeconomic classes.

4. Segregate the young (after elementary school) from persisting intense contacts with individual members of their age group, since students are frequently shuffled from one group to another to meet the needs of rational scheduling.

5. Deprive the young (in departmentalized schools) of intimate contact with individual faculty members.

6. Place the young in environments where they have few occasions to participate in the dramatic, collective release of strong emotions.

7. Fail to encourage young people to participate in cooperative work efforts.

8. Compel the young to work on projects unrelated to proximate social and economic needs.

9. Deprive the young of the chance to receive relatively immediate, tangible, commonly valued reinforcements (e.g., money, punishments, or pats on the back) in exchange for their efforts.

All of these patterns have continuously intensified over the past 20 to 30 years. School and college attendance has increased and has been prolonged. Schools and school districts have become larger, more bureaucratic, and more controlled by forces outside the purview of local parents, teachers, and administrators. Teaching has become more departmentalized and subject-focused. Extracurricular activities have evidently declined in importance, and school activities have been increasingly segregated from local community life. While pupil/teacher ratios have improved (at great economic cost), modern institutional structures encourage teachers to have brief contacts with many different groups of students; they often restrict students to transitory relationships with large numbers of fellow students. Oftentimes, the responsibility for relating emotionally to students has been taken away from the teachers — the adults with whom students spend most of their time — and assigned to "specialists," e.g., counselors and social workers. The present system seems scientifically designed to teach students how not to handle intimacy and, consequently, how to fear and flee from it. But wholesome intimacy is essential to a satisfying life.

Thus far I have presented objective evidence of changes in the nature of 1) adolescent conduct, 2) the attitudes of many adolescents, and 3) our social systems in general and school organization in particular. I have also tied these diverse changes together in a logically related pattern. In the absence of convincing evidence to the contrary, we should assume that distressing youth conduct will continue and increase unless we change the social systems and schools that relate to our young. This analysis of the relationship between contemporary formal education and youth alienation is not essentially novel. A number of reports have presented similar conclusions; the general direction of my recommendations shares some of the emphases of these writings (23).

CONSEQUENCES OF YOUTH ALIENATION

The growing trend toward youth alienation raises the central question of social continuity. Is our society rearing adults who can keep the country going? In the end, the survival of any society depends on its ability to create successive groups of mature adults (i.e., young people who are socialized to adulthood within that society) who are committed to the continuity of its major traditions. Those traditions include the production of goods and services to sustain the young, the aged, and the ill; the maintenance (through taxes and military service) of a necessary defense establishment; the persistence of a decent level of public order; and the commitment of citizens to constructive community and political activities to sustain the country.

The modes of satisfying such traditions are mutable, and they necessarily include adaptations. However, widespread and continuing commitment to the central themes of those traditions is imperative. In other words, a country can "work" only so long as the people in it care about one another as well as about themselves. And that attitude we call caring is both taught and learned. Without such commitments to the whole society, adults of productive age may fail to provide adequately for the emotional and physical needs of the young or the old; society may not maintain an appropriate level of defense; public disorder may pollute social life with fear or make social contacts so unpleasant that we adopt cellular modes of existence; or community and political activities may be abandoned to irresponsible and incompetent leaders/followers and thus be governed by short-sighted egotism. These disastrous outcomes can be the product of excessive personal cynicism, withdrawal, anger, selfishness, and social incompetence among our youths and adults.

As adolescent alienation has increased, so also have signs of alienation among older Americans. The suicide rate, again, invites attention. Essentially, the statistics have always revealed that young males (between 20 and 40) have higher suicide rates than do adolescent males (between 15 and 19). The higher young adult rates are presumably due to factors such as the shifting pressures around young people as they mature, leave their families, and enter into more impersonal environments. In the past 10 to 20 years both the adolescent and the young adult rates have been rising, although the adolescent rate has been rising more rapidly. Presumably, part of the cause for the young adult increase has been the growing proportion of alienated adolescents who carry forward their increasing fragility into adulthood. Another relevant phenomenon is the rising divorce rate, especially among younger married persons. While the steady increase has been a long-term rise, the alienating developments affecting adolescents are also long-term trends. And it is not surprising that increasingly anxious and insecure young adults are less able to make and keep judicious commitments — to make marriages that work. And when those marriages break up children are often left to be reared by one parent. Thus again the personal actions (and shortcomings) of anxious persons affect the lives of others.

We should also look at collective age-group attitudes as well as the conduct of individuals. Attitudinal surveys of adult Americans have found evidence of increasing dissatisfaction with many important public and social institutions. The most careful analysis of these attitudinal statistics undertaken so far — covering the period 1968 to 1972 — concluded that the group between 21 and 24 years of age, the youngest age group consistently surveyed, evinced a comparatively high level of distrust of government (24). The only two groups with higher levels were age 50 to 59 and over 70. Perhaps one cause of this estrangement is not the inadequacy of government per se but the inappropriate socialization of the young. In other words, governments — as well as marriages — can be in trouble if they are held to unrealistically high standards because certain citizens seek to assuage their emotional anxieties by finding villains.

At this point let us return to the phenomenon of student unrest during the Vietnam war. Many adults see this unrest as simply a dramatic response to wrong actions by the government. I can consider here only certain limitations of this interpretation. Many acts of the students involved breaking the law, destroying property paid for by others, disrupting classes, disturbing bystanders, and even injuring (on certain occasions, killing) innocent parties. Of course the violators often offered subtle and elaborate explanations of their transgressions. But how many criminals fail to offer excuses? Is it surprising that articulate and educated persons offer more elaborate justifications? Perhaps it is equally significant to realize that, in general, the violators — as revealed in the statistics presented above — were lonely, filled with unrealistic confidence in their judgment, and members of an age group displaying an increasing disposition to engage in a wide variety of antisocial and self-destructive acts. Is it not conceivable that, for the great majority of the actors — the mass that made the demonstrations feasible — unrest was largely an excuse for the release of latent aggression and the dramatic satisfaction of a variety of starved emotional needs? Of course the unrest eventually subsided, but this is not necessarily evidence that the underlying emotional causes have been satisfied; other measures of youth alienation have continued to show increases despite the end of the war. And perhaps, if another vehicle — real or apparent — as "good" as the war appears, we may have further collective outbreaks among the alienated.

Whether our society, at this time, is uniquely immoral or bad is hard to say — although I do not believe so. Governments will always be imperfect, like all human institutions. But I would contend that many people are applying higher standards to judging this country than ever before in its history. The application of such standards inevitably gives the judges many occasions for expressing anger, and it provides noble-sounding excuses for the display of what would ordinarily appear as selfish and unstable conduct. We cannot ignore this line of analysis as offering one explanation for much of the social dissatisfaction of our times.

Schools are not the only cause of this distressing situation, nor can they be expected to provide a full remedy on their own. The attitudes and conduct of their students reflect the forces that pervade their families, homes, and neighborhoods. Still, school managers do have some choices. Schools not only reflect students' attitudes; they can either try to constructively change those that are harmful or they can intensify them. Unfortunately, the structure of the modern school seems to encourage — almost aggressively — many modern phenomena that are particularly harmful to the young. As a result, the school cannot but aggravate the disabilities the students pick up outside its walls.

What can be done by educators to correct this situation? Essentially, we must strive to change the nature of human interaction in our schools. At the same time, we must increasingly remind the larger society of the limited power to effect change possessed by any one institution. We must also remind the society of the changes that are equally imperative in other social institutions besides schools — businesses, government agencies, neighborhoods, courts — if the challenge of adolescent alienation is to be met. Some of these other necessary changes will occur largely in noneducational contexts, but many will require these extra-school institutions to change their own relationships with schools. Meanwhile, in schools, educators must change or modify the school-related phenomena that cause the current form of inter-personal isolation. Of course not all desired changes can be attempted at once. Most will occur incrementally and take many years to complete. And different patterns of change will be appropriate in different schools and communities.

Many of the proposals presented here are not novel. Still, there may be a special value in seeing them presented in an integrated fashion and in a format that suggests their relationship with many in-school and society-wide patterns.

Some readers may wonder if the changes presage a drift toward a narrower parochialism. As an answer, let me mention the communities in which six of the last seven presidents of the U.S. were raised: Independence, Mo.; Abilene, Kans.; Stonewall, Tex.; Whittier, Calif.; Grand Rapids, Mich.; and Plains, Ga. Evidently, being raised in a small-town environment is not so disabling as cosmopolitans might imagine. Indeed, such a background may even be a source of reassurance to adults who eventually end up dealing with modern complexity. This is why "roots" are so often seen as a precious resource. It may be that, after leaving adolescence, young adults can advance their socialization to adulthood by such means as joining the armed services, attending a university, or otherwise being "broadened." But this broadening perhaps occurs best after a firm and localized foundation has been laid.

One may also wonder about the feasibility of creating more localized institutions, given the many powerful trends toward homogeneity and nationwide institutional structures. Obviously, the question cannot be answered easily. Still, child-rearing systems in all societies have always been somewhat isolated from the total social process. For instance, the family does — and must — create some form of wall or shield to constrain the child's experience. In addition, most cultures prohibit children from participating in or witnessing certain activities. Perhaps we can recognize the need to devise other walls — this time around schools. Such walls should cause schools to become less reflective of the impersonality and bigness that often pervade adult institutions. In other words, perhaps we can create schools that provide more supports for the young (while subjecting them to appropriate demands) until they are ready for more difficult challenges.

Of course one cannot predict whether educational changes of this sort will occur on a large scale over the next five to 20 years. It is simple enough to identify the many sources of resistance to them. However, in spite of such resistance, the pressures for the changes are really very powerful. The data that have been presented imply that present institutional situations are a source of steadily increasing social disorder and suffering. We can predict that, eventually, growing proportions of adults will wonder how the most powerful nation in the world can continue to function with an increasingly erratic and unstable electorate. Indeed, in the perspective of history, all too often large nations have crumbled not so much from raw external attack as from failure to rear mature adult citizens and leaders who know how to work together. After such internal erosion, the society became inviting prey for an external enemy or some power-seeking group of demagogic revolutionaries. But in many ways such decadent societies are already "dead" before their visible downfall. The immediate problem, for America, is that the longer it takes us to get seriously started toward constructive change the longer it will take to reverse the current trends. It is like flying a jet airliner: After the controls have been moved so as to cause the plane to turn, it may still fly several miles before the turn appears to begin. We have built up a great deal of social momentum. How much persisting damage must be done to our social fabric before the effects of improvement begin to show? And how will the effects of that additional damage affect the lives of us all?

FOOTNOTES AND REFERENCES

1. U.S. Department of Health, Education, and Welfare, Public Health Service, personal communication, 1977; Public Health Service, MORTALITY TRENDS FOR LEADING CAUSES OF DEATH. 1950-1969. Washington, D.C.: U.S. Government Printing Office, 1974.

2. U.S. Department of Health, Education and Welfare, Public Health Service, personal communication, 1977.

3. U.S. Department of Justice, Law Enforcement Assistance Administration, SOURCEBOOK ON CRIMINAL JUSTICE STATISTICS, 1973. Washington, D.C.: U.S Government Printing Office, 1973.

4. U.S Department of Justice, Law Enforcement Assistance Administration, SOURCEBOOK ON CRIMINAL JUSTICE STATISTICS, 1976. Washington, D.C.: U.S. Government Printing Office, 1977, p. 436.

5. U.S. Department of Health, Education and Welfare. National Institute on Drug Abuse, MARIJUANA AND HEALTH, FIFTH ANNUAL REPORT. Washington, D.C.: National Institute on Drug Abuse, 1975, p. 63.

6. San Mateo County, Department of Public Health and Welfare, SUMMARY REPORT, 1976: SURVEYS OF STUDENT DRUG USE. San Mateo, Calif.: Department of Public Health, 1976.

7. U.S. Department of Justice, CRIME IN THE UNITED STATES, 1972. Washington, D.C.: U.S. Government Printing Office, 1972, p. 124.

8. U.S. Department of Health, Education, and Welfare, Public Health Service, SECOND SPECIAL REPORT ON ALCOHOL AND HEALTH, pre-print ed. Rockville, Md.: National Institute on Alcohol Abuse and Alcoholism, 1974, p. 128.

9. Daniel Yankelovich, Florence Skelly, and Arthur White, A STUDY OF CIGARETTE SMOKING. Vol. 1. New York: Yankelovich, Skelly, and White, 1976, p. 36.

10. U.S. Department of Health, Education, and Welfare, Public Health Service, TRENDS IN ILLEGITIMACY, U.S., 1940-56, Series 21, No. 15. Washington, D.C.: U.S. Government Printing Office, 1968; U.S. Department of Health, Education, and Welfare, National Center for Health Statistics, MONTHLY VITAL STATISTICS REPORT 25, No. 10, Supplement, December 30, 1976.

11. U.S. Department of Health, Education and Welfare, Health Services Administration, APPROACHES TO ADOLESCENT HEALTH CARE IN THE 1970's. Washington, D.C.: U.S. Government Printing Office, 1975, p. 12.

12. U.S. Department of Justice, SOURCEBOOK, 1976. op. cit. p. 572.

13. U.S. Senate, Ninety-fourth Congress, First Session, Preliminary Report, Committee To Investigate Juvenile Delinquency, OUR NATION'S SCHOOLS. Washington, D.C.: U.S. Government Printing Office, 1975, p. 4. For similar conclusions about in-school crime in one state, see Task Force on the Resolution of Conflict, CONFLICT AND VIOLENCE IN CALIFORNIA'S HIGH SCHOOLS. Sacramento, Calif.: California State Department of Education, 1973.

14. President's Commission on Campus Unrest, REPORT. Washington, D.C.: U.S. Government Printing Office, 1970, p. 387.

15. "Nine Radicals on Most Wanted List," NEW YORK TIMES. November 28, 1970, p. 13.

16. Douglas Heath, GROWING UP IN COLLEGE. San Francisco: Jossey-Bass, 1968, p. 67.

17. Dean R. Hogue, "College Student Values," SOCIOLOGY OF EDUCATION, Vol. 44, 1970, pp. 170-97.

18. Daniel Yankelovich, Inc., THE CHANGING VALUES ON CAMPUS. New York: Pocket Books, 1973, and Daniel Yankelovich, CHANGING YOUTH VALUES IN THE 70's. New York: John D. Rockefeller 3rd Fund, 1974.

19. Dean R. Hogue, COMMITMENT ON CAMPUS: CHANGES IN RELIGION AND VALUES OVER FIVE DECADES. Philadelphia: Westminster Press, 1974.

20. John W. M. Whiting and Beatrice B. Whiting, "Altruistic and Egotistic Behavior in Six Cultures," in Laura Nader and Thomas W. Maretzki, eds., CULTURAL ILLNESS AND HEALTH. Washington, D.C.: American Anthropological Association, 1973, p. 56.

21. Emile Durkheim, SUICIDE. New York: Free Press, 1951, p. 165.

22. U.S. Bureau of the Census, CHARACTERISTICS OF AMERICAN YOUTH, 1974, Series P-23, No. 51. Washington, D.C.: U.S. Government Printing Office, 1975, p. 29.

23. Urie Bronfenbrenner, "The Origins of Alienation," SCIENTIFIC AMERICAN, Vol. 231, 1974, pp. 51-53; B. Frank Brown, THE RE-

FORM OF SECONDARY EDUCATION. New York: McGraw-Hill, 1973; James S. Coleman et al., YOUTH: TRANSITION TO ADULTHOOD. Chicago: University of Chicago Press, 1974; National Panel on High School and Adolescent Education, THE EDUCATION OF ADOLESCENTS. Washington, D.C.: U.S. Government Printing Office, 1976; Frank Newman, REFORM IN HIGHER EDUCATION. Washington, D.C.: U.S. Government Printing Office, 1973; and Edward A. Wynne, GROWING UP SUBURBAN. Austin, Tex.: University of Texas Press, 1977.

24. Arthur H. Miller, Thad A. Brown, and Alden S. Raine, "Social Conflict and Political Estrangement," paper delivered at the 1973 convention of the Midwest Political Science Association, Chicago, May 3, 1973, pp. 44 ff.

SOCIALIZATION
TO WHAT?

David Tyack

There's *that* group. We all know them. They always seem to have time on their hands. They often complain that they don't have enough money, but you rarely see them working. In fact, lots of them loiter around resorts acting as if they owned the place. They don't take care of their bodies the way they should. Lots of them are loners and have trouble relating to people. They are such bad drivers that the insurance companies don't want to sell them policies. More and more of them are living together as man and wife without benefit of marriage. The fact is, they just don't act normal.

Youth? Maybe, but such negative stereotypes are often pinned on old people too. Edward Wynne wants to persuade us that the pathologies of some youth (which he calls "alienation") result from inadequate socialization. Would he also argue that similar pathologies of the elderly be attributed to faulty socialization? Is it not more reasonable to examine the structural characteristics of a society that allocates both youth and retired people to restrictive social niches?

By and large, both youth and retired people are denied meaningful and well-paid jobs in a nation in which work and affluence confer dignity. Both groups suffer age segregation resulting from social rules that define their status — rules relatively new in history. Both connect only marginally to the nuclear family that is still the chief building block of the social system. Both are in important ways *dependents* of society at large, computed as two ends of the demographic "dependency ratio."

Wynne calls attention to facts of age segregation and lack of productive work for youth; but, by posing the issue as a need for effective socialization to adult culture, he implies that this culture is basically sound and that "social continuity" demands that youth be more efficiently transformed into us — that is, present adults. It could equally well be argued that youth actually reflect back, in somewhat exaggerated forms, the bad as well as the good qualities and behaviors of their seniors: their use of drugs and pills, their violence, their obsession with consumption, their conformity to group norms, and their privatism as opposed to social responsibility. Even the conservative study, *Amoral America,* published by the Hoover Institution, marshals convincing evidence about the ethical poverty of major American institutions. It is not only youth, but adults as well, who lack confidence in dominant American organizations, as several recent polls have demonstrated.

This raises a question about Wynne's central concern: alienation. That concept has become obese with conflicting connotations, and Wynne does not help us by giving it precise meaning. By lumping together evidence on suicide, drug use, delinquency, and attitude change, he mixes apples and oranges. These are all serious problems, but are they characteristic of the same people? Is the loner who takes his life the same kind of person as the one who vandalizes a school with his fellow gang members? Can the expressed attitudes of individuals be examined apart from social realities? Is it surprising in the era of Vietnam and Watergate that college students express less patriotism? Is it alienation or an accurate perception of economic life that makes students pessimistic about the chances for meaningful work? Is it healthy or unhealthy for students to place high value on privacy and autonomy in a time when scholars describe the conformity of peer cultures of youth and the timidity of organizational men and women?

Rather than deplore the dissonant values of youth as "alienation" from a beneficent society, one might equally well regard them as accurate perceptions of broader social pathologies and signs of a disaffection that could lead to reform. Changes in attitudes and behavior of youth need to be placed in a broad and deep demographic and economic context.

History offers some illumination here. Neither the recurring discovery of "youth" nor changes in lives of the young take place at random. As John Gillis argues in his book, *Youth and History,* young adults have periodically become visible as a "problem" during recent centuries when their numbers swelled for complex demographic reasons and when they lacked economic opportunities — when, in brief, traditional opportunities disappeared. At such times they often acted out their frustrations and hence were perceived as a threat to society. In the U.S., observers have tended to discover youth during periods of economic depression — during the panic of 1837, when Horace Mann and others became fearful of violence in the streets and the dangerous presence of young men not at work, not in school, and not supervised by parents; during the depression of the 1870s, when there were 10,000 youthful hoboes in New York City alone and when youthful gangs engaged in the violent railroad strikes of 1877; during the 1930s, when the federal government created the Civilian Conservation Corps and the National Youth Administration and countless scholars wrote about the "youth problem"; and during the last decade, when the youth cohort expanded dramatically, when young people rioted in cities, and when unemployment rates of ghetto youth often soared past 50% — reminding policy makers of James Bryant Conant's warning about "social dynamite" in the slums. At present structural unemployment among youth, especially minorities in cities, is a problem that deserves top priority in national policy.

Forty years ago a speaker at the National Student Federation said this:

I must confess that I am a bit puzzled by the current usage of the term "youth problem." There is no one problem that can be shifted upon a certain age group and labeled youth problem without taking into consideration the problem of all age groups. All the so-called youth problems must be seen and solved in view of the problems of business, education, and government for the entire nation.

He went on to argue that "there can be no democracy in America until equality of educational opportunity, equality of economic opportunity, and equality of political opportunity are guaranteed every citizen in America, no matter what age, race, religion, or political belief." In its successive forms, discussion of the "youth problem" has often diverted attention away from basic structural inequalities by focusing attention on the presumed deficiencies of the young — depraved, deprived, or alienated.

Psychologizing issues is a convenient way of avoiding basic changes in the distribution of wealth, income, power, or prestige. Wynne has managed to psychologize away dissent against the Vietnam war: Protesters were (he asserts) "lonely," self-righteous, "anti-social," and "self-destructive." Obviously, he had no need to consider evidence to the contrary about radicals of that era (like the studies of Kenneth Keniston); or to consider the effects of that abhorrent war on those who *did* fight in it. Indeed, in his apocalyptic view, the electorate itself is becoming "erratic and unstable." Perhaps the government should dissolve the people and create a new electorate.

Wynne has made some familiar and relatively sensible suggestions about how schools should become smaller, less bureaucratic, more neighborhood-based. He has urged a renaissance of school spirit, discipline, and patriotism — which will please some people. But he has given no guidance on the really crucial political and economic challenges of actually creating a meaningful place in the economy for youth or using the idealism of youth not just to reaffirm the status quo but to promote social justice. Is he really calling us to an educational Tupperware party, a contrived togetherness for ulterior motives?

The "youth problem" cannot be solved by better socialization procedures in school without at the same time looking at necessary changes in the larger society. Today a guaranteed chance for youth to work is quite as much an *educational* issue as free lunch programs were to an earlier generation. Just as a hungry child finds it hard to learn, so a high school student who sees his older friends unemployed finds little motive to achieve in school. For what kind of world should we socialize youth?

As Joseph Featherstone noticed, American commentators have had a curious ambivalence about youth. "Peter Pan ought to have traveled on an American passport," he wrote, "for in our booster moods we have thought that the rising generation would in its innocence redeem us." Countering the romanticization of the young by Paul Goodman or Charles Reich, other observers have talked about "teen-age tyranny" and the indomitable anti-intellectualism of youth. Now we hear of their "alienation." But generalizing about "youth" as if there were only minor class or cultural differences among them and glossing over the broader social structure in which they live only confuses the root issues of educational and social policy.

ALIENATION:
A CLOSER LOOK

Arturo Pacheco

Edward Wynne has presented a disturbing essay, painting a gloomy portrait of American youth in particular and of American society in general. He sees the trend toward increasing alienation as an indicator of disintegration that may lead to total societal breakdown. Like Durkheim, Wynne argues for steps to increase social cohesion.

There is no denying that something is definitely wrong in American society. I believe Wynne's recital of the data shows that. But I believe that his discussion of alienation and his understanding of Durkheim are faulty, and I will focus on them.

Wynne lumps together a variety of statistics on deviant behavior and attitudes among young people and cites these as evidence of a trend toward increasing alienation. Rather than adding clarity to an already overworked term, Wynne uses the concept of alienation as an umbrella to cover everything from homicide to illegitimate babies to a decrease in feelings of patriotism. Surely some of these woes are more distressing than others. Wynne doesn't help us make these distinctions. In what sense do these ailments constitute alienation? Wynne offers no helpful definitions.

Ever since Marx first used the term in a rather specific way in his critique of capitalist society, the concept of alienation has been much abused. In his early manuscripts of the 1840s, Marx used the concept to examine the basic structure of society. For Marx, the conditions of capitalist political economy and private property are such that the free, spontaneous life-activity (production) that identifies human beings as human is no longer free activity. It is no longer an end but a means. One's life activity is no longer one's own but belongs to another. These are the conditions of alienation, a distorted existence where one is alienated from the products of the productive process, from the productive activity itself, from oneself as a human being, and from other human beings. The point here is that the concept of alienation was used to examine the base structure of society in which it was rooted. For Marx, because something was radically wrong at the base of society, alienation was characteristic of *all* individuals within the society. It wouldn't have made much sense to describe basic aspects of the social structure as affecting only certain subgroups. Yet Wynne, preferring to remain on the surface, joins many other social commentators who have discussed the alienation of youth, poor people, old people, artists and intellectuals — as if both the problem and its solution could be adequately framed in terms of the subgroup alone.

Wynne's focus on youth masks both the source of the problem and its possible remedy. The ailments he describes are as symptomatic of the total society as they are of its young people. Yet Wynne characterizes the problem as one of inadequate socialization of the young. The proposed remedy — improving the socialization of youth through society's major institutions (especially its schools) — is not a new one. Yet where Wynne focuses on the school, Durkheim himself was one of the first to reject such a solution for overcoming the distintegration he saw in his own society. At the conclusion of *Suicide* he discusses the limited role of education:

> *But this is to ascribe to education a power it lacks. It is only the image and reflection of society. It imitates and reproduces the latter in abbreviated form; it does not create it. Education is healthy when people themselves are in a healthy state; but it becomes corrupt with them, being unable to modify itself. If the moral environment is affected, since the teachers themselves dwell in it, they cannot avoid being influenced; how then should they impress on their pupils a different orientation from what they have received? Each new generation is reared by its predecessor; the latter must therefore improve in order to improve its successor.*

Wynne uses only part of Durkheim's analysis and thereby trivializes his views. Although Durkheim himself was much more open to critical examination of the structure of society than he is usually given credit for, Wynne joins the many interpreters of Durkheim (especially those influenced by Parsons) who tend to interpret Durkheim's concern for social cohesion in terms of the need for increased discipline, social control, and the better internalization of societal norms. Thus we can understand Wynne's call for young people committed to the major traditions of American society (production of goods and services, maintenance of a necessary defense establishment, etc.) without a corollary call for a critical examination of these traditions and their place in the social structure.

Given this orientation, it is natural that Wynne would focus his concluding remarks on the schools and on ways of improving socialization through them. Three points need to be made about Wynne's comments in this regard. First, the reforms of the school that Wynne suggests along the lines of localization and return to the less bureaucratic and more intimate

neighborhood school might very well be helpful. They are sound suggestions for making the schools more humane places in which to be, if they are in fact as disintegrating as he suggests. Second, Wynne's romantic characterization of the neighborhood school and small town of the past as contrasted to the modern school, which he sees as encouraging "phenomena that are particularly harmful to the young," is hardly fair or accurate. A look at history often suggests the opposite. There are many ways in which the overcrowded turn-of-the-century schoolhouse constituted a far more alienating experience than the modern school. Third (and most important in this response), Wynne's proposals are at best piecemeal. Wynne might take another look at Durkheim's comments at the conclusion of *Suicide* on the limits of education as the source of reform of society:

> *Besides, even though through some incomprehensible miracle a pedagogical system were constituted in opposition to the social system, this very antagonism would rob it of all effect. If the collective organization whence comes the moral state it is desired to combat is intact, the child is bound to feel its effect from the moment he first has contact with it. The school's artificial environment can protect him only briefly and weakly. To the extent that real life increasingly takes possession of him, it will come to destroy the work of the teacher. Education, therefore, can be reformed only if society itself is reformed. To do that, the evil from which it suffers must be attacked at its source.*

Alienation is the tip of the iceberg, as Wynne suggests, but not in the sense he suggests. Rather, it is much more in the sense that Marx suggested originally. That is, the social problems with which Wynne is concerned lie deep below the surface and have their roots and sources in the very structure and fabric of society. Whether they can best be explained in terms of modes and forces of production is another matter. But it is *here* (and both Marx and Durkheim would agree on this), and not in better socialization of youth as Wynne suggests, that we should direct our attention.

CHANGING THE ENVIRONMENT
FOR YOUTH

James S. Coleman

The statistics Edward Wynne presents give a dismal picture of the psychic state of young people in the United States today. Obviously, many of the statistics refer only to extreme behavior and incidents, affecting only a small fraction of young persons. One's initial reaction may be to dismiss the statistics, despite the staggering increases that many of them show, because they refer only to a minority.

Such a reaction would be, I believe, to miss the central importance of these data. The data show, I believe, the decreasing adequacy of the environment within which young people find themselves growing up. The school is not the principal cause of this inadequacy; but that is not to say that the school cannot act as a partial remedy for it.

An indicator of this inadequacy lies in the "desirable school changes" that Wynne lists in Figure 5. These changes are all in the direction of more "personalized" schools — smaller, less bureaucratic, less insulated from the community. Under what conditions is it valuable to have this kind of school? There are many reasons why schools have gone in the other direction, have become larger, more departmentalized, and more insulated from the community. That direction is the direction of task specialization. It has allowed high schools to give more advanced, more specialized courses, teachers to concentrate in their specialty, and altogether to provide both a broader set of course offerings and more intense concentration on specific courses or programs. The impersonality of the school reduces the teacher's chance of playing favorites. Insulation from the community has made possible more equal treatment of students and lesser impact of the social structure of the adult community on the school.

With all the virtues of large, departmentalized, impersonal schools, insulated from community pressures, why the call for the opposite? What do the small personalized schools, integrated into the community, provide of such importance that it justifies losing the considerable virtues of their opposites?

The answer lies in some of the social phenomena that Wynne lists in his Figure 4, and the consequences they generate within persons who grow up under those conditions — that is, modern society's children. Wynne is correct, I believe, in the distressing set of consequences he sees for young persons' attitudes.

There is one change, however, that I believe is of prime importance in creating the changed environment in which young persons live. This is a change in the family, and Wynne does not discuss it in any detail. The impact of that change is only beginning to be felt. When it is fully upon us it will be of extraordinary magnitude, if I am correct. The very concept of what the family is about has changed; the ethic of self-realization as it grows means that the family is increasingly, for husband and wife, a convenience institution *for themselves*. Children are less and less central to the family, and family life is less and less appropriate for the needs of children and especially young persons emerging from childhood. The extremely high proportion of marriages that end in divorce is only one indicator. Another, more direct, is the great increase in numbers of children who run away from home and live on their own — children aged 12, 13, 14, and up. It is estimated that in the Los Angeles area alone there are 70,000 such youth. And recently newspapers have described how young Midwestern girls, having made their way to Minneapolis, are induced to go to New York to supply the demand for prostitutes.

But runaway young persons are again only a surface indicator of family deficiencies. Along with other indicators, they point to increasing ill-fittedness of many families (or perhaps it is too strong to call them "families"; they might better be called "couples") for teen-aged youth.

This qualitative change in the social-psychological environment provided by many families indicates to me that schools must begin to shoulder a broader set of responsibilities than they have in the past. It also suggests that this broader set of responsibilities is not uniformly required; after all, many families continue to provide better psychic homes for their teen-aged children than schools could, at best. What is suggested, then, is a differentiation: the creation of some schools that do far more, in the way of providing a social-psychological home for youth of high school age, than schools now do. Yet they would be short, except in cases of abandonment, of boarding schools. Some experimental schools, of the form of the Parkway School in Philadelphia and its descendants in other cities, may already have begun to do this, though their manifest purpose was somewhat different. The form that such "broader" or more "comprehensive" schools might take in general is not yet clear, and I will not attempt to speculate on that. I want only to suggest that the essential source of the problem be recognized, and that for some children — not all — schools of a new and broader sort are required to take up where the family has left off.

PART III

A POSITIVE ALTERNATIVE: YOUTH AS COMPETENT PARTICIPANTS

Some of our most prominent social scientists have painted us into the proverbial corner. They have created an updated "Catch-22," arguing that we cannot change the situation of youth until we change society — yet we cannot change society without the political pressures that only young people can apply. Thus we bide time, seemingly paralyzed while conditions deteriorate.

The papers that follow present arguments to suggest that this paralysis is unnecessary. Although the studies described at times offer opposing explanations, they concur that youth policies aimed at correcting alleged incompetencies while preparing youth for distant futures are misguided. This collection of papers, of course, will not in itself produce social change, but it should provide ammunition for those who are working for change.

For example, as Gerald Blake and his co-workers demonstrate, young people can function as "planners" in public transportation, an approach that effectively integrates school and work. The youth involved in this project proved that applying skills to social problems can increase their understanding of the real world. While describing the experiences gained in a project in Portland, the authors also offer some general guidelines for youth participation programs.

In Santa Cruz, young people learned about history and government by mounting a campaign for student rights. In the process, "unmotivated" students became energized and what for them had been dull and deadening began to come alive. There were other positive effects: students from different social groups were drawn together and one serious cause of conflict in school was eliminated. The Santa Cruz experience shows what can be accomplished even by a relatively inexperienced teacher with no resources or special funds.

In Palo Alto, Dick Carey was able to hire students to serve on research teams which successfully completed an important study task. A variety of students was involved and recognition of competence was not restricted to those who normally are rewarded in school. The Palo Alto experiment was especially significant because the funds to pay participating students came from the school operating budget, requiring no special grant monies for implementation.

Participation takes many forms and serves many purposes. One important result of student participation is the acquisition of knowledge about the working world. Stephania Arness describes the Far West Laboratory model of "experience-based career education," which meets graduation requirements while helping students to become proficient in basic skills. The Far West project demonstrates the willingness of youth to learn when they are encouraged to exercise responsibility and choice and when they see the direct relevance of learning to their daily lives.

The background, development, and major ingredients of experience-based career education are described in some detail by Bucknam. He also discusses some of the problems that may be encountered in implementing work programs for youth, such as identifying appropriate work sites and resource persons in the community. Bucknam's analysis of EBCE programs emphasizes the importance of self-directed learning in which students are able to test their interests and abilities against real-life situations. The central role of the "learning coordinator" who assists students in the work/education process is one of the unique features of this integrated curriculum program.

Jennings and Nathan review the literature and research data on both experimental and traditional school programs, coming up with what they term "disturbing" conclusions. Research evaluations of alternative school programs (i.e., those which are innovative in terms of classroom or school structure and curricula) cite "enormous gains" not only for students but for local communities as well. According to these authors, however, evaluations of traditional school programs should cause us to question 95 percent of current educational practices. They conclude that studies challenging the value of a high-school diploma, the need for teaching reading in elementary grades, and the correlation between achievement test scores and later success in life suggest that experimentation and change are needed and should be welcomed in schools.

The Far West project has shown that youth can take responsibility for themselves as individuals. In St. Paul, students demonstrated the ability to accept responsibility as a group. The St. Paul Open School, based on "helping and showing," concentrated some of its efforts on consumer education. Not only were these students effective in rectifying many consumer complaints, they also gained knowledge about their community and became increasingly proficient in reading, writing, and mathematical skills. Their accomplishments are illustrated by the fact that the booklets produced by the class are used by many public organizations and private citizens.

Fascination with technology also can generate youthful enthusiasm and a desire to participate in learning. Increased motivation clearly can alter a student's perception of school; students accustomed to viewing school as a "prison" are able to see it as an exciting place to be. Such changes are described by Lee Conway in his account of a "flying classroom." Twenty-five "unmotivated" eighth-grade boys were provided with ten hours of in-flight instruction in airplanes. Students learned navigation, meteorology, and many other skills that required mastery of reading, writing, and mathematics. Spectacular changes in "character" and "competence" were observed. While the tie to a glamorous profession undoubtedly had something to do with the success of this project, the shift from passive to active learning must also have played a part.

The Howard University project discussed by Pearl showed how active involvement in human services — child care, recreation, and evaluation — could affect both character and competency. Involved in the project were unmotivated young people, many of whom had delinquency backgrounds. As they intensified their involvement in socially useful projects their commitments to antisocial behavior were substantially weakened. The success of this project was due to increased accessibility not only to legitimate incomes, but also to opportunities to establish different group memberships and social outlooks.

Foxfire, a widely recognized success, is a multifaceted enterprise which provides access to many exciting youthful activities. Foxfire began as an educational experience to motivate disinterested students to learn. Eliot Wigginton shares four discoveries from his twelve-year involvement with Foxfire: (1) Students are more competent than their teachers generally acknowledge. (2) Labeling students "incompetent" in school often persuades them to hate learning. (3) Schooling is most effective when it has many linkages to the past and the present of the community, i.e., when it has "roots" and an integrating culture. And (4) schooling must meet the needs of adolescents, among which is a need for self-esteem acquired from peer approval and acceptance.

The concept of the "active community" underlies Ernst Wenk's proposal for tomorrow's education. He describes a Partnership-in-Research experiment in which students identified issues important to them which then became the focal points of eight study groups. As in the other alternative programs described in this section, the student response was highly favorable. Wenk also presents evidence that active learning is superior to passive learning. On the basis of this and other experiences, he calls for an Integrated Community Education System (ICES) that allows the community to "own" its education system. ICES addresses individual as well as social concerns. Flexible and building upon personal success and competence, the active integrative school that Wenk proposes is designed to permit meaningful accomplishments for the individual while also benefitting the community in measurable ways. His proposals stand in stark contrast to current approaches to schooling which render the student passive and label those alienated by the process as unmotivated or incompetent.

There is a clear message in all of these essays. It makes little difference if the "classroom" focuses on one's own culture, an airplane, a project in which older children care for younger ones or study the problem of youthful drug abuse, a public transit system, a political mobilization for student rights, or an effort to help consumers protect themselves. If learning is active, if competence is expected, if there is a social contribution to be made — then students learn. It also appears that when such approaches are used, the differences in achievement often associated with race, social class, and sex are markedly reduced. When organized to learn while involved in projects that help others, students not only benefit — society as a whole also benefits.

RECRUITING UNEMPLOYED YOUTHS AS PLANNERS OF YOUTH EMPLOYMENT

Gerald F. Blake
Lee Penn
James Mason
Dennis Hoffman

INTRODUCTION

Forty years of federal job programs, ranging from conservation work to subsidies for employment and training in the private sector have had little lasting impact on youth employment. One reason for the ineffectiveness of these various efforts is that they have been based on an assumption that youth unemployment could be solved through counter-cyclical programs of a short-term nature. The belief that massive youth unemployment is a temporary phenomenon, and that over time the economy will generate enough jobs for employed youth is widely off the mark. Recent figures presented by Ginzberg (1), and the conclusions reached by the Panel on Youth of the President's Science Advisory Committee (2) lead to the realization that solutions to the youth job problem lie in efforts aimed at job creation and redesigning work to allow for more of a meshing of work and educational experiences.

In the summer of 1977, the Youth Employment Planning Team (YEPT) of the School of Urban Affairs at Portland State University attempted a different approach to the creation of youth jobs. This paper describes the development of the planning team, and how it involved a diverse group of high-school aged youth in the planning of new, long term public service employment for young people. The paper also describes such details as youth recruitment, supervision, training, and generation of strategies for dealing with prospective employers.

The Youth Employment Planning Team philosophy was based on a critique of the prevailing organization and definition of work and education, as they relate to youth. Prominent among these criticisms were that schools rarely allow students to participate in decision-making, and often enforce student passivity and segregation. These actions and policies work to inhibit student development as responsible, self-actualized citizens, and at the same time perpetuate negative stereotypes about youth.

Regarding the world of work, criticism centered around the performance of the private sector of the economy. Private employers, even with heavy government subsidy, have not been willing or able to create adequate numbers of jobs for youth. Moreover, much of the work that has been created can be characterized as dead-end and short-term, allowing only a few youths the opportunity to develop skills, utilize talents or try different lines of work in order to make an informed career decision. Finally, the linkages between educators and employers are tenuous, so that many young workers are denied access to school resources and credit that could help them in a present job, or in preparation for a career.

YOUTH EMPLOYMENT PLANNING TEAM

In order to overcome these problems the Youth Employment Planning Team was organized as a project-oriented learning situation where youth were employed to study a problem and generate solutions, while at the same time receiving strong educational support to carry out project tasks. This method of insuring close cooperation and integration between educators and employers proved useful as a means of assisting youth to make the transition from school or joblessness to productive work that meets widely perceived unmet needs of the community.

It was found that allowing youth to design work and educational programs for themselves promotes effective learning and sound program development. In all phases of the employment planning process youth workers studied aspects of the problem, acted or developed situations using the knowledge gained, and then evaluated their actions, with resource and educational support provided by adult YEPT staff.

This was an effective way for youth to plan jobs within their selected target, the city's public-transit agency, and for generating support for their plan for business, political leaders, schools, human service agencies, and labor unions. Despite end-stage funding and administrative problems which prevented immediate implementation of the YEPT plan for 50 new youth jobs in public transit, the process employed in developing the plan, project-oriented learning, was shown to be a useful way to combine academic curriculum and work experience to combat youth unemployment.

ORGANIZING PERSPECTIVES OF YEPT

One of the central organizing perspectives adhered to by the Youth Employment Planning Team was that society often keeps youth from fulfilling their most urgent need as adolescents, and as human beings: to make a positive contribution to their community. Schools, which have become the primary institution to socialize adolescents, keep youth on "hold" as passive learners, or as potential troublemakers in need of babysitting, until the youth graduate or drop out. Schools often compound the waste of youths' potential by segregating them from the "real world," and by keeping youth divided from each other along race, sex, age and class lines.

The nation loses much by such authoritarian methods of dealing with young people. Youth educated in traditional school settings are often poorly prepared to assume constructive adult roles and responsibilities. Passive education does not adequately prepare youth to make individual or collective decisions, to work responsibly with others to meet social needs, or to find their own identity by testing themselves through legitimate action in the community.

The schools' attempts to link work and education are often unsatisfactory. Students are tracked by race, sex, and class into different curricula (3); the "winners" go to college and the "losers" end up in voc-tech classes that often use obsolete methods and equipment to prepare youth for dead-end jobs.

Linked with the failure of schools to provide options for youth to develop cognitively and affectively as responsible citizens is the economy's failure to achieve full employment and thus allow youth to participate in the world of work. There are too few jobs for youth — especially for blacks, women, and those of high school age. The jobs that are available are usually dead-end, offering employees low pay, insecurity, little hope of advancing in their chosen career, and virtually no way to try different occupations to find the career which fits them best. Vigorous recruiting, as well as removal of explicitly and implicitly discriminatory policies are needed if programs are to aid Blacks, Chicanos, women, ghetto dwellers, high school dropouts, high school and college students, and veterans. Now-prevailing public and private investment and personnel policies (including job training, qualifications, testing, on-the-job discipline, information on job openings, and counseling) have failed to provide enough work for those who seek it, and may instead be contributing to the problems of a mass of unemployable youth. It would seem, then, that those who plan youth jobs must innovate or be doomed to failure.

YEPT PLANNING PRINCIPLES

It is the position of the Youth Employment Planning Team that any effort to plan for youth jobs be guided by certain realities and principles. Job planners should, at the very least, be aware of the following:

- Jobs should be in careers that will not rapidly become obsolete, and that have prospects for steady growth in future employment. With the energy crisis likely to worsen, this seems to dictate a shift in planning orientation away from youth jobs in energy-intensive industries. (Such industries are doubly unpromising for youth in that they produce few jobs of any kind per dollar invested; energy-intensive industries are usually capital-intensive rather than labor-intensive.)

- Employment in private construction and production of durable goods is not optimal, since recessions (which normally occur every three to four years) cause demand in these industries to collapse — sending droves of their workers into the streets. In such cyclical industries, youth are especially vulnerable, since they have little seniority to protect them against layoffs.

- Youth employment programs need to create *new* jobs, with accompanying career ladders. Failure to do this, meaning that government money would be used to steer youth more efficiently into existing jobs, will result in youth competing for scarce jobs with adult breadwinners. Such antagonism would do little to benefit unemployed youth.

- Jobs should be organized so that youth can work and remain in school; this calls for a long-term program of part-time work during the school year and full-time during the summer. School counselors, administrators, and teachers should work with youth and parents to provide and steer youth toward courses that will enhance work experiences in their present and prospective jobs.

- Youth job programs should provide adequate incentives to work, and work well. Incentives should include a decent wage which rises with experience, skill, and proven performance on the job. The personal benefits of work should include feelings of competence, usefulness, belonging, power, and excitement on the job.

- Newly-created jobs should provide youth with the opportunity to help people, and meet needs perceived by them and the community as being important. This will help the community to more readily accept young workers, and should give youths an additional incentive to work well, and to seem themselves as connected with, and important to society — which may reduce youth disaffection and crime.

- The job criteria of satisfying perceived and unmet social needs, creating new permanent jobs, and doing so in industries that are not energy — or capital — intensive dictate an emphasis on creation of public-sector, human service jobs for youth. Such jobs can be planned for and maintained regardless of economic instability or business investment decisions. Furthermore, they do not compete with or swamp the market for the private sector.

PROJECT-ORIENTED LEARNING

The YEPT team in Portland was faced with a difficult set of tasks. They had to first learn how to plan and then plan to learn. That is, the youth had to rapidly learn their planning roles since they had neither experience in planning nor extensive knowledge of the key issues in urban transportation. Moreover, the YEPT staff was interested in creating a working/learning situation in which the youths themselves could benefit.

In response to these two concerns, it was necessary to design work and education programs that embodied what the National Commission on Resources for Youth calls "Youth Participation — the involvement of youth in responsible, challenging action that meets genuine needs, with opportunity for planning and/or decision-making affecting others, in an activity whose impact or consequences extends to others — i.e., outside or beyond the youth participants themselves."

The YEPT participation-oriented employment program included systematic education and training of youth. This occurred through academic courses related to the job and given in conjunction with it, on-the-job training, and discussions by youth and supervisors of their experiences on the job. Such educational support, arranged with close cooperation between the youths' school and the workplace, was essential to the project.

The most effective learning and skill development took place when the youths learned about their work and themselves through a process of action/ reflection/action. The youths acted upon their environment in a constructive project, they discussed and summed up their experience (successes and failures), learned related theory and history and technical skills related to more successful completion of their project, and then returned to the project armed with their new understanding. Such education was directed toward the solution of a particular problem, unlike the prevalent banking model of education, in which teachers deposit "knowledge" in a youth's head and expect him/her to draw it out and apply it many years later.

This type of learning experience developed personal skills (responsibility, decision-making, compassion, cooperation, working in groups, and personal problem-solving) as well as technical, vocationally-related skills. Youths were working at jobs which will hopefully be related to their future careers, and they had a significant voice in deciding what they want to do and how it should be done. Youths also made choices now, rather than learning about making them in the future. Participation in determining project goals was designed for a cross-section of youth, not just a few elected representatives.

Projects do not need to be limited to public transit agencies — they can be established in different settings, from schools to recreation agencies — and involve youths in direct provision of services to others, such as community action, improving a community's physical structures and environment, or in various internship and apprenticeship experiences. The important point is that participating agencies make a long-term commitment to providing youth employment and training; part-time while they are in school, and full-time while they are out of school in the summer. It is also necessary for a project-oriented youth participation program to pay youth workers and to award academic credit. Pay demonstrates that the agency or firm hiring the youth values their work enough to compensate for it. It also enables poor and working-class youths, who need paying jobs, to join in a program that will help them educationally, rather than forcing them to take a dead-end job.

The awarding of academic credit likewise demonstrates that society takes youth participation seriously, and allows students to use school time to work on selected projects. Additionally, unless high schools and colleges give credit for youth participation programs, college-bound youths will avoid this experience in favor of traditional college-prep courses. This would turn youth participation into a new track for those not going to college. The restriction in clientele that would result from refusal to pay or award credit for that program would greatly handicap an effort which has as one of its aims the bringing of youth of diverse backgrounds to work on a common project.

A CRITICAL REVIEW OF THE
ORGANIZATIONAL DYNAMICS OF RUNNING
A YOUTH EMPLOYMENT PROGRAM

This section of the paper describes how the youth employment planning team was set up and how the team leaders and youth participants attempted to create youth jobs within the city's public transit agency — Tri-Met. Included is a detailed description of how the project was organized, and a number of suggestions for others who wish to establish similar youth participation programs.

One point requires strong emphasis at the outset: *Any youth participation project must be carefully planned before being put into operation.* A hastily conceptualized or slipshod effort could kill the project at birth, and discredit the concept of youth participation in that community for years to come. Selection of competent adult project leaders, development of a strategy and tactics to secure work, pay, and credit from schools and potential employers, educational support for participants, and selection and management of youths from diverse backgrounds are all critical elements to a successful project.

Development of a participation-oriented youth program begins with establishment of a youth planning/research team. This helps to develop a core of youths who will be active citizens and future team leaders. It also stimulates lasting and effective learning by the participants, and ensures that a diverse group of youths is involved in planning youth employment. This in turn makes the new project more responsive to youth needs and interests, and attacks the stereotype of shiftless, irresponsible, incompetent youth — a stereotype that needs to fade if youth participation is to become a reality on a large scale. YEPT urges that a youth research team continue in existence alongside a youth employment project during its entire life in order to give youth input into new directions for the program, and to be sure that the program continues to meet needs of youth as participants perceive them.

INTERNAL ORGANIZATION OF THE
YOUTH EMPLOYMENT PLANNING TEAM

For ten youth researchers on the team, three adult leaders were employed — a project strategist, a project coordinator and a learning consultant. The project coordinator supervised the youth workers and organized, with the learning consultant, the training and education, including outside lecturers, for the team. The project strategist coordinated the work of the other two adults, set up meetings between YEPT and other agencies, raised money, and made initial contacts with those who could arrange paid work and school credit for the youths in future youth employment programs.

YEPT found that three adult staff workers were necessary because of some practical considerations. First novice researcher/planners, whatever their age, need to receive a substantial amount of education and training prior to their involvement in paraprofessional planning activities. Second, the bureaucratic inertia of most organizations, such as Tri-Met, suggests the need for additional adult staff to direct (at least initially) group efforts which have a political character.

Youth employment teams operating within a single agency could use these three adult staff to oversee two teams of ten youths working on different projects at the same time. Three adult staff could likewise handle two youth research teams that are evaluating ongoing youth employment projects, since the hard initial work of training the youth and establishing the jobs program in the agencies will already have been done.

RECRUITMENT OF YOUTH
FOR THE PLANNING TEAM

YEPT chose youth researchers who were articulate and able to read and write and who showed interest in, and dedication to the work of the project. School grades, work experience, criminal record, or medical history were not seen as relevant work qualifications. Participants' ages ranged from 14 to 21, although most were high school age. These hiring practices were successful and warrant replication — although, if time permits, applicants to work on the team should write a brief essay on why they are interested in the project. This change would improve the team leaders' screening for reading and writing ability.

YEPT recruited youths from three youth service centers (YSCs), agencies under the direction of the city of Portland's Youth Services Division (YSD), YEPT's main collaborator. Each YSC manager was asked to identify five youths to be interviewed. At the interview, the project was explained and applicants were asked their interest in and experience for the planning jobs. This hiring process for the team was completed within a few days (4).

HIRING A DIVERSE GROUP OF YOUTH

Since the youth service centers each covered a different Portland neighborhood, YEPT hired youths from all parts of the city. The planning team was comprised of blacks, whites, males, females, and working-class and poverty-level people. Educational levels ranged from school dropouts and high school sophomores to high school graduates — two of whom are now in community college.

For future programs, the recruitment process should ensure a geographic mix if the project the youths will be working on is to be city wide. If the new project centers on a neighborhood, hiring should be from youth in local schools, community and citizen action groups, neighborhood associa-

tions, and the juvenile justice/probation system. The intent is to ensure that all classes of youth, including those excluded from society's mainstream, have input into the planning of their neighborhood's future youth participation project.

For any youth employment program, whether it be for a neighborhood or an entire city, it is critical to have researchers represent diverse ages, educational backgrounds, races, sexes, and social classes. This will prevent the youth research group and the ensuing employment project from becoming stigmatized as an upper-class or lower-class activity. Diversity challenges the traditional educational theory that some youth can undertake research and planning activities while others are too dumb or lazy. Rather, diversity substitutes the idea which has been proven in practice — any youth, given meaningful work, educational support and good leadership, can work well in almost any role — even one usually thought to require professional training. Diversity ensures that the needs of all youth are represented in employment planning, and it helps the planners reach all parts of the community. Lastly, a diverse research team will help team leaders evaluate the performance of a mixed group of youth.

LEADERSHIP OF YEPT

Good adult leadership is critical to the success of a youth research/planning team. The Portland experience indicates that these traits and skills are essential:

- Desire to work with youth, and respect for their ideas, ability, and potential.

- Having formed, and being able to act upon, a theory of how people act and learn.

- Ability to teach, to communicate ideas and provide feedback.

- Recognizing that conflict is inevitable in human situations.

- Ability to tolerate and resolve conflicts within a group.

- Ability to cooperate with and lead a youth team that is racially, sexually, educationally and economically diverse.

- Sensitivity to the needs and feelings of youth.

- Acceptance and exercise of natural adult authority to set limits on youth participants' behavior and work habits, while not interfering with youths' ownership of the experience.

- Willingness to say "I don't know" at times, to admit mistakes, rather than bluffing to avoid "loss of face."

These needed qualities show that selection of leaders of youth research/action teams must be done carefully. The special skills, traits, and aptitudes required by a certain project should mesh with those possessed by the chosen leader. It cannot be assumed that an adult will be successfully and thoroughly trained to assume leadership of a youth action team in a few weeks.

Training of the leaders of the YEPT project required discussion of leadership style, learning theory, and the economic and political issues involved in designing youth employment. A list of recommended readings was given to all team leaders.

MANAGEMENT OF THE YOUTH PLANNERS

YEPT developed these procedures to run the youth planning team:

- There was a process to deal with, rather than suppress, conflict within the group. There were some minor race and sex frictions within the youth team. Youths were informed beforehand that this may happen, and put that problem in its social context. The leaders said, "Rise above the conflicts, for if you use them as a way to avoid working on the substance of the project, you will confirm society's negative stereotypes of youth."

- Decision-making was done by the group as a whole.

- Time was set aside for the supervisors to be alone, so that they could plan, reflect, and recoup their energy.

During the course of the project, several pitfalls were identified that adult leaders of youth planning and research teams must be wary of:

- Fear of taking youths into the community or to meetings, because they might do or say something embarrassing.

- Public chastisement of youth participants.

- Adult domination of the project.

151

- Assignment of routine or menial tasks to youth participants.

- Equating "giving youths responsibility" to "leaving them alone"; responsibility increases youth participants' need for feedback from respected adults.

WHAT THE YOUTH EMPLOYMENT PLANNING TEAM DID

Supervisors provided readings to prepare the youths to think about energy, mass transportation, and employment.

Several members of the youth planning team — different ones each time — attended YEPT meetings with the Tri-Met management, the transit workers' union, and the representatives of various youth service agencies. After each of these meetings the youth and leaders who attended discussed with the entire group what had transpired.

In addition, the YEPT team met with a similar youth action team working under Comprehensive Options for Drug Abusers (CODA), and helped them formulate research instruments, and deal with problems occurring within the team. YEPT gave similar consultation to another youth team hired to do traditional, limited-substance youth program planning.

The basis of the YEPT team report comes from the youths themselves, who wrote a draft report. They also reviewed articles, did library research, read and criticized newspaper stories related to employment, energy, and transportation, and kept diaries. A lecture on the project was also presented by YEPT at a graduate and undergraduate class at the University of Oregon at Eugene.

Youths worked 40 hours per week for $2.30 per hour; time for recreation, including a group picnic, was set aside by leaders during the project.

YEPT leaders arranged the following 40-50 minute lectures, usually by guest speakers, as learning support for the youth: mass transit theory, manpower planning, youth employment and unemployment, urban design, problems of the handicapped, light rail transit, research methods (statistics, surveying, and report writing), energy, and ecology.

YEPT completed this youth research/planning project during 10 weeks in the summer of 1977. In general, a summer youth action program is not conducive to causing immediate and major structural changes. There is enough time for consciousness-raising with the youths, but not enough time to fully research a problem, develop a solution, and implement it. Professionals could do the research much more rapidly, but in a youth participation program, it is necessary to train youths in research and planning — and that takes time.

YEPT recommends, as was true in this case, that youth planning and research projects be done in or close to universities, where there is access to a library, lecturers, and other educational support. If projects are to be organized within high schools, it is important that educational support be secured from allies within the university.

YOUTH REACTIONS TO THEIR WORK WITH YEPT

Youths who participated in the YEPT planning effort praised their work and their leadership. Here follow the conclusions that youths who turned in end-of-summer reports reached:

- Participants found their work meaningful because they learned about mass transit, work, and unemployment. In the process, they also learned to study, do research, and write reports. The participants learned while working, helped to create change, and met different people — other youth workers of different backgrounds on the project, and the managers and workers they met in the course of doing their research. As one person said, "We have accomplished something most people would feel youth incapable of."

- Participants found this work experience different from others they had had. The job included education, and would help them get a better job later. People were paid for learning, and for some, it was their first non-manual job. The work environment was relaxed, and one youth said that his interest in the work helped him keep the job.

- Youths learned about data collection and analysis, survey taking, unemployment, pollution, and energy crisis, youth job needs, using the library, understanding bureaucracies, and the political system.

- Youths especially liked meeting and working with new people, including their diverse co-workers, and the many agency heads and workers they met while doing research. They enjoyed planning and pressuring for environmental improvement, and appreciated the relaxed work environment in which youth were treated as equals.

- Youths least liked the personality conflicts that occurred within the team, especially in the last few weeks. Other problems were absenteeism by some — and late paychecks from the City. However, those responding to the questionnaire called their problems with the job "minor."

- When asked what they would have done differently had they been running the project, all said they liked the project as it was, and especially liked the teaching.

- This participation-oriented youth planning team had an impact on its participants' lives. One person plans to seek a career in youth program planning; another feels better informed about the world and feels that the skills learned this summer will help get a better job later. Still another person said, "Having this job made me feel a lot better about myself and my environment . . . there are many things that I can do with myself and I can succeed if I try."

FORMING ALLIANCES WITH OTHER AGENCIES TO IMPLEMENT YOUTH PARTICIPATION

In planning the research and implementing the youth job proposal that resulted, it was critical to establish close formal and informal ties with significant other agencies in the community. YEPT's leaders made such an alliance with the director of Portland's Youth Services Division (YSD) early in the research project. Repeated meetings of YEPT leaders with the head of the YSD led to a general consensus and an alliance based on mutual trust, common goals, and a philosophy shared by the leaders of YEPT and the YSD.

The YSD was the central agency in this planning scenario because it controls $2.5 million of city youth employment money. This department decides the number of youths to be employed, their wage, the duration of employment, and the kind of work the youths will do. Then too, YEPT leaders had been less successful in establishing a relationship with the schools that would induce them to commit school credit and teachers to the new youth jobs plan. There is no doubt that those who seek to establish youth employment programs must establish a friendly working relationship between the employment planners and those who can commit teachers, credit, and pay for the young workers.

The basis of YEPT's unity with the YSD was agreement among the two leaderships about the principles which should govern youth employment, as well as personal trust and liking between the leaders. The principles agreed upon were:

- Youth should have an active, responsible role in planning and evaluating their employment.

- Jobs created should allow youths to transfer from one career to another, and should help them rise the job ladder in that field if they wish.

- Youth workers should not drive adults into unemployment.

- Jobs created should be consistent with energy conservation and preservation of the environment.

- Race and sex discrimination should be actively fought in a youth job program.

- Society needs to put the innovative, creative energy of youth to work in productive ways.

- Youth employment money should create goods and services of significance to society as a whole, not just the youth workers. Therefore, work should meet a perceived and unsatisfactorily met social need.

- For these reasons, existing youth employment programs are often unsatisfactory, and new approaches should be tried.

Generally, what is needed is agreement that the goal of a youth job program is not just to plug youth more efficiently into existing institutions, but also to change those institutions. This shared awareness kept the planners on track, although there were disagreements within YEPT and between YEPT and the YSD over the specifics of implementing the program.

In approaching agencies and dealing with the public, it was important not to be seen as "radical" or "political." Rather, YEPT developed and emphasized acceptable and implementable ideas that deal with specific, concrete needs for human services. Hence, the job proposals were acceptable to most administrators and disadvantaged youth.

DEALING WITH THE PROSPECTIVE AGENCY
OF EMPLOYMENT FOR YOUTHS

After establishing a favorable contact with the agency that could commit resources to build a youth employment program of the type outlined above, YEPT sought to win allies and neutralize opposition to the program within the agencies to be affected and the community at large.

Tri-Met, the local public transit agency, was chosen as the site for job creation because its workers fulfill a still inadequately met social need, and because the agency is likely to have steady employment growth as energy costs, congestion, and pollution force more people to turn to public transit. To date, the agency has had no layoffs, even during recessions. Tri-Met itself plans to triple its ridership by 1990, with corresponding growth in employment. Without active program intervention, youth would be unlikely to benefit from this potential employment growth (at present only 4 employees of Tri-Met's 1,200 workers are under the age of 21).

The intent of the planning effort was to create jobs at Tri-Met, so it was necessary to win the backing of that agency, and those connected to it whose aid we would need: Tri-Met managers, the transit workers' union, and the schools. In these agencies, YEPT identified people who could relate to youths, and the goals of the planning effort.

Support was generated by going to meetings with the people concerned — explaining what YEPT was trying to do, and why their organization's involvement was necessary. Care was taken, from the outset, to rebut the stock objections to youth employment programs: "How can they get pay and school credit too?" and "It will take jobs from adults," etc.

At first, some at Tri-Met would not return YEPT telephone calls. It was apparent that some departments at Tri-Met did not want to undertake the additional work that creating new jobs would entail. YEPT also had to overcome the after-effects of a badly-conceived youth career awareness program of the previous year. In that program, supervision of youths, liability insurance, the youths' relationship to union workers, and the relationship between that program and youth needs and goals were not worked out. That program was a failure and hampered our efforts to begin a soundly-planned youth job program — a clear warning to all who follow us to plan well before acting.

The YEPT strategy featured a multi-faceted approach to dealing with anticipated bureaucratic intransigence. This included arranging meetings with members of Tri-Met's Board of Directors and directors of various departments within Tri-Met. We also approached the leaders of the transit workers' union and sold them the plan. They in turn told us who to approach at Tri-Met and how. YEPT also contacted legislators with knowledge of mass transit in the tri-county area, as well as citizen advocates of better bus service. Together, these sources helped YEPT understand better what makes projects work or stop in the transit agency.

Through the YSD head's contacts with the Mayor of Portland, YEPT got the Mayor to write a letter to Tri-Met's acting general manager. In this letter the Mayor criticized the agency's inadequate response to youth needs in Portland with respect to bus routing, fares, and youth employment. This letter, with other political and labor pressure, moved the general manager and his employees to begin cooperating with YEPT.

Team members then met with the managers at Tri-Met who were most open to the planning goals, sold them the project, and got their agreement to hire 50 youths once the program and its funding were settled. YEPT went around pockets of resistance and offered proposals to answer objections. These included the provision of adult CETA workers to supervise and handle paperwork for new employees.

By September, YEPT and Tri-Met had agreed upon the creation of 50 jobs for youth, age 15-19, in the agency. These were to be part-time during the school year, and full-time during the summer, with academic credit, teacher evaluations, and counseling to take related courses provided. These jobs included escorting elderly and handicapped riders using the special Lift buses, providing information to the public and especially to youth from junior high school through community college to promote bus ridership, and coordinating the provision of artists, dancers, and other performers to entertain those waiting for buses at the downtown Transit Mall.

THE OUTCOME OF YEPT EFFORTS

In early fall, prospects looked good for the creation of new youth jobs. The Tri-Met management was cooperative, and the Youth Services Division of the City of Portland had committed Federal dollars to funding the youth jobs.

However, the project has been temporarily derailed. In the late fall of 1977, the Tri-Met management changed, bringing in a new management that was unwilling to move ahead now on a large scale, innovative youth employment project.

Also, the Youth Services Division has changed its policy, preferring to commit its money to private sector rather than public sector youth jobs.

YEPT believes the rationale for its job proposal remains sound, and will resume negotiations with the City and Tri-Met to create the public-service jobs.

FOOTNOTES AND REFERENCES

1. Eli Ginzberg, "The Job Problem," SCIENTIFIC AMERICAN, November, 1977, pp. 43-51.

2. President's Science Advisory Committee: Panel on Youth, YOUTH: TRANSITION TO ADULTHOOD, Washington, D.C., U.S. Government Printing Office, June 1973.

3. Samuel Bowles and Herbert Gintis, SCHOOLING IN CAPITALIST AMERICA, New York, Basic Books, 1976.

4. One other point warrants mention here. The authors have recruited several youth action teams over the past two years, and have found that teams recruited and hired all at once worked together considerably more smoothly than those where youths were hired over a period of several weeks. Youths for any one action team, whenever possible, should be hired and then put to work at the same time. What this does is eliminate the repetition of the project start-up activities.

A STUDENT
BILL OF RIGHTS

Joe Berney

That some youth are in conflict with established authority is not a new phenomenon. What makes the current situation unique is the magnitude of the problem and the despair. The proportion of youth caught by the juvenile justice system seems to be always increasing. Youthful violence appears to be on the rise. And old solutions apparently no longer work.

School as a positive force in youth's lives is in particular disrepute. John Holt, for example, sees school as an oppressive force, denying youth elemental rights and offering nothing of substance in return (1). Christopher Jencks and his associates conclude (on the basis of massive, although not necessarily appropriate, data) that schools cannot be an important force in reducing inequality (2). In an introduction to a volume that critiques that work, however, one of the co-authors admits:

> . . . Lacking any dynamic model for the educational process — and any reliable evaluations of educational experiments — we cannot know what will happen if we alter the process itself, i.e., the ways in which resources are used. The possibility of significant shifts in the curves of diminishing returns should not be dismissed (3).

What needs to be tested is whether it is possible to change school climates through youth participation in every aspect of school programs, whether this has impact on students' rights, and, ultimately, whether students' long-term life conditions are positively affected. Here we present evidence of youth participation that leads to expanded students' rights, teaching at the same time that rights are won by a political process and those who will benefit from such rights must be involved in the process of winning them.

Yet another problem puzzles experts. There is no clear indication of how delinquency should be treated. Most efforts posit the source of the problem in the individual and try either to cure or to divert youth away from delinquency (4). In recent years some investigators have identified the school as a delinquency-generating force, hypothesizing that the most effective treatment is youth participation in school activities (5).

The study at Soquel High School presented here, while hardly definitive, does lend credence to the notion that changing the nature of schools by expanding youth participation can have a positive effect on antisocial behavior and may also be important in the distribution of justice. This chapter describes a concrete experience in youth participation. Such programs operate on the basis of a theory which suggests that when we generate substantial and real youth ownership of school programs, we can successfully reduce delinquent activities.

In a nutshell, to the degree we can generate meaningful and useful roles for students in schools, and to the degree that youth have the chance to buy into and ultimately "own" programs and goals they have helped to develop, schools will become non-alien institutions. As alienation decreases, so do the myriad youth activities which reflect alienation — drug abuse, alcoholism, burglaries, gang crimes, violence, suicide, truancy, poor school performance, and various other personally and socially destructive behaviors.

SETTING THE STAGE

During the spring semester of the 1974-75 school year at Soquel High School (Santa Cruz City School District) I found myself given the responsibility for teaching a "Z"-track Civics class. While successful completion of a government class at Soquel is required for high-school graduation, this requirement is waived for "Z"-track students. According to policy, school district "Z" students are intellectually incapable of completing a normal curriculum, so they are routed on a curriculum track developed for slower, more marginal students. "Z"-tracked students are identified on the basis of scores on reading and intelligence tests. Once so designated in the track, it is difficult to get out. Teacher, peer, and personal expectations of behavior and ability tend to be consistent with the "Z" designation, and all students respond to the expectations of others.

It is no coincidence that "Z"-tracked students disproportionately demonstrate delinquent activities. They just aren't "into" school. School is a bad place for them to be, yet they have no real alternative. The result generally is delinquent or antisocial behavior. This was especially true of the "Z" students in my Civics course. All students in this class had experienced failures in school. Most of them smoked marijuana; a few used harder drugs. This interfered with their academic performance. Several had been arrested on campus by undercover narcotics officers for possession or sale of drugs, pills, and/or alcohol. Three boys had serious juvenile records. Two girls were unwed mothers. All the students cut classes frequently. As I studied files of students in the class I realized that this group represented the hardcore alienated and destructive students on campus.

I walked into the class as a student teacher. What I witnessed was not a class as much as an uncontrolled zoo. The teacher I was to assist had been assigned the class because this was her first year of teaching and her status was that of the lowest on the totem pole. No one else wanted to teach these students and everyone knew it. In a vain attempt to get some help and sympathy, this teacher video-taped the situation to show the school's principal, vice-principal, and social studies department chairman. After viewing and reflecting upon the situation, only one proposal was offered: "Don't try to teach them anything: just keep them in line." Toward these students, then, all authority in the school had assumed a posture of defeat. For the next twelve weeks of the semester, the only concern was to minimize the problems they caused.

WALKING INTO IT

I came to the class as an aide and student teacher. Already battle-weary by the time third-period Civics rolled around, the teacher would vanish to the faculty room, leaving me to assume responsibility for the class. I had complete flexibility regarding content and format since all responsible school personnel had long since given up on these third-period "animals." Fortunately, the class and I took a liking to one another. I admired their independence and spirit, and I told them so. They explained why and how much they hated school and, to their surprise, I agreed with them. School *was* a bad place for them to be. I suggested they reflect on where they would rather be. While specifics varied, all wanted good jobs, money, and less hassle from the authorities — and all wanted out of school.

We extended our social analysis to help them to plan more desirable futures. We studied in some depth the private and public sectors of the economy and how these operate to provide jobs in specific areas. We analyzed the degree of input citizens have into public sector decisions, as opposed to their influence in private sector employment. We brought in related readings and guest speakers. The students exhibited considerable interest and came to understand their educational potentials and their futures.

A crucial fact remained. Other than third period, school was still a bad place to be. Dope, booze, truancy, and assorted other delinquent behaviors still competed as desirable and more gratifying alternatives.

CITIZEN RIGHTS CURRICULUM

One of the core units of any Civics program is the study of the U.S. Constitution and the Bill of Rights. This class, now an attentive and vocal group, was vitally interested in their own rights. This concern usually translated into their giving me sets of "hypothetical" situations to determine whether the "pigs" had a right to do whatever it was they did to the "hypothetical" citizen victims. But beyond that, I argued, was the whole question of citizen and human rights in our political system. Since they claimed to have so many "bad raps" at school, I suggested they compare the rights and treatment they had received at school — just one of our social institutions — with those rights guaranteed every citizen by the Constitution.

For possibly the first time in their academic careers, most of these students did their homework. They were going to learn that Constitution backwards and forwards until they could prove that not only were teachers and deans and principals and police giving them too many hassles, but legally they shouldn't be! In the next few days this class became the best group of constitutional researchers I have had the pleasure of working with. With the exception of one girl who dropped out to go to a school for pregnant girls, every one of those students checked and double-checked that Constitution — basically because they trusted no one else's interpretation. They wanted it straight from the horse's mouth.

About 90% of the students completed the assignment, which required a substantial amount of class and homework time. Having done their research, they came in ready to do something with it. The assignment was to identify all citizens' rights and protections as provided by the Constitution and to determine where at Soquel High School these rights and protections did and did not exist for its student citizens.

Here I need only point out that the comparisons did not look good for Soquel High School or the public school system. The greatest violations of human rights were found in the areas of freedom of expression, privacy, and due process. And these kids had done their homework. They brought with them to class an impressive amount of data which (despite its unimpressive disorganization) supported their points.

An intense session of bad-mouthing the school was initiated. Now their arguments were backed by research. Room 300 was quite chaotic that day. These students were angry — they had proved how bad school was and there was nothing they could do about it . . . or was there?

THE STUDENTS' RIGHTS MOVEMENT

I suggested that they were doing the same thing they accused the authorities of — taking "cheap shots" — that is, criticizing and condemning a situation without making proposals for improving it. I also told them that if they wanted to learn principles of political organization and governance by doing something about it, I would be glad to provide the class time.

We then jointly began to develop a schedule of study units which responded both to Civics course objectives and to the desire of these students to participate in constructive institutional change. The schedule of units included: Rights in a democratic society; Social Accountability; Types of Political Behavior; How our School System works; Methods of Organizing; and Methods of Governance.

Through these units a project emerged — a students' rights project. Through ''rap'' sessions at brunch and lunch, these students began reaching out to different groups on campus to (1) include them in negotiations for a bill of student rights and (2) to organize a constituency. When it was generally agreed upon that we had no money, they organized power through people. This group of ''delinquents'' and ''truants,'' who previously wouldn't give anyone the time of day, much less participate constructively in class or in any school-related extra-curricular activities, began spearheading a variety of campus activities — discussions, assemblies, interviews, visits to different community groups for support, delegations to other district high schools, letters to the local paper, press releases.

I was amazed at their commitment. Their attendance picked up sharply in all classes not necessarily because the classes became more interesting, but because they did not wish to jeopardize their ability to continue the project. They demanded school and district budgets to analyze. They constructed a flow chart of school system decision-making. It was in their own interest to study, and study they did. They learned how to construct interviews; to code interviews for interpretation; to speak in public; to follow rules of grammar and composition; and to work with other people toward an articulated goal.

Students weren't the only ones involved in this battle. Teachers became very concerned about ''all this students' rights talk,'' suggesting instead that what was needed were guidelines to define student responsibilities! Many faculty saw that it was in their own interest to provide input to the discussions. The students' rights project thus became the students' rights and responsibilities movement. The project moved out of the classroom and into the whole school community. School board members also became involved as consultants.

As organizers, the students were constantly increasing their sphere of participation and impact. A small but significant gain lifted spirits one day during a strategy session. Under "privacy" rights students wanted doors on the toilet stalls in the boys' bathrooms. Apparently when some of the parents heard about this structural condition, they became infuriated and called their elected school board representatives who immediately sent in a work crew to take care of the matter. We discovered that without even getting out a rough draft of the document one of the privacy wrongs had been righted. A victory already!

Our success did not end here. This project, which began in a Civics class with the "bad" kids, escalated into a district-wide movement involving many hundreds of students, teachers, parents, and Board of Education members. After the toughest first few months, even the traditionally "good" student government students wanted it to be their major mission. It was the first time anyone had seen these two groups of students work together. After one year, many meetings, many drafts, redrafts (with the help of County Counsel), and several painful compromises, on November 10, 1975, the Santa Cruz City School Board approved and made into policy 5131.1, the Bill of Student Rights and Responsibilities (6).

Everyone involved learned through experience the necessity of study and of citizen participation in our democracy. In the process, students whom the school had given up on acquired skills and study habits they previously had refused to learn or to demonstrate in their school careers. Students the school had designated as "Z"-track and delinquent demonstrated social accountability, political understanding, and true leadership. Even the "responsible" leaders in student government followed their lead.

It is exciting to see people break out of the institutional roles into which they have been cast. It is exciting to see people given opportunities to develop and demonstrate their potential. It is exciting to see people previously viewed as trouble-makers or "parasites" become useful contributors and have their contributions recognized. When problem students, delinquent students — or any students, for that matter — derive meaning and enjoyment from constructive non-delinquent behavior, only then can such behavior hope to compete with socially destructive activities. In the high school situation, I have seen it happen time and time again.

LONG-TERM RESULTS: ANALYSIS AND REFLECTIONS

It has now been three years since original passage of the Bill of Student Rights and Responsibilities. The issue of student rights seems to be in decline. All of the old-timers — those students who initiated the campaign — are gone. The excitement and impetus of the movement are gone. Today, students seem less politicized, less active, more apathetic and more passive. When the Board of Education voted to make into policy the concerns of the movement, all goals seemed to have been reached and everything seemed to fizzle. Why?

1) **Inadequate follow-through.**
Grass-roots organization developed to negotiate a draft and proposal. As the student government "regulars" and "good kids" moved in, the grass-roots participants lost interest. The movement no longer "belonged" to them. It is not enough that the students become involved; their participation must be ongoing — and that is far more difficult.

2) **Conflicts with the Status Quo.**
Once passed, the student rights bill established a policy base which conflicts with many school practices. Also, students' rights do not exist if no one knows about them and there is a tendency in the school authority structure to avoid publicizing information in such a volatile area.

3) **Lack of Mechanisms for Ongoing Involvement.**
Nowhere in the school offering is there a place for an analysis of the system of education which involves students in the research. Such student involvement is necessary if students are to play instructive roles in developing alternative visions of desirable futures, both for themselves and for the school. Without these visions of desirable educational goals sudents may be involved in the projects spasmodically but their efforts will be fragmented, piecemeal, and dispersed. This, unfortunately, is what happened to students' rights at Soquel High School.

4) **Inadequate school-community linkages.**
School programs do not, at this time, involve students in activities which relate work and learning activities, are flexible enough for meaningful negotiations on curriculum, establish a sound governance system for student-initiated projects, or develop visions of a better school and enable work toward these goals.

IMPLICATIONS

The type of youth participation project described here has broad implications for school programs and structure. The project demonstrated that there can be more joy than pain in participation and, concurrently, that there is likely to be a lot more pain than joy in non-participation. The challenge here is to build continuing student participation into the school program. Token student participation simply will not work, especially if the aim is to compete with delinquent activities. Inadequate also are "simulation games" that allegedly give students a "feel" for real-world participation.

Effective strategies against massive alienation and apathy in schools and in other areas of life must have at their core the involvement of students in curriculum policy decisions (i.e., school governance) and meaningful changes in the relationships between school and community and between school and work. Given the limited sphere of power of school people (students and faculty), the best approach will involve projects in which students share governance with faculty and field placements are integrated into curriculum. Some feasible examples include:

1) Constructing a Bill of Student Rights as a student project in government classes.

2) Intern programs in government agencies or community service[3] groups, in conjunction with social studies courses.

3) Developing projects organized around cultural holidays.

4) Developing peer learning situations, cross-age and cross-ability tutoring programs, student-directed seminars for variable credit, alternative programs around theme areas which double as school resource centers, and student court or grievance committees.

Since currently these activities are not built into the offerings of many school systems, seed money for demonstration projects is desirable and in some situations necessary. Dedicated and knowledgeable leadership, however, is far more important than money. Given the tragedy and cost of youth crime it would appear that avenues which appear to offer the greatest potential should be tested rigorously. One of the most promising solutions to youth problems clearly is youth participation in existing systems.

FOOTNOTES AND REFERENCES

1. John Holt, ESCAPE FROM CHILDHOOD. New York: E.P. Dutton, 1974.

2. Christopher Jencks, et.al. INEQUALITY: A REASSESSMENT OF THE EFFECT OF FAMILY AND SCHOOLING IN AMERICA. New York: Basic Books, 1972.

3. Donald M. LeVine and Mary Jo Bane. Introduction to THE INEQUALITY CONTROVERSY: SCHOOLING AND DISTRIBUTIVE JUSTICE. LeVine and Bane (Eds.) New York: Basic Books, 1975, p. 13.

4. For example, textbooks on adolescents explain delinquency in personality terms. Grinder in his textbook ADOLESCENCE, (New York, John Wiley & Son, Inc., 1973), only cites studies that impute family factors, "high mobility, instability, financial strain," (p. 395) and for middle class youth "discrepancies between parental achievement for the youth and their ability to achieve" (p. 396). Rice, in his work, THE ADOLESCENT, (Boston: Allyn & Bacon, Inc., 1978) summarizes this literature and finds possible sociological, psychological and genetic causes of the problem (p. 256-262). Neither author ever mentions schooling as a cause or contributor to delinquency, although many youths insist that the seeds of their problems with the law began in school.

5. See for example: K. Polk and W. Schafer, SCHOOLS & DELINQUENCY. Englewood Cliffs, N.J.: Prentice-Hall, 1972.

6. Copies of the Bill of Student Rights and Responsibilities and of the evaluation design are available from the author.

STUDENT RESEARCH AS A SOURCE OF PROGRAM DEVELOPMENT: A CASE STUDY

Richard W. Carey

The use of studies of student attitudes and performance as a source of educational program development is not new to the Palo Alto (Calif.) school district. Both philosophically and pragmatically, information obtained from students has been seen as important in developing or revising educational programs. Philosophically, the rationale has been that students' needs are continuously changing and school programs should be developed and modified to reflect these needs. Pragmatically, interpretations of students' needs by parents and school staff often have been colored by preconceived notions, however unconsciously applied. Even the best designed studies in student needs have seemed to leave something to be desired.

One defect in this type of study of student needs is that students are not as involved or given the same rights as other groups studied, such as parents or staff. The latter often have control over, or at least input into, the way their needs are assessed. In fact, they often conduct the study or have it done for them and they generally have rights of review over the data gathered and the power to act upon any recommendations developed. Traditionally, students have not had the political power, organization or training to conduct studies of their own needs or to question the findings of studies by others.

The definition of problems and the production of solutions is greatly enhanced by a feeling of problem ownership. Students' needs and problems "belong" to the students, not to the adults who purport to study them. The chances of meaningful action to meet needs or resolve problems are greatly increased if the client group whose needs are studied feel they are part of the process of designing solutions. The studies described in this paper, however, did not grow out of any such carefully thought-out rationale. They evolved over time and with experience, deriving in large part from frustration with studies that produced less than satisfactory action on student needs as felt by students.

THE RESEARCH SETTING

Gunn Senior High School in Palo Alto, Calif., has a population of about 1470 students in grades 9 through 12. Over its 12 years of existence, many studies of student attitudes and perceptions have been completed. One of these studies, which was completed in June 1971 (1), was different from the others in that it was conducted primarily by students with the help of a research consultant from the school staff. This study was related to student activism and the students who conducted it were among those most concerned about school and its relevance to students. Study findings were widely reported and had some impact upon program development at the school. Although it had been hoped that the study would result in an ongoing student self-study group, the drop in activism ended support of this program.

Much later, in the 1976-77 school year, the district developed a set of recommendations for revision of human services within the school district. This set of recommendations was derived from the recommendations of three groups: (1) a task force studying problems of drug abuse in the community; (2) the district human relations committee concerned with multicultural relationships; and (3) the PTA report on health education, which included sex education and mental health concerns. This report, which was accepted by the Board of Education in February 1977, set forth a series of goals which included: *"We want students to be actively involved in the planning and evaluation of school services."* Among the "events" proposed to achieve this goal were: (1) that a process be established whereby student involvement will be an integral part of program development; and (2) that periodic assessment of students' views on "needed and wanted" programs and activities be made.

In spring 1976, the Director of Human Services met with students in the Tri-School Council and reviewed the recommendations for obtaining student input. At Gunn High School members of the Tri-School Council met to consider how students should participate on the School Advisory Committee for Human Services. As a result of their recommendations, the Assistant Principal established a student advisory group for the school's Human Services department. This was viewed as one means of involving students actively in planning and evaluating human services. However, it did not address itself to the full range of potential areas of student need at the school.

THE STUDENT RESEARCH TEAM

In fall 1977, the school psychologist at Gunn and the district coordinator of research met to discuss how students might be involved in evaluating school services. It was decided to recruit students from psychology and sociology classes to do research at the school. These classes were selected because they reached a wide range of students and course content was related

170

to research on understanding human beings. The "pitch" to the students included a review of earlier studies at the school and how these had resulted in new programs and improvements for students. It also emphasized the importance of learning by doing and the skills that students could learn in this kind of project. In addition, the district's Peer Counseling leaders were asked to add sections on their "Assignment Information" sheet describing the possibilities of working on a research study. One assignment was described as follows:

> *We will be doing a research study on the atmosphere and climate of your school in conjunction with the Director of Research and Human Services team members. We are interested in having some Peer Counselor help with this study. Would you be interested in taking such an assignment?* . . *Yes* . . *No*

As a result of these recruiting efforts, a group of about ten students started meeting with the school psychologist and research coordinator after school from 3:30 to 5:00 one afternoon a week. Since the peer counseling assignment requests came in late, most of the initial group of students were from the psychology and sociology classes. This group was quite diverse in background and cut across interest and identification groups at the school, although it was made up primarily of juniors and seniors.

In the first meeting, "group-building" exercises were a big part of the agenda. Students and their staff consultants got to know each other rather quickly. In addition, they spent time looking at potential research areas. These group-building exercises seemed to be of real value, adding a dimension of closeness and mutual understanding not often provided by a strictly "task-oriented" group or an ordinary classroom project. This may have had some influence upon the project developed by the research team.

THE CAMPUS ATMOSPHERE STUDY

After reviewing previous studies at Gunn, the students decided they wanted to do their own study. They were particularly interested in the social climate at the school since the prevailing opinion was that it was "cold" and that students tended to remain separated in their own little groups. An early activity involved interviews with other students in the group to determine their views on the social climate. Combined with the "group building" exercises, this tended to show the group that they belonged to different cliques and that "outside" students often had quite different and often negative views of their identification group. In fact, one question in the initial interview turned out to be the most revealing, and probably most threatening:

Which groups do you feel you belong to, if any?
Do you belong to more than one group?
How do you feel about joining a group if you are new?
What do you feel you get out of your group (or not belonging to a group)?
What does it cost you in terms of time, independence or good feelings to belong? Is it worth it? If yes, in what ways is it worth it?

From this initial interview, which was used both for skill development and for getting new content, and from the discussions, a research design began to emerge. A questionnaire was developed and a plan was devised for getting a representative sample of student opinion at the school. The questionnaire featured names of the cliques at the school (obtained from the interviews) and the location on the campus that seemed to be associated with each clique. The focus was upon getting descriptors of different locations on campus that were the "habitats" of the cliques during school hours. This questionnaire was tried out on a group of Gunn students to get responses to the instrument. After considerable discussion of the responses received, the group asked two student members to revise the original and at the next meeting final revisions were made.

The problem of sampling was then discussed. After reviewing the various ways in which a representative sample might be obtained, the group decided to sample classes and get about an equal number of male and female 9th, 10th, 11th and 12th grade students. This proved to be a more difficult task than expected because it required locating classes at the right grade level which were not homogeneous in terms of student groupings. For example, sampling an advanced placement class might tend to result in more "brains" than would be representative of the school. Usually, social studies classes were chosen because they tended to have a wide range of students and were not grouped by ability or other factors. Although the group did not get the ideal sample they intended because they had fewer lower classes than they expected, time was running out on completing the study in the spring, so this less than perfect sampling was accepted.

The group then spent some time discussing how best to analyze the completed questionnaires. It was decided to provide some quantitative analysis of the data, but not to lose the flavor of the comments that students had provided in the open-ended questions. The report thus included data showing the "comfort level" of the campus and the degree of association between groups in quantitative terms while giving the flavor of the student comments. The report was prepared by one of the consultants at the direction of the research group.

REPORTING THE INFORMATION TO OTHERS

The written report from the study was presented to the school principal and his administrative staff and a follow-up oral report was made by about half of the study group. At this meeting possible meanings and actions based on the study were discussed. The principal expressed his appreciation for more specific information on cliques and feelings about school climate that had until now been surrounded by rumor and conjecture. Ways in which some of the areas might be made more comfortable were discussed at this meeting.

A district human relations committee reporting to the Superintendent of schools requested that students report to them on their findings. This meeting was attended by most of the study group. Preparations were made so that each student reported on that part of the study in which they had been most involved. The consultants gave a general introduction and remained as resources to the student research group as they made their report. Interestingly, this committee earlier had received a report by a group of student leaders on cliques and inter-student relations. The research group obtained findings which differed in some ways from what had been said at the earlier meeting, which was based on individual student opinions rather than systematic data gatherings. The fact that the research group represented a number of different social groups at the school also helped to lend credibility to their findings. They did not have a stake in some particular position, nor were they so limited in their contacts that they did not have access to a broad range of student "cliques" at the school.

At the end of the school year, the research group wrote an article, took some pictures, and attempted to make their report less academic and more attention-getting for other students. Experience gained in this effort may be important in future studies.

STUDENT WORK AND OTHER OUTCOMES

Because of their research experience and newly developed skills, some members of the research team were asked to help with a study by the district research department undertaken to assess the elementary school climate. The study design called for tape-recorded interviews with elementary school teachers, classified staff, parents, administration, and students. The students were asked to interview representatives of the student groups. For this they were paid the rates for student research assistants. The group interviewing and reporting back was a logical extension of the skills and knowledge developed in the study of their own school climate.

FUTURE DEVELOPMENTS

The final meeting of the group was devoted to discussion of the future and of what had been learned. The group wanted to continue as a research team and certain directions seemed to develop:

1. Credit should be granted (if desired) for this kind of project learning. This might help to validate the educational nature of the experience, making it possible for students to devote more energy without feeling that their other school work was suffering.

2. The consultant model for staff members (teachers, school psychologists, district researchers, etc.) works very well in the project learning situation. Working together on a common problem provides adult input and assistance in a way that encourages student growth and independence as well as insuring the study is directed at student needs, not adult perceptions of those needs.

3. Paid work experience should be a possible result of learning the skills of research and program development. Part-time work can be made a part of the work experience program or of the school's CETA positions for more extensive work.

4. The research teams can develop contracts with other groups, such as the Tri-School Council or groups representing other student interests. The possibility of needs assessments that get beneath the surface to the basics of school environment can help make both the research teams and the groups representing student interests more potent. One of the problems of student governance is that students who become involved often do not know the problems of the full range of students. Since they represent a small portion of the student body, they often are shunted into social and other matters not nearly as important or compelling as they could be.

5. Movement into a full range of student problems would imply a need to involve a full range of students. From this study at Gunn it seemed very clear that in order to study student problems successfully, students should be involved. For example, if part-time work is a problem for many students then the study needs to involve students who have this problem in the definition and study of the problem.

6. Research, program development, and social action all fit into a

model for project work that students can use to their own benefit. The need is for more attention to a curriculum that would make credit granting more clearly related to basic skill areas such as English, composition, or mathematics.

FOOTNOTES AND REFERENCES

1. The Tri-School Council includes students from all three high schools in the district. They represent students' interests and report to the Board of Education.

EXPERIENCE-BASED CAREER EDUCATION

Ronald Bucknam

Unemployment is regarded as one of America's major social problems in the 1970s. Citizens, politicians, and economists debate over the manner in which unemployment can be reduced. Creating new jobs is one controversial solution that has been proposed.

Often ignored is perhaps the more serious problem of employability. For every Bureau of Labor statistic there is a person who is unemployable. He or she may lack needed credentials or job-related skills. Or there may be no market for available skills. Discrimination, value conflict, or poor self-concept also may be reasons for an individual being labelled or labelling themselves unemployable.

Because the quality of education a person receives has a great deal to do with whether or not he or she falls into this "unemployable" category, the National Institute of Education (NIE), and the Office of Education, (OE), since about 1970, have been re-examining public education with respect to the causes of unemployability. A set of conditions and subsequent programmatic recommendations have been identified, which, when realized in schools, have ameliorated some of these causal factors. The Experience-Based Career Education program described in this paper is one educational innovation, developed by NIE, which has resulted from these deliberations (1).

Several theoretical assumptions underlie the EBCE program. One is that students will learn more about careers through direct exposure to the work place and active participation in the economy than they could learn in the classroom. A second assumption is that work experiences reinforce educational competencies. This tenet is similar to that underlying traditional cooperative education, in which students first learn skills and then apply them on the job, but also refers to a series of planned and integrated learning and work activities that clearly went beyond those of traditional cooperative education. Thirdly, the EBCE program holds not only that free choice be maximized, and that students be capable of self-direction in their educational endeavors, but that the development of the capacity to be active and self reliant would benefit students not only in schools but in their lives as well.

Perhaps the major conceptual underpinning of the EBCE is the notion that education is preparation for life. The emphasis upon career, as opposed to vocational training, is an important aspect of the total career-education philosophy. The program aims to encourage student receptivity toward the continuation of both formal and informal education throughout life!

Career means one's progress through life or life path, and not just a nine-to-five segment of it. The goal of EBCE, to borrow Charles Silberman's words, is to prepare people not just to earn a living but to live a life (2).

THE NEW VOCATIONALISM (3)

Concern with how young people are prepared to enter the adult world, particularly the working world, has been a major focus of American education since the founding of the Republic. Ben Franklin's Academy, the Morrill Act forming the Land Grant Colleges, and the Smith-Hughes Act of 1917 are examples in the history of this concern. The past twenty years also have witnessed attention to the success or failure of education to adequately equip young people to enter the work force. The Kennedy Administration's efforts to address this issue culminated in the 1963 Vocational Education Act, which attempted to broaden the range and upgrade the quality of school career education programs. The 1968 and 1976 Vocational Educational Amendments further broadened these opportunities.

Despite this history of concern and legislative support, however, it was reported in 1973 that:

- 61% of a sample of 32,000 11th graders believe that persons never change jobs throughout their adult life (the average person changes jobs five times).
- 43% believe unemployment rates are lower for youths than adults (unemployment rates are almost four times greater for youths than adults).
- 46% believe women never work after getting married (42% of married women are currently in the labor force).
- 59% did not know where to begin to prepare for their own first choices for careers.
- 60% had talked only once or never with workers in the occupation of their first choice, had never taken a course, visited local industries or workplaces related to their choice (4).

The results of a 1973 Gallup poll further highlighted this failure of past efforts: 90% of the American people believed that public schools should give more emphasis to the study of trades, professions, and business to help students decide on careers.

Recent research thus has focused on the contribution of the structure of public schools to the failure of past career education programs. Reports of such bodies as the President's Science Advisory Panel on Youth, the National Commission on the Reform of Secondary Education, and the National Panel on High School have suggested that our high schools are too far removed from the adult world, particularly the world of work. They note that young people are offered insufficient developmental opportunities in the areas of career decision-making and direct interaction with the environment in which they will soon be immersed.

In 1975 the National Association of Secondary School Principals published a report entitled, *This We Believe*. With regard to the high-school curriculum they commented:

> *The Association believes that the secondary school curriculum should be redesigned and placed in a more comprehensive setting. Opportunities for service and work, serious contact with adult institutions, and experiences that span age and ethnicity need to be a part of secondary education. Thus would schools become less exclusively cognitive, egoistic, and segregated by age and culture* (5).

This "new vocationalism," arising out of the heightened concern with and questioning of the purposes of education, has spawned many new programs. One major development has been Experience-Based Career Education. EBCE aims to provide an integrated program that blends experience and knowledge about the world of work with a strong academic education. It attempts to provide a meeting ground for the positive facets of experiential learning, individualized curriculum, use of community resources, and career development with the necessary academic concerns of a strong general education.

EBCE PROGRAM DEVELOPMENT

The EBCE program, as it has been developed (6), takes the subjects students normally study, adds many new ingredients (about people, self, jobs, and the way communities work), and lets high-school students learn about them out in the community, through direct experience with adults. In the process, students obtain academic credit, explore the real dimensions of many careers, learn about who they are and what they want to become, and master some of the skills they will need to successfully negotiate the complex world of adult living.

The direct experience of working with many adults as they perform their daily activities is a key to the EBCE program. Students who are studying politics test their new knowledge against the practical insights of legislators, judges, city managers, and policemen. Students who think they are interested in a career in ecology study and work alongside scientists, technicians, investigators, and secretaries. They discover that "ecology" covers many jobs, that every job has its moments of both boredom and excitement, and that the specific careers that interest them may require far more (or far less) education and experience than they expected.

The entire community, with all its richness, confusion and reality, becomes the school for students enrolled in EBCE. Their goal is not to train for one pre-selected job, but to discover by direct experience what career(s) they find most potentially rewarding; not to use occasional "field trips" to supplement classroom study, but to study within the context of sites and people in the community; not just to learn about responsibility, values, and maturity, but to become more responsible and mature and to begin to develop a consistent set of values.

The Experience-Based Career Education program consists of many programs rather than just one. All students are at different points as they enter the program and each has his or her own unique interests, abilities, academic background, and personal traits. The student enters EBCE as a full-time activity; the total community will be the school, not just the classroom. The topics, people, and jobs which are "for him" or for her are different, totally or partially, from those which are "for" any other student.

One of the two major priorities of EBCE is to create a set of learning experiences uniquely appropriate to each individual. As a result, all students experience their own special community, in terms of the people they meet, where they go, and what and how they learn. The program's other major commitment is to the belief that "courses" do not have to be separate sets of events. The content of social studies, English, science, and career development are inescapably different, yet within the EBCE program they are combined into sets of activities. An EBCE student, for example, may conduct biological research and experimentation (for science credit) while he is exploring a particular career in ecology (for career development credit). He may write reports on both of these activities and have them evaluated for English credit. He may supplement any of these "on-site" activities in a special learning centers. The only criterion is what is best for the individual student, which is a joint decision made by the student, the Learning Coordinator, and frequently parents and community adults.

The Experience-Based Career Education program, in short, is an attempt to provide high-school students with learning opportunities which are both as realistic and as relevant as possible — realistic in terms of the actual demands and possibilities of adult life, and relevant in terms of what each individual student wants and needs to learn.

The EBCE staff recognized from the beginning that they would have to break some new ground in translating EBCE from an idea into an actual program. Many of the ideas behind EBCE were not new; existing programs already were bringing the classroom and the community closer together. EBCE's planners, however, hoped to put the pieces together in new and more effective ways. Vocational, cooperative, and work-study programs have emphasized training for a specific skill rather than learning about many careers, about adult life, and about making many types of decisions. They have kept academic studies in the classroom rather than letting academic learning occur in the community. And they normally limited the students' choices to a single site and a small number of courses, rather than encouraging them to study many things, in many different ways, in a large number of different community sites. One set of problems for the planners, then, was to find ways to blend all aspects of learning (career, academic, and personal growth), to make them occur out in the community, and to provide each student with innumerable choices as to the learning that was most important to his own needs, interests, and abilities.

Doing all of these things, however, would not be enough. Other programs had failed, or been crippled, because they had "lost track" of the students once they were out in the community. EBCE planners recognized that the program could be completely effective and useful only if it could identify precisely what a student was going to learn on a particular site, find out what she or he actually did learn, and then use that learning both to guide the next decisions about learning activities and to establish credits and grades. The EBCE program meets all of these needs in ways that are both practical and effective. The community has become the classroom for junior and senior high-school students (and, more recently, others in the 15-25 age range) and students, community resource persons, parents, staff, and school administrators have all been pleased with the outcome.

The instructional "systems" devised for the EBCE programs are highly complex structures, yet simple to operate. Equally important to many observers of the program is that the components are not unique to any one site. That is, EBCE programs can be installed in communities easily, quickly, and efficiently — in fact, at the local average secondary per-pupil expenditure. Essentially, EBCE programs consist of seven basic ingredients:

- Community experience sites and resource persons, once they have agreed to participate in the program, are thoroughly yet economically analyzed to find out what kinds of things students might learn there, and under what conditions.

- Students' needs, interests, and abilities are individually probed, both initially and throughout the year, to find out the kinds of learning and experiences that are most appropriate for that student.

- Standard course-work has been re-worked into a vast series of concepts and objectives, which a student can tackle in many different ways, depending on overall program needs and choices.

- Information on sites, assessments of student needs, and the concept-oriented curriculum have been systematically cross-referenced so that the ingredients can be mixed and matched to meet the unique needs and desires of each student.

- Each student's specific learning activities are carefully described, followed, and evaluated so that the student is accountable as he or she learns in the community.

- A systematic, multi-level process is used to guide the student as he uses the community to investigate who he is, what the adult community offers him, and how to deal with the life-long series of vocational, avocational, and personal choices which constitute a "career."

- Finally, the traditional "teacher" has been replaced by a "Learning Coordinator" who has full responsibility for coordinating, guiding, and evaluating all aspects of a student's program.

An examination of these seven ingredients will help to identify the most innovative and exciting elements of EBCE programs.

COMMUNITY EXPERIENCE SITES

A grave initial question for planners was whether or not the community would be willing to participate in an EBCE program. Would private businesses, labor unions, or government agencies be interested in having students on their premises? Would they spend time helping students learn, without being paid and without the promise of a trained potential employee at the end?

The environments within which the EBCE programs were to be developed were diverse: two large cities, Philadelphia and Oakland, a state capital, Charleston, W.Va., and a suburb, Tigard, Oregon. EBCE planners adopted several techniques to recruit community resources sites. One of the most successful has become known as a "front-runner" strategy. In essence, this strategy creates an on-going Community Advisory Council, made up of residents with as many business, civic, political, and social contacts as possible. The Advisory Council, which should include prominent labor, business, educational, and civic leaders, has proved indispensable in determining the kinds of programs that would "fly," in obtaining and maintaining community participation, and in critiquing and evaluating the programs as they evolved. This strategy has proved very successful. Less than ten percent of those asked to participate have declined or dropped out after initially agreeing. The number of sites available to EBCE students thus far has been limited primarily by the numbers the programs have needed; there is no evidence that the community loses interest in the program after becoming involved.

Another major concern was what to do with the sites once they agreed to participate. Given EBCE goals, it was not possible simply to turn students loose on sites; it was necessary first to find out what kinds of learning could go on there. On the other hand, it was impractical to obtain every bit of information that could be gathered — a task which might require months of effort and many volumes of information for each site. The procedures which the EBCE programs now use were not developed overnight. About two years were devoted to design, revision, and more revision to achieve the current balance between too much and too little information and effort.

The system for analyzing and documenting what learning can take place on a given community site starts with the garnering of information spelled out on a form. This form (sometimes called a Learning Guide), which can be put together by paraprofessionals after a short training session, contains several basic kinds of information, such as:

- General information about the site (names, phone numbers, location, hours, dress code, etc.);

- General description of the site (kind of business, subdivisions within the organization, etc.);

- Task statements for each Resource Person in each subdivision (what they do, why, with what tools and instructions, etc.);

- Activities which a student may only observe (e.g., a lawyer Resource Person arguing a case in court);

- Activities which a student may do with no prerequisite training or experience (e.g., setting up props in a TV studio under direction);

- Activities a student may do with prerequisite skills (e.g., writing radio scripts); and

- Special activities and projects (discussions, demonstrations, tutoring, etc.).

The first three types of information are relatively cut-and-dried, and depict the general nature of the site without providing too much detail. The last four types are the keys to learning; they respresent more creative efforts on the part of the EBCE staff and site personnel to pinpoint career, academic, and personal development learning activities which the site can offer to students.

Use of Learning Guides gives the staff and students an opportunity to agree on sites and on general activities within a site which match the student's program needs and choices. Once this is done, specific activities can be generated to guide and measure precisely what a student is supposed to do, and what he actually does, on that site. Since site personnel must "sign off" on the Learning Guide, both student and staff know in advance that the learning activities they create will be acceptable to the resource people at that site.

STUDENT NEEDS, INTERESTS, AND ABILITIES

A major activity during the student's first week or two in the EBCE program is to find out as much as possible about what that student needs, wants, and can do. This analysis process takes several forms, ranging from standardized testing and review of the student's high-school transcript through special checklists and one-to-one discussions between the student and his Learning Coordinator. A major concern is to identify the credits the student needs. For seniors, EBCE must assure that each student gets all the formal credits he needs to graduate. To assure this the staff study the transcript and establish the student's credit needs and options.

The first outcome of this analysis is a tentative profile of the student. It might conclude, for example, that a student needs five credits to graduate (English, mathematics, and three electives); is "sort of" interested in careers as a teacher, an auto mechanic, or a lawyer; is slightly below average in standardized tests and in grades; is relatively outgoing and mature; and prefers to work with people rather than things (although he has a knack for machinery).

Staff and student discuss this information, the available EBCE sites, and the interdisciplinary curriculum which EBCE offers. They agree on the academic studies the student will "contract" for during the year, the first site he or she wants to go to, the jobs she or he wants to explore, and the first set of specific activities he or she will undertake. From then on, the student and the Learning Coordinator will reassess this initial set of decisions, and will change or re-interpret them as the student progresses. The key ingredient in such changes is the opportunity for the students to test their interests and abilities against real-life situations and to change their course as they learn more about themselves and the adult world.

A student exploring auto mechanics at a local automobile dealer, for example, gradually (or rapidly) may discover a greater interest in selling or designing machinery than in fixing it. As a result of this discovery, the next site assignment might be in the merchandising or research and development department of an electronics firm. The student might have different activities and objectives specified for this assignment, looking at precise things he or she liked and disliked about those career areas, and perhaps pursuing his or her required math credits through helping procure bids for equipment rather than calculating costs of auto parts. Increasingly, the students settle into a pattern of overall studies as they discover how they "fit" (or want to fit) into the real world about them.

INTEGRATED CURRICULUM

Traditionally, one of the greatest barriers to combining different academic courses has been the fact that such courses have focused on the classroom and on content materials. A chemistry course which emphasizes mixing chemical elements, for example, has been difficult, if not impossible, to unite with an economics course which emphasizes laws of supply and demand. One set of learning activities could not easily accomplish both types of content objectives within a classroom environment.

The EBCE program has been able to blend many apparently discrete subject areas into single sets of activities only because it has avoided a focus on the classroom or on subject-matter content. This does not mean that students have no academic content in their studies; rather it means that content is not the organizing principle for learning. The academic and career curricula within EBCE programs are oriented instead toward what is known as the "concept/inquiry" model of learning. This model, which is both simple and efficient in practice, has two major elements: concepts and the inquiry process.

- **Concepts and objectives.** Essentially, the model states that learning becomes more meaningful for students when they concentrate on key concepts and objectives in a particular area, rather than on a body of knowledge. For example, a student might need a Civics or Social Studies credit. As part of this credit, the student might choose to explore the question: "Are particular groups who are in contact with each other basically cooperative or competitive?" The student could learn about this general question in many ways, through many texts and references, and on many different sites, depending on the nature of the rest of his studies.

  He or she might, for example, be exploring careers (and earning science credits) at a large chemical plant. In the social studies area, it might be learned from a number of people that such large industries are both competitive (in sales and new product development) and cooperative (in basic research, lobbying, etc.). One site, and one set of experiences, could help earn credits in several "courses" while giving some valuable insights into the adult world.

  Within the EBCE program, then, students choose their academic learning objectives on the basis of key concepts, with the specific emphasis and subject matter variable, rather than the other way around.

- **Inquiry Process.** The concepts described above serve essentially as the structure for student learning. The inquiry process provides the key process for learning. A student, for example, may have decided to master some aspect of the concept of cooperation/competition; he or she wants to understand it and to be able to apply it to the things in the community. The inquiry process, as used with EBCE programs, lets students "master" the concept systematically and, at the same time, develop rational thinking skills.

  After a student selects a concept to work on, the student and Learning Coordinator generate specific activities to "get at" that

concept (e.g., obtain opinions from ten persons at the site about whether they are basically competitive or cooperative with rival companies and identify their reasons, values, and priorities in making those judgments; read selected chapters from certain books; analyze the interview results in light of the textual information). Each activity which helps get at the concept is based on the five levels of rational thinking. Cumulatively, each student will have gone through all five steps a number of times during a year in EBCE, thus systematically preparing him or herself to think more rationally in situations that will be met in the future.

Once students have selected their target concepts, then, they can "mix-and-match" concepts, sites, references, and learning materials in ways that are uniquely their own. EBCE programs have developed special manuals, cards, and other materials which cross-reference community sites, texts, possible activities, and other information. This set of cross-referenced, concept/inquiry-based materials lets the student and Learning Coordinator translate general decisions about sites and concepts into a personalized curriculum. Similarly, a student's curriculum can be changed by repeating the simple procedures.

ACCOUNTABILITY

A major outcome of the analysis of sites, student assessment, and cross-referencing curriculum is the fact that, once basic decisions are made, the EBCE staff have the information needed to follow and evaluate precisely what happens to the student as he or she goes out "on site." The major vehicle for that is a student activity sheet.

Once the student and Learning Coordinator have agreed upon the basic thrust of the student's program, they must turn general desires into specific assignments. The student and the Learning Coordinator discuss a number of possible specific activities. Once they agree upon the first activity, an activity sheet is prepared. This sheet specifies the site and duration, the credit range to be given, the products to be produced, and the specific activities to be undertaken. Additionally, the activity sheet indicates the level of inquiry process involved in each activity.

The student activity sheet serves many purposes. It is a binding agreement between the student and Learning Coordinator; it insures that student, Learning Coordinator, and site personnel know what the student will be doing; it establishes the range of credit the student may receive and what must be done to earn maximum credit; it sets a timetable for completion; and it documents the student's work for high-school credit purposes. After the student completes the activity, performance is evaluated by the Learning Coordinator, the site resource person, and him or herself. The amount of credit awarded is negotiated and recorded in the student's permanent file. Every step of the process is carefully followed, coordinated, and evaluated so that students do not simply "get lost" as they make the community their classroom.

CAREER DECISION-MAKING

The only course of study pursued by all EBCE students is Career Development. This curriculum is designed not to aid students in preparing for a pre-selected career but to guide them in learning about possible careers and in mastering basic career decision-making skills. The curriculum is based upon the idea that the most important career-related attribute for high-school students is the ability to make rational career decisions in the future. This, in turn, is based on the belief that a "career" is not a single job, but rather a continuing, life-long series of vocational, avocational, and personal options and decisions.

The Career Development curriculum contains the same type of concepts and objectives listings as do other curricula. The concepts cover such areas as: "What types of behavior usually bring satisfying job advancement?"; "What types of training for a specific job or position are transferable to what other jobs?" and "What are some of the advantages and disadvantages of membership in professional and union groups?" Students pursue the concepts they select through the inquiry process described above.

Additionally, the Career Development curriculum helps the student plan, carry out, and evaluate the career-oriented experiences he or she has on community sites. These focus on three key dimensions of learning: occupational awareness, self-awareness, and career planning and decision-making. Essentially, EBCE students continually play these three dimensions off against each other throughout the year. They use their site experience to learn about occupations, specific jobs, and the generalized "world of work" (getting a job, relations with supervisors, promptness, etc.). They assess the meaning of such information in terms of their growing awareness of who they are — their values, abilities, interests, and temperaments. They then evaluate these insights to find out what implications they have for their career options and plans.

A student involved in this process might discover, for example, that he or she was very "turned on" by a certain kind of job and had the required abilities, but could not stand the amount of travel involved. Such discoveries would help the student to make some initial (and sometimes very difficult) decisions about where to go after high school; for example, how to resolve the conflict between liking and being qualified for the job and the dislike of traveling. More importantly, students should have gained some invaluable attitudes and skills concerning the nature of career choices — isolating the key factors in various jobs, assessing them in terms of their own self-awareness, accepting and reacting to the fact that abilities and interests often conflict with job realities, and recognizing that career decisions are not a one-shot deal but rather involve a lifelong process of insight and re-evaluation.

THE LEARNING COORDINATOR

The final, and perhaps most crucial, element of the EBCE program is the Learning Coordinator (also called Learning Manager, Learning Facilitator, and Counselor). The manuals, catalogs, theories, and site analyses which the program has devised are coordinated by this staff member who has full responsibility for insuring that they serve the needs of each student. Unlike more traditional education programs, the Learning Coordinator does not serve as the primary dispenser of information within the EBCE program. Rather, the Learning Coordinator's primary function is to help the student get to where the information is, get the information, and then make use of it.

Unlike more traditional programs, in which a student must relate to several teachers and counselors, a single Learning Coordinator is totally responsible for each student's program within EBCE. Each student is assigned a Learning Coordinator when he enters the program (changes in assignments can be made if there are strong conflicts or problems). The Learning Coordinator orients the student to the program; helps him make the initial choices of sites, courses, concepts, and activities; monitors the students while on-site; evaluates the results; helps the student plan the next activities; counsels the student as needed; and continues all of these activities for that student throughout the year. All of the manuals, references, and other materials used by the program are designed to provide the Learning Coordinator with the information and procedures they need to perform these functions. At present, EBCE programs have a student/Learning Coordinator ratio of about 20 to 1, but some sites are operating with a 35 to 1 ratio.

Perhaps the primary feature of the Learning Coordinator role is the degree to which the traditionally separate functions of instruction and guidance are blended into a single event. Learning Coordinators within the EBCE programs do, in fact, "teach" their students two things: (1) how to use the real-world community to gain access to learning experiences; and (2) how to organize, assimilate, and draw inferences from those experiences. In effect, these Learning Coordinators are "teaching" their students where to go, and what to do, in order to make rational decisions relating to the outside world.

REQUIREMENTS THE COMMUNITY MUST MEET

Each resource person and site is free to specify reasonable requirements which they impose upon EBCE and its students (e.g., dress code; hours and days of participation). EBCE, in turn, expects its sites and resource persons to adhere to several requirements which are designed to: assure that each student has full opportunity to experience all EBCE community resources; and protect the student, firm, resource person, unions, and other employees against the dangers implicit in any sort of experiential learning program of EBCE's scope. For example, EBCE programs have prepared, and require each site to sign, formal statements which guarantee that the site will be available to all EBCE students without regard to sex, race, creed, or national origin, and that it is in full compliance with all pertinent federal, state, and local equal opportunity, civil rights, and other regulations and policies.

In addition, the EBCE program's instructional systems and requirements are built around the need to adhere to both the letter and the spirit of the Fair Labor Standards Act. The EBCE program, for example, has obtained and twice verified a set of criteria (from the U.S. Department of Labor) which specify that EBCE students who are not paid can have learning experiences on community sites if:

- The training, even though it includes actual operation of the facilities of the employer, is similar to that which would be given in a vocational school.

- The training is for the benefit of the trainees or students.

- The trainees or students do not displace regular employees, but work under their close observation.

- The employer providing the training derives no immediate advantage from the activities of the trainees or students (on occasion his operations actually may be impeded).

- The trainees or students are not necessarily entitled a job at the conclusion of the training period.

- The employer and the trainees or students understand that the trainees or students are not entitled to wages for the time spent in training (7).

These criteria are fully met within EBCE, by both the instructional systems and such policies as limiting student placements to a maximum of 13 weeks at a single site.

All EBCE programs similarly are responsive to and concerned about a variety of other safeguards of both student and worker rights. Site analysis, placement, activity specification, and on-site monitoring practices, for example, are based upon continuing assessment of student activities in relationship to such legislation and policies as the Occupational Safety and Health Act, federal and state child labor laws, Title IX of the Educational Amendment of 1972, and the Civil Rights Act. Full compliance and safeguards are identified in advance, reacted to in learning activities, and continuously monitored by EBCE staff and the Community Advisory Council. Such precautions are necessary to protect both students and workers during program operation. EBCE is fully aware that its scope and nature force it to continually walk the line between organizing student activities and community resources for learning and protecting both the student and the community from exploitation.

THE PROGRAMMATIC EFFECTS OF EBCE

Evaluation of such a complex alternative as Experience-Based Career Education (EBCE) project was not a simple task. There are, in effect, four somewhat similar programs created by the four developer laboratories; and the ideas and concepts from the work of Provus, Stake, Stuffelbean, Scriven, and Ianni have all played a part (8).

The majority of the evaluative effort associated with the EBCE project was formative and designed to better understand and improve the program, its materials, and its implementation. Formative evaluation data, however, although important to the implementer and developer at the time of its collection, tends to lose its usefulness as the findings are incorporated into the on-going program development effort. Thus the focus here is on information more useful to those who have not yet made a decision to implement an EBCE program — that is, information on program outcomes.

There are three areas in which EBCE has sought to measure outcomes. While these are equally important (because without positive findings in each of the areas an innovative program cannot long exist), they are of sequential utility and, therefore, necessity. The first area is *community support*. In order for an innovation to be adopted or adapted by an educational agency, it must be seen to be useful before it is tried. Consequently, community support for the continuation of the program must be generated long before measurable programmatic outcomes are available.

The second area is *academic quality*. That is, students in the experimental program cannot be hurt academically, especially in terms of reading and math achievement, by being involved in the programs. If academic consistency cannot be shown, then either (1) the programs will not be utilized, regardless of quality in other areas, or (2) they will be used only with students for whom academics are relatively unimportant. Both alternatives should be avoided since they adversely limit the program's educational value.

The third area is *programmatic effect*. Normally, this might be thought of as the most important area and, for the program developer, it is. However, for the potential program adopter/adapter, the level of local support for the program usually is most important, since outcomes become apparent and measurable only after a program has been in operation for as much as two or three years. In addition, lay persons generally weigh the testimony of other parents and community members more heavily than the formal results of written tests and questionnaires so often associated with programmatic outcomes.

COMMUNITY SUPPORT

Two basic sources of commuity support are associated with EBCE programs. One is the group of parents of the students enrolled in or graduated from the program. The second is comprised of the resource persons associated with the operations of the program. These resource persons may be from private industry, labor unions, governmental service, public services, volunteer organizations, etc.

Ninety per cent of the parents questioned rated the EBCE program as "much better" or "somewhat better" than the past school experiences of their children. Only 2.8% compared it unfavorably. Over 96% of parents saw no negative changes in their children that they could associate with the EBCE program. The resource persons associated with the programs also respond favorably. Only four percent said their resource organization would probably not continue working with EBCE programs and 96% said they would recommend, either without reservations or with some reservations, EBCE program involvement to other resource persons and organizations.

ACADEMIC ACHIEVEMENT

Academic achievement is important to include in a discussion of the outcomes of EBCE because one might question whether or not students who spend up to 80% of their time out of a school building will suffer academically. Results of reading comprehension and arithmetic skills instruments indicated that there were no significant differences between EBCE students' scores and those of control group students. In the areas tested, student academic achievement was shown not to be harmed by involvement in the EBCE programs.

PROGRAMMATIC OUTCOMES

The experimental group of EBCE students scored significantly higher on oral communication skills and improved attitudes toward career planning than the control group. Student attitudes toward education in general and the total learning environment had improved significantly over those of the controls since involvement with the EBCE program.

Eighty-two percent of EBCE graduates indicate that the program had a positive effect on their educational preparation, while 87 percent indicated that their experience in the program had a positive effect on their future employment.

In conclusion, the evidence briefly summarized here shows that there is strong support for the EBCE programs from the parents of students, and from the resource persons and organizations associated with the program and from past graduates. Students are not academically hurt by their involvement with EBCE programs; and the evidence points to increasing benefits the longer they remain in the EBCE program. Assessments also show that the programmatic effects are positive, in line with expectations, and that they become more positive the longer a student stays in the program. In addition, school dropout rates have been found to be significantly lower for students involved in EBCE programs.

Dr. Keith Goldhammer, who headed an independent review group that spent more than a month in 1974 at the four projects, commented on the future of EBCE:

Somewhere at sometime someone said, 'I have seen the future, and it works!' I think that is how I felt as I had this opportunity to see the EBCE programs in operation. Can you picture randomly selecting 150 students from any high school within the country and finding genuine enthusiasm, a feeling of belonging, a feeling that school exists for them, a feeling that they were recognized as human beings and they can do within the schools what is important for them to do? We did interview approximately 150 EBCE students, and we didn't find one who was disaffected by what she/he was doing (9).

FOOTNOTES AND REFERENCES

1. The concept of an experience-based career education program (first called employer-based) emerged late in 1970 in the Office of Education's National Center for Educational Research and Development (NCERD). In June, 1971, feasibility study contracts were awarded to Research for Better Schools, Inc., in Philadelphia, and the Far West Laboratory, then in Berkeley, California, for data collection, analysis, and elaboration of the EBCE concept and ramifications. In May-June, 1972, four laboratories (Appalachia Educational Laboratory, Far West Laboratory, Northwest Regional Educational Laboratory, and Research for Better Schools) were authorized to begin operational sites in Fall 1972. Students were enrolled and completed a first developmental year in June 1973. The second developmental year began in September 1973, and the third in September 1974.

   To give the reader some idea of the present scope of EBCE (August, 1978) there are over 150 school districts with one or more EBCE programs, over 25,000 students that are or have been in EBCE programs, over 16,000 community persons involved with EBCE and more than 15 state Departments of Education that are in the process of having their staff trained to be able to provide EBCE services to local educational agencies. In addition, a new National Experience-Based Career Education Association (NEBCEA) has begun.

2. The author wishes to express his appreciation to David H. Hampson for his permission to draw upon his short article published in the ILLINOIS CAREER EDUCATION JOURNAL, Vol. 33, No. 3, on "The New Vocationalism."

3. Far West Laboratory for Educational Research and Development, THE FEASIBILITY OF EMPLOYER-BASED CAREER EDUCATION: A SUMMARY, February 20, 1973, pp. 17-32.

4. D.J. Prediger, et al., NATIONWIDE STUDY OF STUDENT CAREER DEVELOPMENT: SUMMARY OF RESULTS, American College Testing Program, Report No. 61, November, 1973.

5. National Association of Secondary School Principals, THIS WE BELIEVE: A STATEMENT ON SECONDARY EDUCATION. Task Force on Secondary Schools in a Changing Society. Reston, Va.: NASSP, 1975.

6. In the interest of simplicity, the discussion on program development focuses on only one of the four EBCE models. The objective is to be general enough to encompass all four models while keeping the focus specific enough to be clear. The writer is indebted to Dr. Harold Henderson of the Appalachia Educational Laboratory for his permission to draw upon a paper he wrote in 1974 describing the AEL/EBCE model program.

7. Department of Labor publication OH-1297, 1973, pp. 2-3.

8. A more extensive description of the programmatic effects of the EBCE was published originally by the author as a chapter in the ILLINOIS CAREER EDUCATION JOURNAL, Vol. 33 No. 3, Spring, 1976.

9. Keith Goldhammer, "Extending Career Education Beyond the Schoolhouse Walls," lecture delivered at the Center for Vocational and Technical Education, Ohio State University, May 24, 1974.

EXPERIENCE-BASED CAREER EDUCATION
FAR WEST HIGH SCHOOL
OAKLAND, CALIFORNIA

Stephania Arness

Of all the problems that young people face, the one that is most pressing, personal, and far-reaching is that of selecting a livelihood. In the wake of the industrial revolution and the introduction of mass production and computerization, one no longer becomes a shoemaker because one's father is a shoemaker. One must select an occupation from an increasingly complex array of possibilities. The choice is even more difficult because an occupation chosen today may well become obsolete before one's retirement, making it essential that a young person select an occupation that is not an end in itself, but may also lead to other related positions: a career.

Making a decision has never been so important or so risky. In schools, values clarification and decision-making are gaining status in the curriculum. It is becoming increasingly evident that the life skills that help a young person make a successful career choice must be included in a basic education.

The Far West Model of Experience-Based Career Education (1) is one of the current efforts to help young people develop these skills and learn about the choices available, while meeting high-school graduation requirements. Far West High School provides students with opportunities to investigate their own values, to set goals according to those values, and to make decisions that will help them reach those goals. Students also are exposed to a wide range of potential role models. The amenities of a traditional high school that duplicate available community resources are omitted; students instead are provided information about and access to such community resources. Academic credit is granted for the successful completion of "projects," which include first-hand career exploration, library research, problem-solving, and communication skills development.

VALUES, GOALS AND DECISIONS

Clarifying values, setting goals, and making decisions that lead to those goals are continuous processes in adult life. At Far West High School they begin with the student's decision to leave his neighborhood school. He must be willing to give up the glamour and excitement of interscholastic athletics, the social setting, and all the amenities of a traditional high school. He must be successful in convincing a parent to come to the school for an informational interview.

Once that decision has been made, the student discovers that he is no longer dependent upon the counseling office for his academic program, but is fully responsible for it himself. He begins to make decisions about the next two or three years of his life in his first meeting with his Learning Coordinator. The Learning Coordinator (LC) acts as the student's personal counselor, homeroom teacher, and academic supervisor. The LC hands the student a copy of the district graduation requirements and a copy of the student's own transcript, saying something to the effect of "Well, here's what you look like on paper. What do you want to do about it?" It's the first time most students have thought more than a couple months ahead about their own lives, so it can be a fairly grueling experience. It may take two or three weeks to make even the major decisions.

This long-term planning includes several steps. The student subtracts courses already completed from the graduation requirements to determine what he still needs and adds college entrance requirements and special interests of his own. He divides the total units needed in each subject area by the number of terms before he proposes to graduate, and sketches out a tentative study schedule for each of the remaining terms. This plan may change at any time, but putting it all on paper gives the student a focus on his immediate goals. This process requires the student to reaffirm his long-term goal of graduating from high school, consider post-high-school plans, and decide what to do right now that will help him progress in the direction he has chosen.

Even proficiency in basic skills becomes the responsibility of the Far West student. With the help of the staff Skills Specialist, the student assesses his own skill development in reading, writing, mathematics, and foreign languages, and requests appropriate small group or individual meetings with a tutor. Advanced students may take courses at local community colleges or the university.

The LC helps the student to coordinate his academic needs with his career and other interests and to select resource persons from the file of cooperating volunteers in the working community whose careers include the academic area the student needs to study. A student working on credit in governmental social science may work at the local assemblyman's office, the District Attorney's office, and the Housing Authority office, learning

198

how the government operates while exploring various careers in these offices.

Working closely with his LC, the student develops academic and career goals and determines how he will demonstrate that he has met them. Demonstration might include a formal research paper, a tape-recorded series of interviews interspersed with the student's own commentary, a video tape, a photo essay, other art work, or any combination of forms that will demonstrate what he has learned. Each Far West project includes academic subject matter, career information, problem-solving, and communication skills development.

The student assesses each career he explores in terms of his own values. He may meet a woman in charge of quality control for the local sewer district whose job entails dipping her bare hands into the partially processed sludge to inspect for a particular characteristic. The student's initial repulsion to the job may disappear when he learns that her salary provides an expensive home and a sailboat. The informal nature of the student's encounter with the resource allows him to become familiar with the personality of the resource and the lifestyle the job allows, while the formal report of the encounter requires the student to learn about the person's reasons for having this particular job, how he or she came to this position, what kind of planning, preparation and previous experience were required, and whether the resource person sees the job as a lifetime career or a step toward a more preferable position. Each of these aspects is evaluated by the student according to his current values, giving these values tangible dimensions.

ROLE MODELS

Most values, goals, and decision-making processes are learned from the examples of parents and other role models. The more varied the potential role models, the more alternatives a young person may be able to see when facing a decision. Most young people have their families, adult friends, and school personnel as role models. The Far West student has the entire range of the local working community on whom to pattern his value system, goal selection, and decision-making processes.

The Far West student meets most of his potential role models as school resource persons. They are volunteers in the community who have the time, energy, and inclination to share their working worlds with high-school students. During any school year a student may come in contact with such varied resources as a mortician, a printer, a bank executive, an interior designer, an accountant, and a restaurateur. Students are encouraged to compare careers that have similar aspects, such as graphic artist with a portrait painter. A student earning credit in World Studies may explore careers in the international banking component of a major bank while researching how the international money market affects social and industrial developments in various parts of the world.

Another group of potential roles is provided by the tutorial staff, who are students at the local university, hired and supervised by the staff Skills Specialist to teach the basic academic skills that require a classroom or tutorial setting. Tutorial staff teach all levels of reading, writing, mathematics, and foreign languages to individuals or small groups of students. University students are ideal as role models in that they are only a few years older than the high-school students, but have already established some of their own values and are in the process of achieving some of their personal and career goals. Even their jobs at the high school are part of that process in that they are financing their educations and providing work experience or, for some, university credit and possible entry to the college of education. Involved in meeting the short-term goals of their university course work and making decisions that will lead to their long-term career goals, these tutors are natural role models for high-school students.

Although an LC's day includes more student contact hours than a typical classroom teacher's, his actual number of students is smaller, allowing him to develop closer relationships with them. Whereas a traditional teacher has five or six groups of 35 students rotating through his or her classroom each day and meets individually with students only during "conference periods", an LC is responsible for only one group of 35 students for an entire day. This increase in contact hours fosters the development of personal relationships and thus increases the likelihood and intensity of potential role modeling.

COMMUNITY RESOURCES

Far West eliminates several of the expenses of a traditional high school by making use of community resources. Since many of the amenities in a traditional high school are duplications of resources already available in the community, paid for by the same taxpayers who provide the schools, Far West's costs are comparable because it utilizes the community resources.

Local tax money provides an excellent library system, and for more scholarly work, the University library is available to any state resident. The City Parks and Recreation Department sponsors a complete range of athletic, musical, and dramatic classes and events. Museums, art galleries, and civic musical groups provide a wide range of cultural and instructional resources. Rather than duplicating these resources within the schools, Far West provides telephones and bus tickets so students can participate in community programs.

Since they work with only 30 students, the LCs are able to counsel and coordinate student interests and needs with available resources, including community organizations, volunteer resource persons, and tutors. Rather than being one of 100 or more students each of his teachers sees during the day, a Far West student is one of 30 students developing projects with his LC, one of not more than 15 working on academic skills with a tutor, and one of not more than ten learning about careers with a resource person.

Intelligent and creative use of human and community resources can result in a highly personalized education that develops the skills a young person needs to deal with the most difficult tasks of adult life. Besides mastering basic reading, writing, and math, the Far West Student learns the basic life skills — how to establish values, set goals, and make decisions that will help him make a successful career selection.

Experience-Based Career Education has different benefits for different students. One student may attend Far West all three years of high school, exploring some 50 different careers, many of which are related to the field in which he has already developed some interest. Another student may also explore 50 careers, and decide that none of them is exactly what he wants to do. This student will have made 50 valid decisions about his own life and avoided 50 less than satisfactory career choices. Still another student may spend only a semester in the program before deciding that this is not the way he wants to prepare for adult life — that he really prefers the regular schedule of classes and activities in a traditional high school. In order to make this decision, the student must look at his own values and consider what high school might do for him. Even in leaving the program, a student must practice those life skills that are the focus of the program.

FOOTNOTES AND REFERENCES

1. The program was developed in 1972-75 in Oakland, CA, under an NIE contract with Far West Educational Laboratory, San Francisco, CA. In 1975 the emergent Far West High School was absorbed by the Oakland Unified School District. It now operates with about 200 students entirely on conventional public funds, with no special status. Students in grades 10-12 who otherwise would attend any other district school may attend.

SOME DISTURBING RESEARCH ON
SCHOOL PROGRAM EFFECTIVENESS

Wayne Jennings and Joe Nathan

At the turn of the century, when there was no mass media and few people subscribed to the weekly newspapers or magazines, schools performed a valuable function of information sharing and dispensing. Children of that era had many important responsibilities in the home, family business, or on the farm as workers and could see the direct relationship of their efforts to the well-being of the family.

James Coleman (1) argues that the current situation is reversed: society is now information rich and responsibility poor. The schools should re-examine their goals, Coleman argues, and, rather than dispense information, should provide diverse experiences and opportunities for youth to learn to assume responsibility in important matters.

Coleman is just one of many writers who have criticized the public schools for being seriously out of phase with the rest of society. And although alternative theories and innovative model education programs exist, they are little known.

This chapter attempts to summarize an impressive body of literature which documents the effectiveness of non-traditional school programs in the United States and also the serious shortcomings of existing educational arrangements and theories (2). The disturbing research results presented should cause us to question 95 percent of current educational practice and should modify educational history to reflect the important new directions which have been evolving in this field.

I. EXPERIMENTAL PRACTICES

One of the most extraordinary experiments ever conducted in American education was the Eight-Year Study (3), once widely cited in the literature but neglected in recent years. In this study, conducted during the 1930's, thirty high schools signed an agreement with 300 colleges to exempt their graduates from the usual college entrance requirements. This meant that the high schools did not have to use grades, class rank, required courses, credits, etc. They could experiment with curriculum and organization.

Some 1,500 students from the experimental schools were paired with

1,500 from similar but non-experimental schools and were matched by sex, age, intelligence, family background, race, and other factors. The students from experimental schools did as well as the others or better at college in grades, participation, critical thinking, aesthetic judgment, and knowledge of contemporary affairs.

Further analysis yielded some startling results: When students from the six *most experimental* schools were compared with those from traditional schools there were great differences in college attainment. Finally, graduates of the two most extremely experimental schools (where practices were indeed different — e.g., extensive learning in the community; outside volunteers working with students; advisor-advisee systems; students teaching other students; interdisciplinary problem-solving curricula; etc.) were found to be "strikingly more successful" (4).

The Eight-Year Study was one of the most significant and exciting studies in the history of American education. Subsequent studies of a similar type have yielded essentially the same results.

One of the schools in the Eight-Year Study was the Ohio State University Lab School. The students who graduated in 1938 wrote a book called *Were We Guinea Pigs?* In general, they liked their school, but of course had little to compare it with, since most of them had gone to the Lab School throughout their high school careers. Many years later a thorough follow-up study of the "guinea pigs" was reported in *Guinea Pigs 20 Years Later* (1961) (5). The Lab School graduates were then between 35 and 40 years old. The study found that the "guinea pigs" had been strikingly successful in life. When they were compared with subjects in the Lewis Terman study of genius and with graduates of Princeton University, where a similar follow-up had been conducted, the experimental school graduates came out ahead. They more often expressed satisfaction with life, were judged leaders in their professions, had more stable family lives, possessed better self-accepting attitudes, and were mentioned more frequently in *Who's Who*.

Six major studies completed by national groups between 1972 and 1975 provide sweeping suggestions for change in our schools. Though each of these studies was conducted independently, there is a remarkable similarity in their final recommendations. In general, they conclude that schools are inflexible (students who know a subject still have to take a course in it); most activities in school are done in lock-step, group-paced fashion; the products of high school are not very competent as citizens, consumers, parents, or workers, and seem poorly informed about the current world while possessing troubling undemocratic attitudes (6).

One of the many strategies recommended by the six studies has come to be known as "action learning," which requires students to engage in projects that enhance their lives in the school or society. The studies also recommend that students become deeply involved in the community — i.e., in business, internships, social service experiences, and the like. A further recommendation is that schools operate on an extended day and year basis, so that learning is increasingly seen as a life-long process, and that secondary studies insist that students and parents have a variety of programs from which to choose — i.e., alternatives.

Reports recommending participation in community/action service projects as part of classroom investigations make fascinating reading. Groups which have accepted these suggestions report exciting results. First, specific recommendations of the U.S. Office of Education National Panel on High School and Adolescent Education:

> *Education programs should be inaugurated for the joint participation of adolescents and other interested and qualified adults in the community-pedagogical programs which may be designated participatory education (learning by doing what is socially useful, personally satisfying and health supporting for the individual and the community).*

> *The Panel sees three major areas of education that lend themselves to such combined participation — education in the arts, vocational education and education in the operations of government . . . The Panel recommends that adolescents, in addition to the academic study of the social sciences and their methodology, should be involved in government in all appropriate agencies within the larger community. The preparation of citizens for a Republic is as central to the concept of education for us as it was for Plato. This involvement should be diverse: as volunteers, including internships, as aides, as part time employees...* (7).

The National Task Force on Citizenship Education points out that: *An abundance of research data indicates that the nation's young people have scant knowledge about the responsibilities of citizenship or how to become involved in government . . . neither school nor society presently considers citizenship preparation to be an important function of the schools. This is in sharp contrast to the attitude of the founding fathers who assigned to public education a primary political purpose — to promote the values, the ideas, the knowledge and the obligations required of citizens in a democratic/republican society* (8).

This Task Force recommended:

Among the experiences required for high school graduation should be a practicum in civic education . . . Community service experience should be related to work in the classroom and monitored by teaching personnel . . . Civic education courses should involve a broad range of participants from the community in addition to school staff (9).

The National Organization of Social Studies Teachers has accepted these recommendations and agreed: "Students should become involved in community problems as part of their social studies investigations, rather than being insulated from them" (10).

Now, what results have been obtained when education programs carried out these recommendations? The results demonstrate that action learning and youth participation programs can produce enormous gains for individual students, their communities and society.

For example, New Jersey developed the Institute for Political and Legal Education (IPLE). Originally operating in a single classroom in Burlington City, New Jersey, IPLE has been nationally validated by the U.S. Office of Education and recognized as "a carefully evaluated proven innovation worthy of national replication." IPLE trains teachers to help students design and carry out community service/action programs as part of their study of government. Students have conducted research for legislators, worked on specific projects such as obtaining a traffic light for an intersection, lobbying for a bill, and conducting voter registration drives, or working as interns with political activists.

Careful comparisons between experimental and control groups "have consistently shown that IPLE students have more knowledge and political awareness than other students." IPLE students also "generally take civic responsibilities more seriously . . . and are more involved in community activities" (11). The IPLE has worked with over 200 communities in 30 other states to help them adapt these ideas, and the research done in the sites reaffirms the outstanding results obtained.

Another attempt to integrate community and classroom learning has been carried out for several years by North-Central High School, near Indianapolis. In Learning Unlimited (a school within a school), students carry out community service projects as part of their graduation requirements. A careful evaluation funded by the Lilly Endowment (12) determined that the wide use of community-based learning experiences and independent structure results in:

a. students improving their feelings about their own ability to cope in the adult world;

b. students developing ability to connect practical experiences with formalized text and classroom endeavors;

c. improved students' independent motivation and internalized responsibility for academic and social existence;

d. improved students' feelings about themselves and a trust in their own ability to make decisions, deal with consequences and solve problems.

Another program which follows some of the recommendations of these reports is the Experience-Based Career Education (EBCE) project (13), described on page 177.

Careful research by outside evaluators showed the program had enormous benefits for participating students and was viewed enthusiastically by participating students, their parents, and community members who worked with the students.

Numerous other evaluations could be cited of the relatively few programs which have adopted and implemented these recommendations. The results are clear. Youth participation enriches learning, increases students' feelings of control of their own lives, and encourages them to remain concerned about and active in their community.

TODAY'S ALTERNATIVE SCHOOLS

Since 1970 a number of schools have been established which make use of curriculum and organization ideas developed either by the experimental schools in the thirties or even earlier by John Dewey and other progressive educators. Virtually every evaluation of these contemporary alternative schools show students doing as well as or better than students in traditional schools, when standardized tests are the evaluation instrument. Perhaps more important, they feel much better about themselves and are confident of their ability to accomplish things for themselves. They also demonstrate more positive attitudes toward school and learning. These results come from alternative schools in various cities — Cambridge, Chicago, Hartford, Los

Angeles, Minneapolis, Providence, Philadelphia, and St. Paul, for example.

One might wonder if alternative schools have atypical populations. Educators associated with the National Alternative Schools Program studied 300 public alternative schools and found that the average student body was more diverse racially and economically than the country's population. They also reported an average of two applicants for every alternative school opening.

A number of schools work specifically with students who are rejects from traditional schools. Harlem Prep in New York City was established for dropouts of other schools, yet 95% of its graduates go on to college.

The Career Study Center in St. Paul, Minnesota, was created for students who are unsuccessful in the city's traditional high schools, where they are typically truant half the time. Some 70 percent of CSC candidates are in trouble with the law, and schools and parents are at their wits' end. After some time in the progressively designed program at CSC, attendance rises to 80 percent. Youngsters then get out of trouble — and their parents can hardly believe the change in attitude toward schooling. Ninety percent graduate, although the original prognosis was that only 10 percent would do so. Career Study Center I was so successful that a second has been established.

It is too early to tell whether these alternative programs will yield long-term results as satisfactory as those of the experimental schools in the Eight-Year Study. However, there is reason to believe that today's alternative schools will produce effective, competent, and stable adults.

PREDICTIVE STUDIES

Recent studies challenge traditional notions about how one predicts success in later life. Consider, for example, the national mania for graduation from high school. Is graduation important to later success? One study reports on students enrolled in California colleges which accepted anyone who applied, disregarding high school diplomas (14). Seven percent of 32,000 whose records were examined (2,240 students) had not received a diploma. The grade-point average for these students was 2.56; for all students it was 2.51. The data were then corrected for age, sex, marital status, veteran status, family income, etc. Results remained the same: The nongraduates were doing as well or better than the graduates.

Even more startling is a pair of studies which question even the value of grades and test scores in predicting success. The American College Testing Services recently completed a study of itself which compared the value of four factors in predicting success (as measured by self-satisfaction and participation in a variety of community activities two years after college) (15). The factors were: 1) major achievement in what most high schools call extracurricular activity (debate, speech, journalism, etc.), 2) high grades in high school, 3) high grades in college, 4) high scores on the ACT. Three of the four factors were found to have no predictive value. The only factor which could be used to predict success in later life was achievement in "extracurricular" activities.

The College Entrance Examination Board's Scholastic Aptitude Test was examined for its accuracy in predicting how successful a person might be at a chosen career upon graduation from college. Results show that "the SATs offered virtually no clue to capacity for significant intellectual or creative contributions in mature life" (16). That is, there was virtually no correlation between high scores on the SAT and success in life. This study also found that the best predictor of creativity in mature life was a person's performance during youth, in independent self-sustained ventures. Those youngsters who had many hobbies, interests, and jobs, or were active in extracurricular activities, were more likely to be successful in later life. This study also found that admissions officers relied increasingly upon SAT scores. In other words, they were making mistakes.

Both studies show that test scores predict who will get good grades in college but that such academic success has *almost nothing* to do with success in later life.

Many other studies reveal nearly a zero correlation between college grades and later success in such fields as medicine, law, education, engineering, etc. (17).

For Project TALENT, one thousand 30-year-olds were interviewed in one of our most nationally representative follow-up studies. Robert Gagne summarized the findings in one terse sentence: "The evidence of these interviews suggests that high school education as a whole serves no very useful purpose" (18).

NEW WAYS OF ORGANIZING SCHOOLS

There is ample evidence that organizing total schools in very different ways makes sense. The studies we have mentioned were made where alternative schools are "total systems." But it is important to look at results of studies which deal only with parts of a program.

An international study of mathematics achievement is of particular interest. Ordinarily, the beginning age for studying math is 6. The study shows that in some countries math instruction is delayed until age 7, and in a few instances to age 8. The study found that students who are taught math late quickly catch up with those who are taught earlier. Differences of as much as two years of instruction made no difference in math achievement. Moreover, those who have the latest initial math instruction have fewer negative attitudes toward school and themselves (19).

In the area of remedial reading, a number of studies indicate a substantial gain in achievement after remedial instruction. Within a year these gains disappear and the child appears to have made only the progress one would expect without the remedial instruction (20).

It has been known for a long time that scores on standardized achievement tests are very stable. Considerable reductions in time spent on reading, math, and spelling (the basics!) did not reduce achievement scores, according to a 1932 review of studies (21). This result has been affirmed many times since.

The Plowden Report in England found that the integrated-day approach became increasingly prevalent in English primary schools after World War II. Students who did not have the usual long, thorough, carefully graded and sequenced reading, math, and writing instruction did as well as students where lesson hearing and workbooks were emphasized (22). That stunning finding led to much interest in the open classroom in the U.S.

Numerous studies indicate that children can be very effective at teaching other students in a one-to-one situation. Typically, the studies show that the student being taught (usually younger) learns better than would be expected and that the older student or tutor learns a good deal more, even when initially weak in the subject. Teaching what one has learned to another appears to be a very effective learning reinforcement (23).

There is a growing acceptance of different organizations for learning. Public alternative schools have increased from fewer than 10 in 1970 to 1,200 by 1975 (24). Parents and students who have participated in these programs are often their best advocates. The research done on alternatives indicates that hopes have been fulfilled. At least one regional accreditation association (the North Central Association) has developed new standards so that alternative schools could be evaluated and accredited. Three alternatives in the Midwest received accreditation last year under these standards. Thus the people who are pushing for new kinds of learning have strong support. In a recent review, Robert A. Horwitz compared the performance of about 75 studies of open classroom and traditional classroom students in these areas: academic achievement, self-concept, attitudes toward school, creativity, adjustment and anxiety, locus of control, and co-operation (25). In every area the open school children did as well or better than the traditional school students. If the open schools cost no more (and the researchers say they don't), and if the parents and children like them better (the researchers say they do), then why shouldn't the open schools have the right to exist as an alternative?

II. TRADITIONAL SCHOOLS/LEARNING

Many commonly held beliefs about the effectiveness of our traditional schools are questionable. Among those beliefs are that children need to be in school five days per week, that increased expenditures to do more of the same thing will make a significant difference, that schools prepare students well for our society, and that the environment of most schools is conducive to learning.

Two little-known studies pose major questions about the necessity of so much formal school time. The Unity (Maine) School District found itself in financial trouble four years ago and decided to institute a four-day week for students to save money on busing and cafeteria costs. The staff continued with a five-day week, devoting one day to inservice training. The Maine Department of Education was upset and gave its approval for the plan only with the stipulation that extensive tests be given to compare student achievement with previous years. These tests were conducted by the University of Maine. The evaluation director's conclusion was that, with the four-day student week, "gains clearly outweighed losses when considering the grade-equivalent scores of all students tested" (26). The Maine commissioner of education congratulated the district on its "foresight and initiative."

Similar results were obtained from a study following the Philadelphia teachers' strike in 1972-73. The strike lasted eight weeks. Some schools were closed and others were open the entire time. At the end of the year, scores of students who attended full time during the strike were compared with those of students who were out the entire eight weeks. No significant differences in achievement were found between the two groups (27).

BEHIND THE CLASSROOM DOOR

Attitude investigations show that by late elementary school age nearly

20 percent of children dislike school; the remaining majority "do not feel strongly about their classroom experience one way or another." One study found that even children classified as satisfied with their school experience describe it with such adjectives as "boring," "dull," or "inadequate." The children themselves may be "uncertain," or "restless" (28).

Such results lead to questions about what is happening in traditional schools "behind the classroom door." A study which used that phrase as its title listed well-known principles of learning. Researchers went into the schools to see to what extent these principles of learning were practiced. The answer was, to put it succinctly, "inadequately" (29). This study's findings are similar to others in which teachers have been questioned about their knowledge of modern principles of learning, i.e., students should be actively involved in their own learning, students can learn from a variety of people, success leads to future success, etc. In each case, teachers appeared to know very little about the principles. Even when teachers can verbalize them, the principles are seldom applied in their classrooms.

Given such facts, it is not surprising that observers entering the average U.S. classroom find a good deal of boring activity and a sense of program dullness. In one recent study, researchers found that attitudes toward most school subjects became measurably more negative in the course of a single year (30). Other studies have shown that, with each advancing year in school, children's evaluations of teachers and curricula as well as of themselves as people, became increasingly less favorable (31).

This finding reminds us of mental health studies which indicate that about one-third of U.S. adults are seriously ill, while another third need some attention. Only about one-third have good mental health (32). It's not a happy record for our society — or for the schools, which are supposed to help people achieve their potential.

Clearly, people's learning and achievement capabilities are not being realized. A recent U.S Office of Education study asked 7,500 adults questions to see if they were competent at tasks the researchers considered necessary for survival in our society. The tasks included knowing where to apply for social security benefits; how to figure which is a better bargain: one-half gallon of milk for 79 cents or a gallon for $1.10; how to read a sample ballot; etc.The study found that from 20-33 percent of adults could not achieve minimum levels (depending on the tasks) and that another 20-30 percent functioned but without proficiency (33).

Numerous studies have looked behind adults' skills to assess their attitudes toward society. Philip Jacob tested for open-mindedness and political literacy. He found that only 20-30 percent of college graduates possess these characteristics of a liberal education. There was no difference in these qualities between liberal arts college graduates and those of technical colleges. Nor was there any difference between freshmen and seniors. The college experience had simply made no difference — except in the case of a very few progressive colleges (34).

Studies of youth of high school age indicate that rather high numbers have seriously undemocratic views and tend to reject typical American ideals of liberty and opportunity for all (35). This finding seems related to experiences of people who have used the Bill of Rights disguised as a petition to be signed. They found few takers; some people commented that it looked like a Communist document. This should not be a surprising finding, in view of the systematic denial of democratic decision making which characterizes virtually every public school in the U.S.

In some localities expensive efforts have been made to improve the schools. A few years ago John Henry Martin became superintendent of an affluent suburb near New York City. He persuaded the school board to increase the budget by 35 percent in order to make many school improvements. Class size was reduced, various specialists were hired, training programs were started for staff, new materials were purchased, and so on. In all, some 60 improvements were made; but the basic organization and curriculum methods of traditional schools were retained. After two years psychometricians were hired to see what difference these expenditures had made in student achievement. They found no difference (36).

THE CONCERN WITH READING

It is hard to understand why schools go to such lengths to make excellent readers out of all students. One might as well try to make all students excellent musicians. The effort would be better spent in developing good learners, for there are many ways to learn. Unfortunately, schools concentrate on literary and academic achievement. Reading is a talent or aptitude distributed on a normal curve, just as music or art talent is distributed, and the beginning age for reading ranges from 3 to 14. In an extraordinarily valuable article, Neil Postman points out the highly political nature of reading instruction in this country (37). Fortunes continue to be made by companies which produce massive quantities of reading curriculum material. In fact, the reading instruction materials industry is the largest single sub-industry in education. But learning to read is not nearly as difficult as it has been made out to be in this country. Cynthia Brown documents the fact that Paulo Freire helped Brazilian adults learn to read in 30 hours or less with extraordinarily simple, low-cost materials (38).

Freire's work suggests that learning to decode or learning to change symbols into words, i.e., the act of reading, amounts to a few hours of actual teaching or learning. The acts of learning addition, subtraction, and other basic arithmetic functions may require only a few hours if we work with children when they are interested in learning, have the capacity, and have a background of concrete experiences that make that learning a simple, final conceptualization of some earlier intuitive learnings. William Rohwer says that the timing on instruction is probably inappropriate for 40-50 percent of the students who attend our schools. This seems conservative (39). Rohwer suggests that the prime time for most formal kinds of learning might be adolescence. Informal learning — interaction with materials, experimentation, observation, trial and error, and interaction with older and younger people — will provide an enormously potent background of intuitive learnings for the time when formal instruction begins.

CONCLUSION

Reformers pushing for change in public schools have had remarkably little help from professors of education. Most of the research mentioned in this article is never discussed or even cited in college and university classes. Harold Taylor studied a representative cross-section of colleges and universities where teachers are educated and concluded that the typical teacher education graduate is expected to "learn what he is taught from texts which raise few fundamental questions, by teachers who are older versions of himself and what he will someday be" (40). Taylor also found that college educational experiences typically encourage teachers to continue to function within a simple concept of curriculum — a prescribed pattern of courses distributed among various subjects supposedly covering specific topics which are prerequisite for courses to follow.

With relatively few major exceptions, college people offer very little help to those trying to make fundamental changes and improvements in learning systems. Indeed, scholars often frustrate changes within their own institutions as well as in schools (41). Yet change must come. The research summarized in this article suggests that we should not be upset by experiments in education but should welcome them. We should support program and curriculum experimentation. We should not be afraid to be open to ideas. Each of us should try our own experiments.

It may be that current practice is the worst possible arrangement for the education of the young. Research suggests that scores on standardized achievement tests are not likely to drop in school experiments. To us, these findings suggest that the state of educational research is primitive and that our schools resemble factories turning out identical products, not programs designed to help individuals realize their unique potentials.

Educators should view the curriculum not only as those experiences which the schools control for youth; the curriculum is all of life, irrespective of time and place. It needs to be recognized that learning is a life-long process, best when self-directed.

FOOTNOTES AND REFERENCES

1. James S. Coleman, "The Children Have Outgrown the Schools," PSYCHOLOGY TODAY, February, 1972, pp. 72-76.

2. A version of this chapter appeared in the March, 1977 PHI DELTA KAPPAN and in Herb Kohl, ON TEACHING. New York: Schocken, 1976.

3. Wilford Aikin, STORY OF THE EIGHT-YEAR STUDY. New York: Harper & Brothers, 1942.

4. Ibid, p. 113.

5. Margaret Willis, GUINEA PIGS 20 YEARS LATER. Columbus, O.: Ohio State University Press, 1961.

6. Panel on Youth of the President's Science Advisory Committee, YOUTH. TRANSITION TO ADULTHOOD. Washington, D.C.: Superintendent of Documents, U.S. Government Printing Office, 1973; National Association of Secondary School Principals, AMERICAN YOUTH IN THE MID-SEVENTIES. Reston, Va.: NASSP, 1972; California Commission for Reform of Intermediate and Secondary Education, RISE REPORT. Sacramento: California State Department of Education, 1975.

7. THE EDUCATION OF ADOLESCENTS, U.S. National Panel on High School and Adolescent Education, Washington, 1976.

8. EDUCATION FOR RESPONSIBLE CITIZENSHIP, Report of the National Task Force on Citizenship Education, cosponsored by the Danforth and Charles Kettering Foundations, New York, 1977.

9. Ibid.

10. GUIDELINES, National Council for the Social Studies, Washington, 1971.

11. Charles Harrison, "The Proper Study of Government," AMERICAN EDUCATION, July 1977, p. 14.

12. EVALUATION REPORT: LEARNING UNLIMITED, North Central High School, Washington County Township Board of Education, June 30, 1976.

13. EVALUATING EXPERIENCE-BASED CAREER EDUCATION PILOT AND DEMONSTRATION SITES 1975-76, Washington, D.C.: National Institute of Education, p. 2 (available from Far West Regional Laboratory, San Francisco).

14. Donald Feldstein, "Who Needs High School?" SOCIAL POLICY, May/June, 1974, p. 20.

15. L.A. Mundy and J.C. Davis, VARIETIES OF ACCOMPLISHMENT AFTER COLLEGE: PERSPECTIVES ON THE MEANING OF ACADEMIC TALENT, ACT Research Report No. 62. Iowa City, Ia.: American College Testing Service, 1974.

16. Michael Wallach, "Psychology of Talent and Graduate Education," paper presented at International Conference on Cognitive Styles and Creativity in Higher Education sponsored by the Graduate Record Examinations Board, Montreal, November, 1972.

17. D.P. Hoyt, RELATIONSHIP BETWEEN COLLEGE GRADES AND ADULT ACHIEVEMENT: A REVIEW OF THE LITERATURE, ACT Research Report No. 7. Iowa City, Ia.: American College Testing Service, 1965.

18. Reported in THE SCHOOL ADMINISTRATOR, American Asociation of School Administrators, February, 1976, p. 2.

19. Torsten Husen, INTERNATIONAL STUDY OF ACHIEVEMENT IN MATHEMATICS, vol. 2. Uppsala, Sweden: Almquist & Wilsells, 1967.

20. Margaret Silberburg and Norman Silberburg, "Myths in Remedial Education," JOURNAL OF LEARNING DISABILITIES, April, 1969, pp. 209-17.

21. Bancroft Beatly, ACHIEVEMENT IN JUNIOR HIGH SCHOOL. Cambridge, Mass.: Harvard University Press, 1932.

22. Central Advisory Council for Education (England). CHILDREN AND THEIR PRIMARY SCHOOLS, two volumes. London: Her Majesty's Stationery Office, 1967.

23. Alan Gartner, Mary Kohler, and Frank Riesman, CHILDREN TEACH CHILDREN. New York: Harper and Row, 1971.

24. Robert D. Barr, "Growth of Public Alternative Schools," CHANGING SCHOOLS, no. 12, 1975, p. 3.

25. Robert A. Horwitz, PSYCHOLOGICAL EFFECTS OF OPEN CLASSROOM TEACHING ON PRIMARY SCHOOL CHILDREN: A REVIEW OF THE RESEARCH, a North Dakota Study Group on Evaluation publication. Grand Forks, N.D.: University of North Dakota Press, 1976.

26. Robert Drummond, "Preliminary Report — Research and Evaluation Team," University of Maine, Orono Achievement Testing Program for MSAD No. 3, mimeographed, 1972.

27. James H. Lytle and Jay M. Yanoff, "The Effects (if Any) of a Teacher Strike on Student Achievement," PHI DELTA KAPPAN, December, 1973, p. 270.

28. P.W. Jackson, LIFE IN CLASSROOMS. New York: Holt, Rinehart & Winston, 1968.

29. John I. Goodlad, BEHIND THE CLASSROOM DOOR. Belmont, Calif.: Wadsworth, 1970.

30. D.C. Neale, N. Gill, and W. Tismer, "Relationship Between Attitudes

Toward School Subjects and School Achievement," JOURNAL OF EDUCATIONAL RESEARCH, vol. 63, 1970, pp. 232-37.

31. D.C. Neale and J.M. Proshek, "School-Related Attitudes of Culturally Disadvantaged Elementary School Children," JOURNAL OF EDUCATIONAL PSYCHOLOGY, vol. 58, 1967, pp. 238-44.

32. August B. Hollingshead and Frederick C. Redlich, SOCIAL CLASS AND MENTAL ILLNESS. New York: Wiley, 1958.

33. Norvell Northcutt, ADULT FUNCTIONAL COMPETENCY: A SUMMARY. Washington, D.C.: Department of Health, Education, and Welfare, 1975.

34. Philip E. Jacob, CHANGING VALUES IN COLLEGE. New York: Harper & Brothers, 1957.

35. H.H. Remmers and D.H. Radler, AMERICAN TEEN-AGER. Indianapolis: Bobbs Merrill, 1957.

36. John Henry Martin and Charles Harrison, FREE TO LEARN. Englewood Cliffs, N.J.: Prentice Hall, 1972.

37. Neil Postman, "The Politics of Reading," HARVARD EDUCATIONAL REVIEW, May, 1970.

38. Cynthia Brown, LITERACY IN 30 HOURS. London: Expression Printers, Ltd., 1975. Available from the Center for Open Learning and Teaching, Berkeley, Calif.

39. William Rohwer, "Prime Time for Education: Early Childhood or Adolescence?" HARVARD EDUCATIONAL REVIEW, August, 1971.

40. Harold Taylor, THE WORLD AS TEACHER. Garden City, N.J.: Doubleday, 1969.

41. Gail Thain Parker, "While Alma Mater Burns," ATLANTIC, September, 1976.

CONSUMER ACTION SERVICE: HOW YOU CAN DO IT!

Students of
St. Paul Open School
St. Paul, Minnesota

INTRODUCTION

Students can help other people as they develop survival skills such as letter-writing, reading for comprehension, getting along with others in a group and perseverance. That's the basic idea of the Consumer Action Service, a project of the Protect Your Rights and Money class at St. Paul Open School. In its two years, the class has worked on about 75 problems and successfully resolved about 70% of them.

Helping and sharing are basic ideas of the St. Paul Open School, a public alternative for 500 students, ages 5-18. The first edition of this booklet was produced by the 1975-76 class. In less than a year, all 1000 copies of that edition were exhausted. The second edition was revised by 1976-77 Consumer Action students. It includes new developments (1).

HOW WE WORK ON CASES

Almost everyone has been taken advantage of, but most people don't know how to handle it. One of the best ways to ''handle it'' is to avoid it. We tried to learn how to avoid getting into a problem situation. However, sometimes, you find yourself with a problem despite all the care you've taken. That's when the following steps help.

We found the first and most important step in solving consumer problems to be preparing for them. For example, we learned the importance of habitually getting receipts for *everything* we buy. We saw several cases (including one at Small Claims Court) decided because one side kept a copy of the receipt and the other side couldn't find its copy and had forgotten the exact terms of the agreement.

A second way of preparing is to make sure you understand *everything* in contracts you sign. Have salespeople explain the contract until there is no doubt in your mind as to what it says. Often people are embarrassed to ask questions. Sometimes they're even more embarrassed when they learn what they've signed and are now obligated to do! Sometimes people say, ''well, my brother, or wife, or husband handles all the financial affairs for us." If your name is on a contract or policy, you better understand it, even if other people in the family are the experts.

A third way to prepare is to have all agreements in writing. Anything written is ten times better than words. Disputes are common enough about the meaning of written words in a contract. We found people almost always have different recollections of what they decided if they only talked and didn't write down anything.

Another good way to prepare is to know the local and state groups and agencies which work with consumers. We were surprised and fascinated to learn the variety of people who help consumers: private groups like the Better Business Bureau and newspaper and television "Action Lines, Action News, Column 1, etc."; and governmental groups like our Mayor's Office of Information and Complaint, City Attorney's Office, Minnesota Insurance Commission, Minnesota Attorney General's Office, Minnesota Consumer Services Offices, and Small Claims Court. These are just examples. It's definitely worth writing to these agencies to find out what they do, and if possible visiting them to learn how they operate and the limits of their power. We found talking with representatives of these offices to be extremely helpful (2).

The final way to prepare ourselves for problems is to know as much as possible about our own rights and responsibilities. We read a number of books and periodicals which helped. The people in our class feel each student should have a chance to learn about this before graduating.

So far we've talked about preparation. What can you do when you've prepared but still find yourself with a problem? We developed a number of steps which helped us successfully resolve about 70% of the cases brought to us.

1. If you have a problem, try to think clearly and specifically about exactly what it is you want. Instead of sulking and calling up your friends to complain, write down precisely what you hope to obtain (such as a properly functioning radio which the repair shop didn't fix, the security deposit you put down when moving into an apartment, or reduction of a charge you think is unjustified, etc.).

2. List people and agencies you think might be able to help you reach your goal. At this point you shouldn't try to decide who to go to first. You're

only listing options. Make sure you list talking directly with the person who you see as causing the problem. Sometimes disagreements are caused by simple misunderstandings.

3. Think about advantages and disadvantages to various strategies. Generally, we've tried to stay away from legal proceedings if possible. (They can take a long time and be expensive, unless you go to Small Claims Court. Also, people usually are quite upset about being taken to Court. You may want to keep on good terms with a repair shop or a person you know. That will be difficult after taking them to Court.)

Usually our first strategy is to get the views of the person or agency about whom the complaint is being made. Sometimes getting their view convinced us that they were not at fault. We may decide that we need to know more about the law involved, or the kind of service being performed. (One case involved a complaint about a piano that was out of tune. We decided to start by calling several piano dealers to learn more about how often tuning should occur.)

We found that a calm, unbiased approach sometimes brought quick action. Each group that we talked with stressed the necessity of not taking sides. We found (as they had) that sometimes, after investigation, consumers' complaints seem unjustified, or that the consumers themselves were at least partially at fault. If we automatically assumed the person doing the complaint was right, we lost our credibility with outside groups, and thus would not be able to help other people. We found governmental agencies we worked with asking to make sure we'd heard 2 or 3 views of the case before calling them.

We usually didn't go to another agency (BBB, Minnesota Attorney General's Office, etc.) unless we couldn't get any action within a month. After all, they have plenty to do already. Sometimes we'd call just to get quick information about a particular law. Then we'd proceed with another step.

4. Decide on a strategy after thinking about all the alternatives. Remember that you may have to try several different strategies before resolving the case. In a case described in the next section concerning water damage, we tried at least 8 different strategies over a period of 6 months before meeting success.

5. Make any necessary preparations to carry out the strategy. In the

case of phone calls, we always rehearse before making them. We've learned that the first few times people make calls, they should have the problem and several proposed solutions, plus questions to ask, on a piece of paper in front of them as they talk. Also, our teacher was on the phone (at another extension) the first time each of us called just in case there were problems. This helped give us confidence.

Prior to going to the law library to check on some facts, people had to find out about bus routes in order to get there. Once at the law library, we had to learn how to look up laws (hint: it isn't the same as looking up a book at your neighborhood library). Of course we studied contracts, warranties, guarantees, as well as rights and responsibilities of landlords, tenants, sellers and buyers, etc. during the class so we had some knowledge of all this. It's important to understand that only part of the time was spent working directly on cases. Sometimes we read, or watched movies or filmstrips, or talked with people from the Better Business Bureau or Consumer Protection Agency or talked about laws, courts, etc.

6. Carry out the strategy. Remember that this requires being as fair-minded and unbiased as possible, despite the anger and apparent injustice done to the person making the complaint. We also kept records on our actions (i.e., keeping a copy of all letters sent, and writing down the name of people we talked with at a business).

7. Evaluate the results. In most cases we found that the first strategy helped but didn't solve the problem by itself. Thus, as a total class we decided on a first step. Then a few students volunteered to carry out that step. After doing it, they reported back to the class. We discussed the results. Sometimes our goal changed after hearing the results of the first step; sometimes we decided to try a different strategy. (After hearing what music dealers said about tuning pianos, we decided a woman was unjustified in complaining about her piano being out of tune after several months. In another case, after trying unsuccessfully to get a refund for water damage from an apartment manager, we called the manager's boss. Ultimately, we were able to get some money for the person who had complained.)

8. Decide whether new goals or strategies are needed, and write up what you've done. The goal and strategy-choosing methods are described above. We learned to keep a file on each case, which included copies of all correspondence plus a summary sheet. The sheet explained who had complained to us, which students were working on the case, how we tried to get action, and what the result was. Files really helped us stay organized.

SAMPLE CASES

The next several pages are intended to give examples of the successes and failures we've had as we worked on 75 cases so far. We hope the discussion will give you ideas, and that you'll learn from our mistakes and successes (as we have)!

* * *

The Problem: Mrs. P. of Truman, Mn. wrote to say that her family had been unable to get a car radio they felt was owed to them. Mrs. P said the family bought a van from a Twin Cities area car dealer in October 1975. "The radio had been taken out but the salesman promised to have one sent to replace it free of charge since we could not come in later to have it installed. He did make a notation on our contract to have it mailed." The family tried unsuccessfully for three months to get the radio and then wrote us.

What We Did: We wrote back to Mrs. P asking for a copy of her contract. She sent the original. We made a copy and sent the original back to her. Then we called the dealership's owner (his name was the same as the company). We reached him immediately. He apologized and promised to look into it right away. He suggested that we call back later in the day. We said, "sure." When we called back, he said that we and the lady were right and that he had tried to call the family all day. He promised to call until reaching them and have them come in over the weekend if possible to get the radio. We asked if we could check back in a week. He said sure. We wrote to Mrs. P. to tell her what happened and to ask that she let us know if she heard from the dealer.

Results: Five days later we received a nice note from Mrs. P. saying the dealer had called. The family drove in to get the radio, which was installed. The family was very happy.

We Learned That: 1. Keeping a copy of one's contract is extremely important.
2. Making sure all terms of a contract are in writing is vital.
3. Sometimes going directly to the owner of a business is helpful, particularly when the business is relatively small.

* * *

The Problem: Mrs. Z, parent of an Open School student, believed her land-

224

lord owed her some money for damage she said was caused by a leaking pipe. She said the pipe leaked after the landlord did some repairs, turning off and then turning on the water.

What We Did: This was by far our longest, and most complex case. We began by calling the apartment manager. She said they (the housing authority) had no insurance to cover the situation. Then we called the central office. They asked for a written statement. We went back to Mrs. Z and wrote such a statement with her. After a month, this was rejected. At Mrs. Z's request, we made an appointment with Legal Aide. The law student who met with Mrs. Z at Legal Aide promised to look into it. We asked if we should continue working with the housing authority since legal action took so long. He said, "Fine, go ahead." Eventually, we appeared at the Housing Authority Board meeting. We had called and been assured that we were on the agenda. When we got to the meeting there was a disagreement and the case wasn't allowed to be presented. The Board chairperson suggested that Mrs. Z's attorney meet with the housing authority attorney. We were very angry.

Results: After several months, a compromise was reached. Mrs. Z said the damage was over $1200. The Housing Authority originally felt the damage was caused by a drain Mrs. Z allowed to become clogged. However, they eventually compromised and offered her $425. Because she needed the money and didn't want the case to drag on, she accepted.

What We Learned: 1. It's vital to investigate carefully to get all sides of a case.
2. Some groups would rather deal with attorneys than students.
3. When trying to get on an agenda, it's vital to get written confirmation that you are on the agenda.
4. It may be important to have a written statement from the person who came to you authorizing you to act for them.

* * *

The Problem: A White Bear Lake woman called trying to get a skin or her money back. Her husband took a moose to a local taxidermist in September, 1973. The moose was to be tanned and stuffed. The man paid $50, with the balance of $100 due when the skin was returned. The skin had not been returned as of November, 1975 and the taxidermist could give no estimate about when it might be returned. He refused to tell the woman where he'd sent the skin.

What We Did: We called the taxidermist to find out his side of the story. He said the lady's story was correct. He refused to tell us where the hide was. We explained that we might have to turn the case over to the Attorney General's office. He said that was fine with him - the skin would be returned when he got it back, and no sooner.

Results: We turned the case over to the Minnesota Attorney General's office for investigation. The case is pending.

What We Learned: You can't bluff everyone - some people aren't scared of the Attorney General. Once people get your money, they may not be concerned about getting the work done quickly. If possible, don't pay until the work has been done. Be sure to check the reputation of a merchant if at all possible. (This one has a terrible record with the Better Business Bureau.)

* * *

The Problem: Early in January we learned that the Open School might be moved by the school system from its building on University Avenue to a building near the State Capitol then occupied by Mechanical Arts Junior-Senior High School. Numerous student-parent-staff meetings were held to discuss the move and make recommendations about needed modifications. One major suggestion was that a traffic light be installed on Robert Street at Central Avenue, where students would cross from the building to an athletic field across the street. The Open School Director asked our class to see if that could be done.

What We Did: First we called the School System Engineering and Design Office. They suggested that we have a staff member at the Open School call one of their staff members to describe the use we would make of the athletic field. We asked a staff member to do this. Then, at their suggestion, we wrote to the Director of Transportation and Food Services for St. Paul Public Schools. He responded immediately and invited us to attend a meeting of the Committee on Hazardous Crossings. He said that he had placed our request on the agenda. After discussing the situation with the Open School Director, we decided to take a traffic count and tell the director about the meeting. He said he'd go with us.

Results: The committee agreed to put up warning signs, paint a crosswalk and possibly put up a flashing amber light. It felt that the intersection was not a good place for a stop and go light as most drivers wouldn't expect it there. Also, we wouldn't be able to get it for at least 18 months and possibly 2 years. The other steps could be taken sooner.

What We Learned:
1. When communicating on the telephone, it's vital to be prepared with as many facts as possible.
2. We saw how a formal meeting takes place and how to take part in one.
3. Sometimes you don't get exactly what you want, but you can get something else as a compromise.

* * *

The Problem: Mrs. K asked us to work with her to help resolve a disagreement over repair of her car's transmission. She'd taken the car to a transmission repair shop and asked how much it would cost to fix (she'd chosen the shop because it had the largest Yellow Pages ad). She said the mechanic had asked to drive it for a short time. After he drove it, she recalled that he estimated repair costs of $175-$200. However, she understood him to say that a complete estimate would require more time and the final cost might be $30-$40 more. She understood the mechanic to ask if she wanted him to do a complete estimate and call her the next day with the final estimate. She said "Yes." When he called back the next day, he said the charge would be $350, or $100 to put the car back the way it was when brought in (he said it was apart at the time).

What We Did: We called the Minnesota Attorney General's Office to find out how to proceed. The lawyer there asked that we write down the facts as Mrs. K remembered them. We typed up a summary which was taken to his office. The next day the transmission shop's owner called Ms. K to ask if she was trying to put him out of business! She said "no, just trying to get fair treatment."

According to the owner, the mechanic felt Mrs. K had authorized not just an estimate but actually doing the work. Mrs. K said that wasn't her understanding. The shop's owner said the AG's Office attorney had called to see what was happening and to encourage a just settlement. The owner offered Mrs. K three choices, which he said had been worked out with the Attorney General's office. They were that 1. the mechanic would put the car back together for $25; 2. the shop would buy the car in its present state for $50; or 3.

the shop would do the needed repairs for $270 and give her a 1 year warranty on their work. Mrs. K discussed the options with us. We called the Ag's Office to check on whether the options were acceptable to them. The attorney explained that there was no written agreement and thus no way to tell exactly what had happened. The company felt the repairs were more extensive than originally estimated and that they could charge her $270. The attorney thought the options relatively fair.

Results: After much thought, Mrs. K decided to have the car fixed. She felt the car wasn't worth much more than several hundred dollars but that she wouldn't be able to get a replacement for $50. She sent a note thanking us for our help in getting the repairs reduced $80. Eight months later she reported the car was working well.

What We Learned:
1. Check with the Better Business Bureau or others before choosing a place to get your car repaired. *Don't decide* on the basis of large ads.
2. Make sure all agreements for estimates or repairs are in writing.
3. The Minnesota Attorney General Office is willing to move very quickly on complaints. They're willing to work with students, and they have a good deal of influence.
4. Before calling the Attorney General's office, we should have called the transmission repair shop to get their side of the story.

* * *

The Problem: Mr. D complained about what he saw as false or deceptive advertising. He gave us copies of a coupon put on his doorstep advertising special prices for slide and movie film processing. When he took the coupons to his neighborhood drugstore with film, the drugstore clerk insisted that the coupons were good only for Kodak film. The man pointed out that the coupon said nothing about brand of film, but the drug store still refused to honor the coupon except for Kodak film.

What We Did: We called the drugstore to get their version of the story. Their view matched that of Mr. D who had complained to us. The drugstore said the film processor would reimburse them only for Kodak film. We then called the processor, who was named on the coupon. An official of this firm explained that a mistake had been made on the coupon. The coupon was to have specified only Kodak film. However, the official agreed that his company would have to take responsibility for the mistake and would call the drug store and tell them to accept any brand of film. The processor agreed to reimburse the drugstore. We called the drugstore several days later. They had received a call from the processor and were willing to accept any brand of film with the coupon.

Results: People were able to use the coupon to get processing of any brand of film at a special price.

What We Learned:
1. Sometimes problems are the results of someone's failure to check carefully what has been written (in this case, the processor didn't check the coupon before sending it out).
2. It's important to stand up for your rights.

* * *

The Problem: Mrs. Y, an elderly woman in Minneapolis wrote to say that her insurance company was unfairly terminating her homeowner's insurance. She asked us to investigate as she didn't want to shop around for a new policy.

What We Did: First we carefully read the letter Mrs. Y had received from her insurance company. (She sent us a copy). We agreed that it was extremely difficult to understand. We went over it with the attorney who was meeting with us. It seemed that the company was canceling her old policy but giving her a new one in line with overall company changes. We called the insurance agent who sent the letter. He agreed with our interpretation of the letter and explained that the lady's home would still be insured with all the old policy's terms except that her premiums would be $2 less per year.

We wrote the lady back, explaining what her agent said.

Results: Mrs. Y was very happy to learn her home was still insured and at $2 less.

What We Learned: Communications from insurance companies can be very difficult to understand (even attorneys may disagree). It's important to check out every detail in an insurance policy. Sometimes people are intimidated (frightened) by insurance agents.

The Problem: A woman contacted us regarding a disagreement with her insurance company. In 1956, her husband bought life insurance policies on their two daughters. The policies were to last 20 years, with payments made 4 times per year. The policy stipulated that if the husband died and the daughters were still under 21, no payments would have to be made to the company though the policy would be in effect until they were 21.

The man died in 1972 and his wife didn't know about these provisions until her agent pointed them out to her three years after he died. He tried to get back the $200 she paid to the company since her husband died, but the company would not refund the money.

What We Did: We asked for the policies. When she gave them to us, we made copies and returned the originals to her. Then we tried to understand their provisions. They were *extremely* difficult to understand, frequently written in language full of "whereas" and "party of the first part," etc. We went over the policies line by line with the lawyer who met with us occasionally. It seemed to us that the company did owe the woman some money as she had paid in about $140 before both her daughters turned 21. However, the policy also said she was to notify the company within 6 months after her husband died and ask for the premiums to be waived. Apparently her agent hadn't done this. Her agent kept promising to give her the money but hadn't done so for five months.

We called the Minnesota Insurance Commission and explained the situation, after trying a number of times without success to discuss the case with the agent. The Insurance Commission asked for a letter explaining the situation and copies of the policies. We wrote a letter and enclosed copies of the policies.

Results: Five days after the Insurance Commission received information from us, they wrote to the company asking for reimbursement of the $140. (They also sent us a copy of the letter to the company.) One week later, a check for $140 arrived. The company said it was not legally obligated to refund the money because it had not been notified, but was willing to do so to keep good faith with the woman.

The woman was very pleased with the $140 but felt her agent still should give her the other $60 she had paid because she said he'd promised to refund everything. We tried unsuccessfully to get in touch with him, while questioning whether the last $60 could be obtained. This money had been paid after the daughters turned 21. Ultimately, the woman was very pleased that she received $140 and very displeased with her agent.

What We Learned: 1. You should keep up with your insurance policies, no matter how difficult it is to understand them.
2. Don't count on salespeople or agents to keep up with your policies.
3. Minnesota Insurance Commission staff members act quickly.
4. Sometimes a letter from a state agency will have a powerful effect on a business.

* * *

The Problem: Mrs. X of Delano, Mn., wrote, complaining about a piano she bought from a St. Paul man. She said after 15 hours playing time the piano keys stuck. She asked him to fix the keys which were sticking. He insisted that the piano simply needed tuning. Ultimately she tried to sell the piano back to him, but he refused to buy it back. She reported that he gave her no guarantee on the piano as it was used but that he stated a great deal of reconditioning had been done on the piano. Mrs. X asked if we would try to get the dealer to buy back the piano.

What We Did: It sounded like the piano might be out of tune, so we called several local piano dealers to find out how long it would take to get a piano out of tune. Each said it could happen immediately, but definitely within several months. Then we called the dealer to get his side. He explained that he had been dealing for 6 months with Mrs. X. He explained that the piano had no guarantee. It sounded to him like the only problem was that the piano was out of tune. He'd explained this to Mrs. X but she wasn't satisfied. The dealer also said that originally the customer was to pick up the piano at his shop, but that later as a special favor he had agreed to deliver the piano to Delano. When the piano was delivered and placed in the house, the dealer had tuned it.

Results: The dealer said he would be willing to return to the customer's house and retune the piano for $30. ($25 tuning, $5 gas). He recommended that she get someone closer to her to tune. We wrote to Mrs. X explaining that he seemed to be fair but that since she had no warranty or guarantee, she had no claim. We also told her that other experts thought the problem probably was with the piano's tuning and not with the dealer.

231

What We Learned: 1. People who complain may not tell you the whole story.
2. People buying something and expecting free service after the sale should make sure it's in the contract.
3. Pianos can go out of tune rapidly.

* * *

The Problem: Ms. S. had a disagreement with her landlord over the security deposit. She was moving out of her apartment and had asked for the full $100 back. The landlord refused to return all but $15, saying there were wall marks and spots above the stove.

What We Did: We asked Mrs. S. to write a statement describing the apartment condition before she moved in and now that she was ready to leave. We encouraged Sue to talk with other people with more authority in the landlord's company (one of the largest in St. Paul). This was unsuccessful. Then we encouraged her to go to Small Claims Court while we did some research about the security deposit law. We contacted the Minnesota Apartment Association which gave us a copy of the law: Minnesota 504.20, subd. 3. The law states landlords can withhold security deposit for money needed to "restore the premises to their condition" prior to the tenant coming in, "ordinary wear and tear excepted." We gave Ms. S a copy of the law and information about Small Claims Court, as she had never been there. We explained what she would find useful.

Results: Sue did go to Small Claims Court and received a judgment for $85. This meant she got all the money back she'd originally given for a security deposit.

What We Learned: 1. Landlords can't withhold security deposit money to fix what can be fairly described as "ordinary wear and tear."
2. It's very helpful to be well prepared with witnesses and knowledge of appropriate laws when going to Small Claims Court.

BASIC LESSONS

Visitors often are interested in what Protect Your Rights and Money class students feel they are learning. The answers to this question are fascinating and helpful in making suggestions to others considering establishing a similar program. Students in this class have written that they are learning about their world, and themselves. They learned:

- The rights I have. How I can use them for me and how other people can use them against me.
- How to understand a contract.
- How to watch for false advertising and other deceptive methods sometimes used by businesses and salespeople.
- What agencies you can go to for help
- That you should always get something in writing
- How to use the law library and Small Claims Court
- How to ask effective questions, write clear business letters and talk on the telephone
- About helping other people. I feel that it is more important for me to help people than to sit around thinking about it.
- Independence! Joe really didn't want us to come to him for answers. He asked us for our comments and suggestions instead of him telling us what he thought.
- That the majority of these problems are caused by misunderstanding. Being able to work objectively and look at both sides solves them faster. Usually everyone's first reaction is ''I'' am getting ripped off by ''Them.'' But in many cases this wasn't so and a compromise is what's needed.

SUGGESTIONS FOR ESTABLISHING
A CONSUMER ACTION SERVICE

Students have many suggestions for those starting such a program. These include:

- Print up a simple brochure (ours was 2 pages) describing what you can do and reminding people you aren't attorneys and can't guarantee that you'll be successful. Distribute this through libraries and in your neighborhood (stores, businesses, community agencies).
- Get as much publicity as possible. This helps in obtaining cases. After a while the word spreads and cases come in, though this may take time.
- Try to find an attorney who will volunteer to help you with legal questions from time to time. This might be a parent, law student or someone the Bar Association suggests.
- Keep files on each case. If people send you their original contract, make a copy and return it. Write down the major parts of each case.
- Make sure parents and administrators know what is going on and under-

stand what you're learning. This can be very helpful.

- Learn as much as you can about legal procedures, rights and responsibilities of consumers, business people, landlords and tenants. It's very important to be informed.
- Don't be too upset if some people don't followup after you've written back to them. Sometimes people just decide that their problems aren't worth working on. You may be ready to work on their problems, but ultimately it's their decision. Some people just like to complain.

FOOTNOTES AND REFERENCES

1. Complete booklet available for $1.00 from: Consumer Action Service, St. Paul Open School, 97 E. Central, St. Paul, MN 55101.
2. One group suggested we expand our caseload by setting up a booth in the Skyway system of downtown St. Paul. We went to a bank in the skyway (walkway over streets) and asked if they would allow us to set up a table. They said "Yes" for three months. We made a couple of signs out of plywood and the bank let us use one of their tables.

   At first we didn't get many new cases, but then people started stopping and talking. After three months, we decided the booth wasn't worth the time we put in. However, other groups wrote us to say they tried setting up booths in shopping centers on Saturday, and it worked really well. Perhaps it will work better for you than it did for us.

CLASSROOM IN THE SKY:
A POWER TRIP FOR
DISADVANTAGED YOUTH

Lee Conway

Few educators comprehend the powerful role the airplane plays in their lives and the profound impact of flying machines in the institutional, educational, and aesthetic spheres of everyday life. The monetary costs have been enormous. In the Air Force Museum at Dayton, Ohio, an experimental bomber, the XB-70, stands hangared and useless. It cost the taxpayer over $3 billion. Commercial jet travel is possible only because taxpayers have poured billions of dollars into aeronautic research and development. The public spends billions annually to subsidize aerospace contractors and to maintain our national complex of airfields and communication facilities for monitoring the airways. Almost all airline pilots were trained by the Navy or Air Force — maintained by taxpayers who get to fly only rarely or expensively.

In sum, the airplane is possibly the single most expensive technological development in the history of man. But, from the Stukas that dive-bombed Guernica to the Concorde fleet now ready to destroy the ozone layer, the sociology of flight has been characterized by the expropriation of the most costly invention of the twentieth century by the relatively few.

My purpose here is not to denigrate man's mastery of flight, however. Rather, it is to describe an unusual use of flight by one imaginative California school. This unique flight project, begun in 1968, made the airplane a tool for the education of disadvantaged youth. A light, 150-horsepower, single-engine airplane generated basic behavioral changes in an inner-city junior high school class.

The 25 disadvantaged boys in the study came from segregated schools located in the low SES area of a California metropolis. The group was 80% black. They had attended the typical sixth grade still attended by children from black, Chicano, and poor white families from across the nation. These are sixth grades where at least 70% of all children evidence reading failure by the time they are old enough for junior high school.

As unmotivated, failing, inadequately prepared students, the flight project youths would have been shunted into remedial courses (when available) and a vocational or shop curriculum. As disadvantaged area students, they would have been sorted or tracked into low-status, dead-end courses, thereby lowering their self-esteem still further and depressing their aspiration level.

The flight group class averaged 13.3 years of age at the time of their selection. Many were slow readers. Not a single student was in the above-average or fast-reading category.

All the youths had one or more significant behavioral problems associated primarily with school and/or family background; all showed the progressive decline in reading ability typical of youths who are stigmatized and deprived.

Flight group pupils came from families with an average of 5.5 children. Nine of these families (36%) were receiving welfare assistance. In an additional eight families (32%), the breadwinner was either a laborer or doing other unskilled work. In the case of 15 (60%) of the flight model youths, a desirable role model, in the form of a regularly employed father or successful older brother, was absent.

THE SCHOOL

The high-risk group of pupils represented a fair sample of a black, segregated junior high population, one characterized by disaffection with the educational system, low self-confidence, belief that the teachers were prejudiced, and slight faith in the future.

The pupils referred to Roberts Junior High School as "the prison." The combination of ancient, drab architecture, closed campus rules, and numerous security devices bore out the label. Any student caught leaving the building without specific permission was suspended from school. Teachers at other schools referred to Roberts as a place for tired teachers, those no longer committed to education. An overworked counseling staff was forced to spend most of its time on discipline rather than constructive counseling. Parents knew that few of Roberts' 900 students made it to college or a career.

The negative influence of a stigmatized school on the expectations of parents, pupils, and an instructional staff cannot be underestimated in assessing the effects of an educational innovation such as the flight project.

THE FLIGHT MODEL

The flight project was planned as a "hands-on" flight experience to

236

produce high motivation among youths theretofore destined for failure. The Rosenberg Foundation of San Francisco supplied the basic grant for flying time. The rationale accepted by the grantors was best expressed by Alfred North Whitehead:

> *I lay it down as an educational axiom that teaching comes to grief as soon as you forget that your pupils have bodies . . . Book learning conveys secondhand information, and as such can never rise to the importance of immediate practice. Our goal is to see the immediate events of our lives as instances of our general ideas . . . The learned world tends to offer . . . secondhand scraps of information illustrating ideas derived from another secondhand scrap of information.*

The flight project class, composed of 25 eighth-grade boys, provided 10 hours of dual in-flight instruction for each boy at Buchanan Field near Concord, California. The project consisted of four instructionally related educational units. Unit 1 was an in-school series of classes which segregated the flight group youths in a special aerospace program. This unit was managed by four classroom teachers. Unit 2 included a large number of field trips. Locations visited included a Naval Air Station, an airline maintenance shop, an airport weather bureau, an FAA control center, several Air Force bases, and the University of California. Unit 3 was the small-group tutoring phase, during which a student tutor helped the youngsters with navigation, mathematics problems, and computational exercises. Unit 4 consisted of instruction in a light, single-engine aircraft. Student pilots received a regulation private flying course, including preflight inspection, tower communication, traffic patterns, instrumentation, and of course actual piloting of the craft.

The airport experiences proved to be highly successful. While one student flew, three of his classmates worked with the tutor-counselor, analyzing their flights, solving navigation problems, learning meteorology, etc. They had the opportunity to interact with aviation personnel, people who love flying and earn their bread and butter around airplanes.

Experiences and goals of the flight project youths came to be rooted in vocational-technical work spheres rather than in the abstract world of the high-status professional and the formal course requirements laid upon the secondary school by the universities.

THE FLIGHT PROGRAM

The major invention of the flight project was to conceive a new role for the airplane — as a flying classroom. The plane, 3290 Juliet, was a sleek, retrimmed, aluminum two-place machine which the flight group students came to know and love. Their instructor, Butch, a boyish-looking pilot in his middle twenties, was an expert pilot. More important, he had an easy, relaxed teaching style.

The following observations came from notes I made on an evaluation visit to the airport four months after the project began.

Now the pilot instructor, Butch, is talking:

You can see them checking all the important parts, such as the actuator rod, cotter pins, static system, surface controls. I allow each guy to handle the preflight completely by himself now. I only observe. The kids climb all over each other to show me the points they are checking. This is the only problem — over-competition.

Asked about the optimum time for flight instruction and his objectives, Butch responded:

We believe at least 30-minute in-flight sessions are needed to maximize the learning experience. Now, they complain that the sessions are too short. But our prime objective is to motivate the boys. I believe the program is succeeding in this respect. Our prime objective is not to teach the fellows to solo.

All of our flights are cross-country. We are not teaching the kids to fly in itself, but to stimulate them toward school. During these cross-country flights, the kids learn radio operation, study the terrain, use of the compass, use their math for time and distance. They fly as much as possible.

Confidence is one of the objectives. The boys are encouraged to handle the controls as much as possible during flight. They have made take-offs and landings, with the instructor close to the controls, of course. We teach them to use power if needed. Then we teach flight altitude. They learn, if they're sinking too fast during the landing, to give a short blast of throttle. This has made them more aggressive in the use of power.

I observed Butch continually encouraging the pupils' curiosity:

No matter how stupid the question might be, I get them to ask it. As they get more confidence in me, they are increasingly unafraid to ask questions. So they ask: 'What is this?' and I say: 'Now that's a good question.' This results in their increasing their questions. I tell them, 'You're dumb for only one moment if you ask it,' and I tell them that one answer might be the key which makes everything fit.

The following week I asked Butch to comment on the relationship of formal education to flying. His reply:

Formal education means little in flying. I instruct doctors, attorneys, and Ph.D.s, and they are no better than the project kids at learning to fly. In fact, the kids do better as a group. I have some guys with several degrees who are so afraid to make mistakes they can't learn to fly. Of course, formal education helps in study. An A average is no sign anyone will be a good pilot, although I tell the boys the smarter you can get, the better. But you don't need great academic learning to fly. Flying is a great equalizer, I feel.

The instructor, who was by now called "Butch" by the students, encouraged them to study more. His post-flight quizzes included such questions as, How do you turn an airplane? Why do you lead with the rudder? Why trim? What is torque?

FLIGHT PROJECT OUTCOMES

During the year preceding the project, fully 60% of the boys had been suspended from school at least once. During that year, the number of disciplinary infractions per student ranged from a low of 20 to a high of 23. Some 29% of the boys admitted to having been sent out of the room by their teachers several times; for an additional 35%, it was at least once or twice.

The boys did not become angels when the project began. Quite the contrary. In early fall the flight class won the dubious distinction of being the first entire class suspended in the history of the district. Rather than perceive themselves as something special, an elite class, the group thought at first that they had been placed in a "dummy" project, a class for the retarded. Most such classes are filled with disadvantaged boys; this fact was not lost on the flight group. Additionally, an all-male class, loaded with youths having histories of behavioral problems, placed a heavy burden on the teacher.

But after several difficult months for all concerned, the class settled down. By the end of the first year of the project, I could report in my evaluation that suspensions had dropped dramatically and the boys were attending school even when they were ill.

239

The tutor-counselor, a graduate student in nuclear engineering at the University of California, Berkeley, spent an average of 17 hours each week with the boys. In May, near the end of the first year of flying, he commented:

> *Each one of the boys is more confident of himself. You can see this. They are freer in their conversations . . . more punctual, getting to school in time for the airport trip. They can now sit down before I do and sit for an hour at a time. This was impossible at the beginning. It took the better part of a year for them to learn to sit. But they're grown up now and have an important attitude toward themselves.*

The tutor claimed to notice remarkable changes in the boys, although many of them still required additional help. He found that they had a great need to talk to him about their problems, especially problems of their families, including lacks in their home lives.

The pilot-instructor and the tutor-counselor roles were crucial to the success of the flight project. They were able to impart knowledge and expertise, while remaining flexible and empathetic. Both of them liked youngsters, both believed the flight kids had potential, and neither was constrained to act as a political agent of the school system.

FIRST-YEAR COMPARISONS

At the time the original flight group was chosen, a control group was also selected. Any available data on the control group were collected for comparative purposes. Important gains occurred in many areas in the first year:

1. *Attendance*. Flight group pupils had an absence rate averaging only three days. The control group averaged 14 days of absence. Teachers commented that the flight group boys came to school even when they were sick.

2. *Suspensions*. No project student was suspended, compared with 48% of the control group. Before beginning the project, 60% indicated that at some time they had been suspended before reaching the eighth grade.

3. *Behavioral competence*. At the beginning of the project year, the on-campus flight classes exhibited a high level of disruptive — at times chaotic — behavior. By January, the instructional vice principal could state that profound changes had occurred: "Compared with September and October, the boys are a thousand percent improved, all around. They are mostly attentive and involved for the first time. I am generally elated at the change in the flight boys."

4. *Reading and math ability.* Reading ability increased remarkably for all flight-group students. One instructor commented: "The students now impress me with their ability to read rather complex adult-level material which I have given them in the form of Civil Air Patrol books and magazine articles on aviation."

At the inception of the project, the group was composed of nine slow readers, 13 average readers, and three boys who were considered to be retarded in reading. By the end of the second year of the project, none of these youths was considered a retarded reader and only three were deemed slow. As their grades in the table below illustrate, the flight group had made excellent progress:

Overall Grade-Point Average in Four
Senior High School Solid Subjects
First Quarter, 1968

	A	B	C	D	F
Flight group — (Ninth Grade)	13%	25%	37%	25%	0%
Control Group — (Ninth Grade)	0%	0%	59%	23%	18%

LONGITUDINAL STUDY OUTCOMES

In February, 1975, I began a follow-up evaluation of the project students and the control group. As the data which follow indicate, the former flight group youths, now averaging 21 years of age, had made important gains. Remarkable transformation in the character and competence of these young men had occurred.

1. *Academic progress.* Fourteen (56%) of the flight group youths are presently enrolled either in institutions of higher education or armed forces training schools. Two are attending the University of California. Two are enrolled at state universities and six are in junior colleges. Three of the youths state that they are saving money so that they can return to college. Two have earned private pilot licenses since graduating from high school.

The group attending universities and colleges is presently averaging 3.0 — a B average. Three of the youths, with grade-point averages of up to 3.5, have won scholarships because of superior work. By comparison, only 20% of the control group are attending junior colleges and none are at four-year institutions.

According to most recent census figures, 24% of the U.S. black male population age 20-21 is enrolled in school. Thus the flight project students are greatly exceeding academic expectations for their age group. In contrast to the flight group, the control students are in line with national averages.

Interest areas and specializations among the flight group are the following: biochemistry, economics, business administration, marketing, real estate management, education, special education, social science teaching, construction engineering, pharmacology, dentistry, and coaching. Five of the youths have no firm career aspirations as yet and are taking general courses.

2. *Parental backing*. Black males constitute 28% of all college dropouts in the 18 to 19 age bracket. This means that vast numbers of these youths are forced to quit short of graduation. A primary reason for this attrition is lack of money. The cost of attending college now runs to over $4,000 per year. This sum represents a little less than two-thirds of the median black family income in America and exceeds the total income of a third of all black families.

Flight project youths come from families similarly impoverished, yet they had a college dropout rate of only 12% from age 18 to the present. This low dropout rate appears to be attributable to their families' willingness to sacrifice financially to keep their sons in school, and of course it testifies to the high value these youths now place on education.

Parental participation in the flight project was encouraged from the beginning. At the inception of the project, all parents were invited to a meeting at the airport where they were able to discuss all aspects of the proposed program with flight personnel and take free rides in light planes. Later, parents were participants in the Project Advisory Committee which met regularly during the life of the project.

In interviews, parents appeared to be elated that the district had chosen their sons, feeling that there must be something special, indeed, about them. All the parents were enthusiastic and very positive about the flight program. Here are samples of their comments:

> *I was very excited and thrilled about the program. All the neighbors and friends of ours were very happy for Elmer and wished their sons could have been chosen.*

> *Joe likes it. He does his homework steadily now. This is a new habit.*

. . . The neighbors and relatives envy us. We are very proud . . . Joe writes his brother in Vietnam about his flying and his brother writes him back to do well because it's an opportunity he never had.

The flying and all made a difference for Melvin. It kept him out of trouble all year. He is looking forward to being in the flight program again and wants very much to become a pilot . . .

Kelly now wants to have an aviation job. My husband feels that his chances in life are greater now. He is more capable. The neighbors think it is great . . . but I think some of them are even jealous and act hostile to us.

3. *Employment.* As this is written (fall, 1975), young men, especially blacks, face a severely depressed job market. Yet, only two of these flight group youths (8%) are unemployed. By comparison, 40% of the control group youth are out of work. The table below shows the occupational and academic distribution of former project students:

Fall, 1975 Occupational and Academic Distribution of Former Flight Project Youths (N=25)

Armed Forces		5
Air Force	4	
Army	1	
Higher Education		10
University of California	2	
State universities	2	
Junior colleges	6	
Oil Companies		3
Steam plant operator	1	
Catalytic technician	1	
Operational specialist	1	
Mechanics		2
Automotive	1	
Heavy trucks	1	
Stock clerk (studying religion)		1
Musician		1
Unemployed		2
Unknown		1

Those youths serving in the armed forces are participating in advanced training courses in the following areas: power plant specialist, communications specialist, pharmacology, and meteorology.

Former project youths attending college were found to be involved in the following kinds of part-time work: antibiotics research assistant, elementary teacher trainee, chemistry laboratory aide, turret lathe operator, grocery store clerk, janitor, and watchman.

Since graduation from high school in 1971, members of the group have had extensive job experience. Their overall employment history illustrates great industry and an overwhelming desire to succeed.

Last fall five of the students were involved in the aviation or aerospace industries. Four were with the Air Force and one was involved in rocketry. A large percentage of the flight project youths are still searching for their occupational niche in life. Of those who have found it, one is a catalytic technician, earning $22,000 per year. Another youth earns almost $20,000 as a diesel truck driver. A third is a cashier/clerk whose life goal is to become a religious elder in the Jehovah's Witnesses Church. And the fourth, an under-employed musician, wants to do nothing else for a living.

4. *Self-esteem*. The self-esteem of poor, stigmatized youths is continually, relentlessly attacked in the public schools. At the inception of the flight project, the majority of our 25 students had low self-esteem. When asked to respond to the statement, "I do not have too much to be proud of," one-third of the group agreed and almost as many were undecided. Only 38% disagreed with the statement.

Questioned again in 1968, after one year in the project, only 10% of the flight group agreed that they did not have much to be proud of.

When we questioned the former flight group students in the spring of 1975, only two stated that they did not have too much to be proud of. A dramatic elevation in self-esteem had occurred. By contrast, 36% of the control group presently state that they do not have much to be proud of.

In the spring, 1975 interviews, typical responses by former flight group youths were: "I used to feel inferior about books and academics. Now I feel an obligation to get the most out of myself." "I still remember the complete control I had over myself . . . my own life and death, when I flew the 150."

5. *Sense of mastery*. Closely related to self-esteem is a sense of control or mastery over one's fate. Again, the project youths indicated that they now definitely believe they possess a great measure of control over their future:

"I'll never forget how to fly and the fantastic feeling that you can control things that goes with it." "My grades even improved after I got into the aerospace program. It was a big boost. It changed my attitudes toward education."

In the spring of 1967, we asked these youths to respond to the statement: "You should expect more out of life." Nearly half of the boys (48%) disagreed with the statement at that time, 39% agreed, and 13% were undecided.

In the spring of 1975, we asked these youths to respond to the identical statement. There was definite, positive response, a complete reversal in attitude. Now, 94% agreed that indeed they should expect more out of life. Representative responses from those interviewed included the following: "I can get what I want. I have a lot of confidence in my ability." "If I want to become something, I will." "I have the self-motivation now. I can accomplish my personal goals."

In the spring, 1975 follow-up interviews, both the flight group and the control group were asked to respond to the statement: "What is going to happen to me will probably happen, no matter what I do." In 1967, 45% of the flight group agreed with this statement, 43% disagreed, and 12% were undecided. Questioned again in 1975, none agreed, 86% disagreed, and 14% were undecided. By comparison, 37% of the control group voiced agreement, indicating their greater belief in fate, in forces beyond their control.

6. *Deviance*. Youths from impoverished subcultures, especially black males, must fight hard to avoid getting enmeshed in delinquent or criminal activities. Merely engaging in such victimless social acts as drinking or gambling can bring arrest. The middle- and upper-class individual is immune; he generally confines these activities to private clubs and residences.

Thus the highly vulnerable youth from a disadvantaged community must somehow rise above the normal tendency to get into trouble. Those incapable of escape will almost automatically become further stigmatized; a criminal record often closes off opportunity forever. As Kelly N. informed us: "My life since high school has been going in the wrong direction . . . toward crime. I want to turn it around. I know they let me in the Air Force because of the flight project. I know the Air Force will help me straighten out my life."

Melvin W. is regularly employed and a devout church member. He

246

believes that he has won his struggle against the odds: "After high school I had a bad period. I broke my ankle and lost my athletic scholarship . . . then started drinking heavily. Getting close to religion helped me out. But you know, I think the flight program could curb delinquency. Especially if it went on for, like, four years."

Although it has not been possible to obtain thorough interviews with control group youths, we believe they were concealing a high number of deviant activities. It was determined that their frequency of arrest was exactly twice as high as that of the flight group.

The ability of former flight project youths to overcome overwhelming pressures to commit deviant acts must constitute one of the most crucial of the positive outcomes of the flight project. Recognizing the terrible problems socially "different" individuals face, Gabriel Tarde said 70 years ago: "To innovate, to discover, to awake for an instant, the individual must escape, for the time being, from his social surroundings. Such unusual audacity makes him super-social, rather than social."

CONCLUSION

Aviation experiences — in airport hangars and workshops, weather stations, flight lines, and cockpits — opened up a wide spectrum of imagery and opportunity to the flight project youths. As student pilots, these boys were involved in personal as well as job exploration while obtaining empirical training. They were exposed to new and basic techniques in the process of gaining image-building experiences. They could learn firsthand the types of talents and interpersonal competencies required to earn a living. And these boys could obtain direct contact with positive role models; if they could not identify with these models, they could at least imitate them. A 1972 interview with Butch, the pilot-instructor, identified some of the important flight-related experiences:

> When we first picked the boys up they were about 13 . . . just a bunch of good-natured kids, having a good time. Right? And then, as we had a chance to get into the actual flying of the airplane, their attitudes and concepts started to change. It wasn't a game anymore.

> Then there began a lot of keen competition to show me that they know why they're draining the sumps and everybody is kind of running on top of one another to point out a wire, a bolt, a cotter pin.

> Then, as we continued into the program our main objective was not to

teach the boys how to fly, but to show a practical relationship — how an airplane fits into everyday life. The vehicle shows them the practical application of mathematics, science, communication . . . (They learn) the reason for speaking very clearly on the radio when talking to the tower. And geography. You know, you are flying across country and you are looking down and there is a steel factory there . . . or a cotton field.

There are many successes of the flight project and its unexpected positive results appear to be caused by the youths' involvement in a high-status activity, elimination of the fear of failure, changed expectations on the part of significant others in their lives, acquisition of unique skills, and the opportunity for significant achievement in the dominant culture.

This longitudinal study has produced considerable ''hard'' data as well as qualitative results supportive of the flight project concept. Former project youths are demonstrably better off than controls in the areas of employment, advanced education, and avoidance of deviance. Finally, project youths appear to have grasped the linkage between advanced schooling and career potential as their essential and available source of power.

Flight brought a sense of joy to these youths and overcame their pervasive feelings of alienation and worthlessness. Their flight instructor's noncritical, nonthreatening evaluation of their abilities gave them a sense of ''specialness'' which overcame the judgmental, negative attitudes to which they had grown accustomed.

Our evaluation data appear to prove that moral and imaginative capacity, not measured achievement or tested intelligence (IQ), are the real defining characteristics of human beings.

Are there other similar models? Probably, and they might include: soaring; mountain climbing and ballet; activities which feature risk, sensory stimulation, speed, spatial imagery, and the opportunity to master high-status, technially complex enterprises. But, clearly, for disadvantaged youth, flight captures and captivates. It is a genuine power trip.

YOUTH IN
LOWER CLASS SETTINGS

Arthur Pearl

The actions, life patterns, and characteristics of the poor have intrigued social scientists for a good many years. A major avenue of interest and study has been the social groups that emerge among the lower classes. A mountain of data has been amassed on the academic performance and failure, the incidence of deviance and social pathology among poor youth, together with a spate of theory and quasi-theory to explain the statistics. Since in this chapter I intend to argue against a number of the apparent findings, a brief review of some conclusions derived from various studies of the poor is in order.

There appears to be general consensus that low-income youth, when contrasted with more affluent counterparts, are characterized by the following: a poorer self-image, a greater sense of powerlessness, a more fatalistic attitude toward life, a lack of future orientation, a greater potential for impulsive "acting out." Most studies have found low-income youth to be nonverbal, anti-intellectual, and at best primitive in conceptual ability. The young lower class person is held to have unrealistically high aspirations and at the same time more depressed expectations than his middle-class counterpart (1).

The attitudes and outlooks listed above are supposedly responsible for a complex of behaviors which further hamper the expectations of poor youth. Low-income youth tend to be more likely to leave school prematurely and to achieve little even when they persist in their schooling (2). The poor, in disproportionate numbers, are remanded to correctional and mental institutions (3).

Students of social problems usually assume that intrapsychic variables — attitudes, identifications, and values — are the independent variables, while the indices of social pathology are the dependent variables. They draw the conclusion that a change in the way of life of the poor would produce significant changes in behavior.

Empey and Rabow (4), in their Provo experiment, state this quite explicitly. The goal of the Provo experiment is to convince lower class gang youth that conventional behavior has greater utility than delinquent ways. Such a goal may be possible in Utah, but it is not truly meaningful for the youth of New York, Chicago, Washington, D.C., or Los Angeles, for reasons which will be described later in this chapter.

This interpretation and suggested solution for the problems of low-income youth places the onus on the poor and calls for the non-poor to provide services to produce changes in their self-concept, aspiration, and style. There is, however, a more parsimonious explanation of the available data, which is that the aforementioned styles of life among the underprivileged are dependent variables stemming from their efforts to deal with an insoluble problem, the essence of which is forced exclusion from functioning society. It is only when this dilemma facing the poor is analyzed that it is possible to make sense of their behavior and styles. Our solutions for changing behavior must lie in opening up the *possibilities* for a different existence — possibilities which are currently nonexistent.

The poor of today are faced with a situation uniquely different from that faced by the lowest classes of previous generations. The traditional mechanisms for absorbing the unschooled and unskilled into the productive fabric of society are no longer operative. To indicate the nature of this situation, a number of economic and social factors must be identified, if only in the simplest terms.

The year 1963 was a magnificent one for the general economy. There was a healthy increase in gross national product; a new high was set for median income. But in this same year, rising unemployment widened an even greater economic gap between the poor and non-poor, the Negro and the non-Negro. Between 1957 and 1962, 500,000 fewer workers produced significantly more goods, and one million jobs were eliminated in agriculture although farm surpluses continued to accumulate (5).

Automation must be recognized for what it is, a permanent fixture in American life which will enable private industry to produce efficiently, increase the gross national product, and — eliminate jobs. John I. Snyder, president and chairman of U.S. Industries, Inc., estimates that two million jobs are eradicated a year by automation. Most relevant to the issue of low-income youth is that the jobs that are being eliminated are those which the poor can perform; whereas, the jobs that are being created in our society are those to which the poor are denied access. The result of this is as Snyder states:

We are already feeling the enormous impact of the clash of what I regard as the two surging forces of our time: the growth of automation and the eruption of the Negro's demand for equality. It seems to me

250

there is little doubt that in eliminating the jobs of youth who have not yet even come into the labor market, the technological revolution has intensified the social revolution (6).

The impact of the changes wrought by programs of cybernation and automation is reflected in the coping mechanisms of low-income youth today, in the action and reaction surrounding civil rights, and in new expressions of national concern over poverty in this land of affluence.

THE NEW ELEMENT IN POVERTY

Poverty is not new — but there is something new in poverty — there is no way out. In the not-too-distant past the poor could enter functioning society by three paths. The *unskilled labor market* was open to many, since all technological change then took place at the expense of skilled labor, actually increasing the relative number of unskilled jobs. Today, however, the technological impact of automation is felt most severely by the unskilled, whose functions are fast becoming obsolete. The unskilled poor can no longer use their labor to gain entrance into productive society in significant numbers.

In the past, little capital was needed to make a start in agriculture, sales, or even small-scale manufacturing. Individual members of the lower classes could venture into *entrepreneurial enterprises* with some hope of achieving success. Technology and current business practice has erased this possibility too. Small business mortality — even for established enterprises — is extremely high in this country, and the capital and "know-how" necessary to implement even modest ventures are beyond the means of today's current poor.

Education for professional and business roles was in the past the third way for aspiring lower-class youth to improve their economic and social status. Higher education for some members of lower-class families was often made possible because other family members had attained an economic toehold through the other productive avenues described above. But today education of the extent and quality required for most rewarding occupations is systematically denied the poor.

To obtain a marketable skill, youth of today must be prepared to stay in school four or five years beyond high school. For most of the poor, this is not a possibility. Even if scholarships were provided, the indirect costs would make college prohibitive. However, most of the poor do not even have this choice. They are simply not offered a secondary education which can lead to

251

college. They are neatly detached from the educational through train and shunted off onto tracks which lead nowhere.

One of these "educational" sidetracks is vocational training. In many cases the trades for which training is intended are rapidly being made obsolete by automation. In other instances modern tooling, equipment, and techniques are lacking in a secondary trade school, and an already inadequate technical schooling is compounded by failure to provide even the minimum basic skills — reading and mathematics — necessary to face the current scene. Another fallacy of vocational education is its tendency to be occupation-specific. The vocational student is securely "locked" into a job for life, which means, conversely, that he is *locked out* of opportunities to gain entrance into other fields. The products of an occupation-specific vocational curriculum who lack adequate basic learning skills must become casualties when there is technological change and dislocation.

"Special ability classes," "basic tracks," or "slow learner's classes" are various names for another means of systematically denying the poor adequate access to education. These special programs rarely yield literacy and they most certainly do not prepare the student for any productive role in society. Students assigned to the "basic track" in most metropolitan schools are simply counted and kept in order; they have been relegated to the academic boneyard and eventual economic oblivion. In certain high schools over 40 per cent of the student population has been assigned to the basic track.

It is not fully appreciated that present teaching procedures are insuring and even accelerating a trend to segregation in our society. The inequities of open racial segregation in schools have been brought to public consciousness, but other kinds of segregation are creating similar inequities. Segregation by alleged ability brings with it the same lack of stimulation and dearth of association that the Supreme Court proscribed in declaring racial school segregation unconstitutional.

Nor is it generally recognized that from another viewpoint there is virtually total segregation in the school systems of this country. Nearly all persons currently teaching school are middle class by income, identification, and residence. The entire administrative and teaching staffs of schools in urban slums are alien to the population which they serve — identification and rapport between pupil and teacher is characteristically absent in this situation.

Teachers of the urban poor are discouraged by their students' lack of response to curricula which are geared to neither their interests or experience. Students are oppressed by what is for them an alien imposition — dull and uninspiring at best. City schools typically provide poor youth with little opportunity for developing status, dignity, or a sense of self. The school, in microcosm, represents the dilemma which faces the poor in society. They are not a part of it, it is simply an oppressive authority.

The school is an integral part of the insoluble problem of low-income youth. On the one hand, the school denies them education with any promise for access to success, yet they are urged and warned that they must stay on to graduation if they expect to get any job. They are lectured about democratic processes but have little or no choice in determining their own course of study. In the process they are denied dignity and often stigmatized or ostracized.

REACTIONS TO AN INSOLUBLE PROBLEM

The response of low-income youth to schools which present such bitter contradictions resembles the behavior of other organisms presented with insoluble problems. When rats are placed on a platform and subjected to electric shock whether they remain still or jump, they cease to attend the problem, engage in random behaviors, and sometimes flail out wildly, biting the cages and even the experimenter (7). Studies with human subjects who have been asked to resolve insoluble problems show that their response is variously regressive or aggressive behavior (8). In both social and experimental settings, the behavior of subjects is understandable when the nature of their problem is fully appreciated. In both contexts we note that a variety of apparently irrational behavioral responses are generated from the same problem.

The problem for poor youth is not that they lack future orientation but, indeed, that they lack a future. They are made aware of this early because there is so little meaning in their present. A limited gratification exists in striving for the impossible, and as a consequence poor youth create styles, coping mechanisms, and groups in relation to the systems which they can and cannot negotiate. Group values and identifications emerge in relation to the forces opposing them. Poor youth develop a basic pessimism because they have a fair fix on reality. They rely on fate because no rational transition system is open to them. They react against schools because schools are characteristically hostile to them.

Despite the seeming hopelessness of their chances in life, poor youth do develop coping skills and strengths. It is a mistake, for instance, to characterize them as inarticulate, or non-verbal. Although their academic command of language may be lamentable, urban low-income youth possess a colorful and complex verbal style (9). In the face of a forbidding system in which they seem to have no stake, they struggle to establish codes, groups, values, and goals which will provide a basis for identity, a standard for behavior, a status, a competence.

The problem facing the poor is simply that they lack the skills and education necessary to make a living in society which is becoming ever more technological and specialized. They are unable to take the hurdle into productive existences since their sole commodity, unskilled labor, is not in demand, and no amount of pluck or hope will change this. They are increasingly relegated to the sidelines as spectators of society.

A QUICK CRITICAL LOOK AT
SOME PROPOSED SOLUTIONS

Proposed solutions to the problem of the poor take several forms and we shall briefly consider those with most current importance.

1. *Economic Manipulation* — One solution to poverty is the proposition that stimulation of the economy is beneficial to all classes. Economic manipulation of tax schedules and interest rates is often the method advanced, but it is safe to say that the poor are not the beneficiaries of such measures (10). They have neither the income base nor the credit status to profit by them. And since inflation is a likely after-effect of tax reduction, the poor may actually be disadvantaged by having to pay more for goods with no increase in income.

2. *Educational Reform* — A more widely acknowledged approach to solving the problem of the poor is that of improving educational techniques and staff and providing compensatory education. Advocates of this solution argue that there are plenty of jobs for people with proper training but that the poor are not equipped to fill the unmet needs of the modern labor market. Therefore, by improving school facilities and training of teachers — by increasing the status of teachers to attract and hold the best qualified — the poor can be educated out of their current dilemma. Galbraith (11) suggests that the solution to poverty rests in paying teachers a salary of $12,000 to work with the poor children of Appalachia and Harlem.

Even allowing that paying teachers more will insure the poor an improved education (which is somewhat unlikely since most able teachers prefer closer-to-home assignments in middle-class areas), there is no assurance that the poor will find a future in the economic system.

3. *Compensatory Education* — A more alluring variation on the educational theme is proposed by advocates of compensatory education. It is claimed that the poor fail to negotiate the educational system because they enter it with an acute cultural handicap. Further, if remedial education is not initiated at a very early age, the proponents of this theory state, poor children can never bridge the ever-increasing cultural and academic gap which separates them from more economically favored youth.

Martin Deutsch (12) has marshalled an impressive array of data to support this thesis. He demonstrates conclusively that the poor are already at a comparative disadvantage at school-entering age and that this comparative disadvantage increases as they progress through school. Deutsch suggests that poor children must be stimulated and trained starting at pre-school age — prepared for reading and the development of intellectual interests — if they are to overcome the strictures which seemingly doom them to academic failure. He has devised exciting tasks for the children in his experiments and clearly substantiates that markedly improved accomplishment results from use of these techniques. The incontrovertible evidence to be drawn from Deutsch's work is that a potential for enterprise and achievement exists in the poor.

It is possible, however, to contest his conclusion that the cumulative or increasing differential in achievement is a simple progression stemming from initial lack of stimulation. The growing failure or increasing deficit exhibited as poor children grow older is not necessarily due only to accumulated environmental deficit. Their growing failure may be also in part due to a growing recognition that there is no pay-off in the system for them. Motivation is crucial in inspiring the poor child to make the necessary effort to master skills which are perhaps harder for him than for the youth with more solvent parents, who receives encouragement and rewards within the family for his success.

THEORETICAL FOUNDATION FOR COMPENSATORY EDUCATION

The underlying theoretical formulations in the compensatory education thesis deserve to be examined in some detail. The basic thesis has its foundation in experiments in sensory deprivation. Laboratory studies with primates have provided evidence that pronounced deprivation of stimulation from a very early age has devastating results (13).

Primates kept in total darkness for their first two years may develop irreversible retinal abnormalities. Harlow, in a series of interesting and profound studies, has shown that denial of peer or maternal association from birth will produce hopelessly psychotic monkeys.

Deutsch and his co-workers see an analogy between these studies and the conditions which surround poor children. The poor child, they insist, is starved and stunted by lack of intellectual stimulation; he has parents who do not engage in complicated verbal interactions; his home contains no books; and the environmental noise level is so high that adaptation to it produces a functional hearing disorder in the child. They hold that, if not soon counteracted, the effects of such an environment are irreversible (14).

While this formulation is enticing and seductive, it is based primarily on argument from analogy. Sensory deprivation means denial of stimulation, which to date has only been systematically induced experimentally by rearing or maintaining subjects in isolation. The poor are not reared in isolation; the opposite is true — poverty is characterized by over-crowding. Not only is there no evidence of lack of sensory input, it has not even been conclusively demonstrated that the poor are victimized by an analogous condition — sensory overload. All that can be stated definitely is that the poor child is stimulated *differently* than the non-poor child.

CHANGING EDUCATION TO MEET THE CHILD

The poor child learns to negotiate his world. That world stresses physical accomplishments and downgrades styles which are not functional. The differences between social strata, however, are relative, not absolute. The low-income child is not isolated from verbal exchange and cognitive excitation. He might not get as much, and what he gets may be different from the middle-class child (15).

If his skills and coping abilities lead him toward physical activity rather than verbal manipulation in his adaptation to environment, then why must they be judged inferior or worthless? It is suggested that learning experiences in the early grades be amended to fit the special abilities and approaches of the poor child (16). Why must the child be reshaped to negotiate even the initiation into education when the system might more easily be adapted to appreciate and build on his experience?

Schools should be prepared to meet and treat with poor children on their own level as they enter. If physical activity is the means by which the child has learned to negotiate his environment, then it must be utilized as a skill rather than suppressed. If the child's attention span is limited, then this may need to be an area of special training. If tempo and language styles of poor children are widely variant from middle-class norms, then teachers must be prepared to start by accepting what a child has and stimulating his interest in acquiring new and strange language skills. The incredulity and dismay, the total rejection of his small arsenal of abilities and modes, with which the average middle class teacher initiates the poor child into the school system could hardly be better calculated to stultify inquiry and pride in learning. The work of Sylvia Ashton-Warner (17) has special relevance — a model of what it is possible to do with children of special backgrounds.

However welcome such changes in the approach of the school system might be, this is still begging the issue. Although the schools might be less defeat-ridden, the basic point is that, given society as it is evolving and lacking the negotiable skill necessary to enter it, poor youth still face ultimate defeat. There is increasingly less opportunity for them to enter viable society from the public secondary school.

PUBLIC WORKS

Other proposals calling for structural change to meet the problems of the poor include an expanded public works program and a revival of youth training camps in conservation, forestry and the like. Although the results of such programs might benefit society as a whole by the creation of schools, roads, parks, and renewed urban areas, the problems facing the poor would remain constant. Public works projects will tend to enforce relative inequality. The poor and unskilled will dig the ditches, while the planners and engineers for the programs will come from the affluent sectors of society; meanwhile, over the horizon lurks the shadow of the automatic ditchdigger, ready to displace the unskilled yet again.

NEW CAREERS

In addition to examining and criticizing various current theories and programs in aid of the poor, this chapter intends to advance an alternative proposal and draw attention to a pilot experimental intervention established to implement it.

Background for the proposal

A basic tenet of this proposal is the necessity for providing the poor with a chance for life careers as opposed to the dwindling supply of menial, dead-end niches which are their current lot. The poor need jobs which offer some avenues for personal realization, dignity and improvement of skills and status — careers which would give them a stake in the system. It is important, initially, to recognize where the opportunities lie. As previously stated, the private sector of the economy is committed to increased efficiency of production, which results in more automation and increasingly fewer opportunities for the entrance of untrained personnel.

In the past five years rates of employment growth have slowed or declined in the various industries of the private sector. Trade, manufacturing, construction, mining, and transportation have shown actual decreases in employment. The public sector claimed 64 per cent of the job growth between 1947 and 1962, with the greatest increases occurring in the field of health, education and sanitation in local and state governments (18). These activities, influenced greatly by an expanding population and relatively unaffected by automation, provide a means by which millions of poor can be put to work. Details of how this can be done can be found in Pearl and Reissman (19).

In brief, however, the argument is: (1) there are more jobs than people in the helping professions (education, welfare, health, etc.); (2) these professions contain functions which require little formal training; (3) these functions can be performed by the poor.

Placing the poor in low-paying jobs must be regarded only as a first step of *inducting* the poor into the labor market. Such a program by itself would hardly be expected to affect the life styles of the poor. If life station is to be improved, then training must be provided *after* the poor are placed on jobs. The pay-off of the training would be eligibility for a series of intermediate positions created between initial function and professional duties. Thus, the insoluble aspect of the problem can be obviated by hiring first, training afterward, and making possible access to full professional status by negotiable steps. Only when both entrance jobs and opportunities for advancement exist is there true career potential for the poor.

Many factors must be considered if "new careers" are to be an integral part of American economic life. These include:

1. *Establishment of self-sustaining training groups among the young people starting new careers* — The function of such groups would be to develop morale and goal identification, to discuss and seek solutions for problems arising in the course of work and training, and to render mutual assistance among group members.

2. *Development of multi-level training programs to be utilized while on the job* — These would include remedial courses in basic learning skills, self-study courses in academic and technical subjects, extension classroom courses in community colleges and universities, and on-the-job sessions with professional supervisors. Negotiations with accredited educational institutions should arrange to give academic credit for experience and knowledge gained on the job as verified by examinations and work records.

3. *Training professionals to maximize the utilization of the new personnel at their disposal* — The professional, whose duties would include more training, consultation, administration, and supervision functions, must be provided with skills to better perform an altered responsibility.

4. *Rapid change in policy and form of governmental agencies* — Such metastasis will not come easily. There is need to encounter every bureaucratic control. New positions must be approved and budgeted. Civil service merit systems must be considered, since there is no assurance that, with current practice, many of the poor would survive entrance tests. Many of the youth will have a history of extra-legal activities, and social agencies have shown a disinclination to hire persons with delinquency records.

There is obvious risk in any new undertaking. Agency heads, for a variety of understandable reasons, do not relish risks. Established procedures have been tempered and improved by continual trial and reappraisal. They will not readily succumb to change.

5. *Use of demonstration for agency change* — Sponsoring innovative programs as a demonstration is the responsibility of some government agencies and private foundations. Unfortunately, insufficient attention is given to the use of demonstration for establishing agency change. Independent entities are, in fact, formed to sponsor demonstration to by-pass the tedious regulations of the appropriate agency. Demonstrations of new careers must include a strategy for increasing the commitment of the agency. Initially expense must be borne by outside funds, but agency investment must be phased in and continually increased until fully absorbed as an integral part of agency operation.

CAN THE POOR DO THE JOBS?

What has been proposed as a solution to a chronic problem is placing the poor where jobs are most plentiful. One basic issue must be considered — do the poor have sufficient capacity to perform even the low-level entry jobs? Or phrased differently, can society afford the luxury of entrusting the education and health of the nation, even in subordinate roles, to the nation's poor? There is some evidence that there is potential, even among those with the least achievements.

In Flint, Michigan, a group of fourth grade pupils with reading problems were assigned to the tutelage of sixth grade pupils who were also experiencing reading difficulties. While the fourth graders made significant progress, the sixth graders also learned from the experience (20). This is in accord with what Frank Riessman (21) has called "the helper principal." Persons who are given a stake or concern in a system tend to become committed to the task in a way that brings about meaningful development of their own abilities.

In Chicago, gang leaders have been employed as directors of lower-class youth in recreational and social facilities. Their talents for leadership and ability to identify with young people of their own class and background made them especially useful (22).

The New York State Division for Youth employed a number of delinquents on a research team which conducted interviews of other delinquents. Unanticipated benefits were realized from their employment. When graduate students conducted the tape-recorded interviews, they confirmed the usual conclusion that lower-class youth were inarticulate. But when lower-class interviewers canvassed the same persons, responses were entirely different. The subjects were animated and highly verbal.

Mobilization for Youth has demonstrated that women from welfare rolls can be used as "homemakers" aiding other women receiving welfare (23). The California Department of Corrections has employed inmates and former inmates in a variety of treatment and research roles (24).

In education the employment of the poor has particular significance. As previously described, schools are usually an alien imposition in poor neighborhoods, having all the elements of colonialism. Education takes place in a charged atmosphere. Surrounded by fear and distrust, there is little in the way of a true community base for education. The system "belongs" to the non-residents.

If community residents are offered a stake in the system by way of the employment of indigenous youth, the whole relationship between school and community should begin to change. Pupils will have models to identify with and aspire toward. The problems of poor children and their families would be interpreted by new careerists with a foot in both camps. The dynamics of the relationship between the community and the school should be profoundly affected by a program which obviously can *accept* something from the community.

A PILOT STUDY

At Howard University in Washington, D.C., ten young people from disadvantaged backgrounds were the subject for a pilot study designed to test the feasibility of new career development (25). The only qualifications for entrance into the program were that the youth could not have more than a high school education, could have no pending legal action which might remove them from the study, could pass a physical examination (which only really disqualified those with an active tuberculosis or venereal disease), and could fill out an entrance application form keyed to a fourth grade reading level.

The aims of the study were to determine if youth would volunteer for the program; persist in it; be trained to have usable skills in day care, recreation, and research; and, upon completion of training, be hired by agencies in the community.

The program had, in addition, the purpose of creating a group of ten to establish new norms of acceptable behavior; a group that would be responsible for sanctioning or proscribing behavior; a group that would have a sizable measure of self-determination.

Twenty-eight youth were referred to the program; they came primarily from a youth employment center. Of these, twenty-four appeared for an initial interview, and nineteen returned for the health examination, all but two passing the examination. Fourteen of the seventeen who remained were pair-matched according to age, sex, grade attained in school, employment history, and arrest record. One member of each pair was randomly assigned to the program, and the three without a matched pair were added to complete the team. The seven not selected constituted a contrast group to be used to obtain preliminary gross appraisal of the job experience that could have been expected had this program not been attempted.

All youth referred were Negro. Of the seventeen who survived the screening procedures, six were girls. The group ranged in age from sixteen to twenty, in school attainment from the eighth to the eleventh grade. Six of the eleven boys had extensive arrest records; three of the six girls had children born out of wedlock. None of the youth had stable work histories.

The program began with all ten receiving a minimal orientation of three days in all of the job areas (recreation, day care, research). In research they were instructed in use of a desk calculator and a tape recorder, taught how to calculate percentages, how to interview, how to administer sociometric choice check lists, and how to observe and record processes and activities. In day care the youth were oriented to the organization of the day-care center; the basic principles of growth and development; the supervising technique with young children; and the particulars of specific games, arts, and crafts. In recreation they were advised about the administration and purposes of the center, recruitment of youth to the program, rules of various recreation pursuits, adolescent development, and supervision techniques to be used with older children and young adolescents.

At the end of the two weeks, the young people were given job assignments (although it was stressed that each had the responsibility of briefing the others on the details of their duties, since it was not at all clear in which categories job placements could be established). Four were assigned to a day care center (Friendship House); four to a Howard University Community Mental Health Center (Baker's Dozen) to be part of the recreation program there; and two to the research team at the Howard University Center for Youth and Community Studies.

Training was established as a group experience. The young people were given job assignments for half a day and assembled as a group of ten for half a day to discuss and critically review job performances. Lectures, motion pictures, trips, etc., were scheduled in the context of group discussion. (Fluidity in the organization of such instruction is crucial. Lectures, motion pictures, trips, etc., should be decided on by the youth themselves, and be part of group responsibility. The staff must be adaptable without losing sight of program goals. In the study described here, efforts to attain such disciplined flexibility were only partially successful.)

After four weeks the youth were placed full time on the job except for three-hour-a-week group meetings to discuss policy issues, *e.g.*, rules for excused absences or grievance procedures and disciplining practices. The group was encouraged to meet additionally on its own time. To add structure, a club was formed, dues collected, and a fund established to provide short-term loans to youth caught short between pay days.

During the first six weeks, youth were provided stipends of $20 per week; after the sixth week this was raised to $50 per week. During the first six weeks there were no excusable absences or tardiness. For every fraction of an hour missed, fifty cents was deducted from the youth's pay. After the sixth week the group established a policy which allowed pay for some absences (prearranged appointments with doctor or welfare worker), and allowed some to be made up by overtime work (only if prearranged); on those occasions where no prearrangements and agreements with supervisors were made, absences and tardiness would result in loss of pay.

At the end of the tenth week, all ten of the youth were still in the program. They had demonstrated abilities to perform a variety of tasks; they had had no serious involvement with the law. They were increasingly responsive and prompt.

On the negative side, despite efforts to establish a group reference, these youth largely use the group only when presented with problems that they *must* solve. Cliques composed of the same youth who "ran" together prior to the program remain, and basic attitudes appear much the same; however, perception of self as one who helps others has been tenuously engendered.

GROUP RESPONSIBILITY — SOME ILLUSTRATIVE ANECDOTES

The new career was designed as a group experience in which much of the program responsibility would be referred to the group. The importance of group decision-making cannot be overemphasized. It must be understood that the poor are denied opportunity to express initiative and self-determination in formal structures and organizations. Their group values reflect the range of possibilities open to them. In the new career program the group was to provide a reference for a changed life situation. The group was explicitly told that staff members could not be norm determiners since relationships would have to be relatively distant and transient.

Group references and group identification need to be established because the youth are placed in an uncomfortable situation. On the one hand, they are asked to renounce, as non-functional, the ways of their erstwhile peers; but on the other hand, they do not possess the trappings, the style, or the credentials that would permit them entrance into the establishment.

It is to be anticipated that the group members would meet some unpleasantness and taxing challenges in attempting to gain a foothold in the pursuit of their new careers. Without a group to provide support, the probabilities of success would appear to be extremely small. Without the support of others in a similar situation, old friends and old ways would be extremely difficult to resist at times of discouragement.

However, merely announcing the necessity of a group function does not guarantee a functioning group. In fact, if great care is not taken, a program designed to develop initiative and self-determination could easily be corrupted into mere recapitulation of previous alienating encounters with welfare workers, school personnel, police, etc. The program starts with a handicap. It has been constructed by outsiders. It therefore bears a stamp of colonialism. The youth have no precommitment to the program. Not developed by them, the program is not perceived as being their own. They expect expertness in the staff; they expect direction from it. They expect that to earn their pay, they must do as they are told; and if the program demands that they change attitudes, they are prepared to state what they believe to be the appropriate sentiment. They shirk from responsibility for the program. They do not want to be blamed for failure. They do not want to be held liable for the behavior of others. Lack of authoritarian posture of the staff is viewed with distrust; it might reflect weakness, an invitation to anarchy, an abdication of responsibility, or it might be some kind of trap.

The staff also views the group members with trepidation. If authority is renounced, how can order be re-established? It is possible that group members vying for leadership, unless given a role model, could turn the program against the staff. These youths have turned to violence before; without firm adult leadership it could happen again.

The staff is not completely comfortable with group meetings. Three to four hours can be a fearfully long time. Sometimes the group "grits it out" (refuses to discuss anything). Sometimes the group turns unmercifully upon one of its marginal members, to the discomfort of the staff member. Most of the time the group appears to be bored. Sometimes the staff member wonders whether he isn't more involved in trying to convince the group that he is a "good guy" than he is in trying to present issues for deliberation and policy determination. Most of the time there do not appear to be any issues which require deliberation.

The staff sometimes becomes overly solicitous. They undermine group responsibility by overidentifying with particular individuals. They are overwhelmed by apparent pathology and overtly express shock at peer callousness and brutality. However, despite staff intrusion, the group did make decisions.

During the third week of the program, a girl assigned to research was given a tape recorder and asked to interview one of the other youth. She was given a "hard way to go" by the interviewee and, taking the tape recorder home, she did not return to the program for three days. Staff then offered these alternatives to the group: (1) the police could be called and the girl charged with theft; (2) staff could go visit her and at least get the tape recorder back; (3) the group could assume responsibility for the situation. The group accepted the challenge and, in teams, visited the girl's residence, found her, and convinced her to return to the program.

Establishing policy for excusable absence presented the biggest challenge to the youth. They were conflicted by two diverse impulses. On the one hand, many had been "docked" during the first weeks of the program and wanted others to have a similar fate. On the other hand, the group was tempted to let everyone get away with as much as he could. Superimposed on these options was the desire to reward friends and punish those not in the dominant clique. Ultimately, after much discussion and insistence upon an operational policy, the youth did come up with a workable formula.

Probably the most important decision the youth were asked to make was assignment to jobs. Contrary to the expectations and desires of staff, the boys assigned the boys with the most serious delinquency backgrounds to day care; assigned a girl with seemingly no propensity for athletics to recreation; and assigned, according to the director of the day care agency, the youth best suited for day care to research.

The director of the day care center, with misgivings and after some wrangling, acceded to the decision of the group. The two boys in question made remarkable contributions to the day care center.

The choice made by the group in this instance is important because it contrasted sharply with staff preferences. Complying with the group decision might not only have been best for establishing group responsibility, but also best for recruitment of staff for the day care center. Day care is a female-dominated field. It needs men for a variety of reasons, not the least of which is that many of the children are from broken homes and have little contact with adult males. Yet, had staff made the decision, the boys would have been rejected. Part of the staff problem was a fear of alienating the boys by assigning them to "girls' work." This instance accentuates, given the current state of knowledge, the danger of prejudgment.

All but one of the group were in favor of the assignments — the one exception was a boy who opted for research but was given a recreation assignment. The reasons offered by the group members for the choices gave some insight into their thought processes. They had made their decision that the youths with delinquent backgrounds would go to day care because during the orientation period these two boys had been most active with little children. Unlike the others, who stood around and watched, they had participated in activities with the children. When asked about their decision to do "women's work" rather than recreation, they replied that they had appreciated the children's enthusiastic response. One of the two pointed out that recreation presented a problem. He would return to the playgrounds where he had earned a "rep" as a troublemaker and would have to confront his friends. Inevitably, his friends would engage in disruptive activities, and he would be placed in a position where he could either violate a deeply ingrained code and "drop the dime" (call the police); or he could ignore the disruption and thereby jeopardize his job; or he could attempt to establish control through the use of physical force (and thereby also jeopardize his job). He felt he could maintain control with three- to five-year-olds without such conflicts.

The other youth asserted that he felt the children truly needed him, and that this was the dominant reason for his choice.

DISCUSSION — SOME CONCEPTUAL ISSUES

There has been an attempt, in this chapter, to demonstrate the need for structural change in our society if the poor are to play a more viable role. It must be stressed, however, that mere creation of employment possibilities does not guarantee a change in the values or even the life style of the poor. Any change in structure must also bring with it dignity for the individual. Dignity and status and concept of self are determined by group standards. The group values are guided by reality and limited by setting.

It has been stated here that group values of poor youth emerge in response to attempts to solve the insoluble. Merely raising them to the status of middle-class youth is no solution. To a lesser degree all adolescents are denied meaningful function and self-respect in our society. As Friedenberg points out: "Adolescents lack reserves of self-esteem to sustain them under humiliating conditions" (26). Although Friedenberg stresses the school as an agency of humiliation, his observations hold true for other institutions. He argues that the classroom situation, the guidance office, and the extracurricular activities of the school intrude upon the adolescent with the goal of exacting conformity rather than stimulating growth.

A further failure of the school is the denial of the development of a youth culture that has continuity with adult responsibility. To obtain a measure of dignity, youth must develop peer groupings which are not under the control of adult authority.

The growth in middle-class delinquency also reflects the adolescent's reaction to a difficult problem — a problem described by Friedenberg to be "the terrifying emptiness of the world he must deal with, which gives him no hint of any reason why people might be valuable" (27).

There has been recognition of the chronicity and severity of youth problems. However, there is too much reliance on standard measures without reflection on their utility. Too often proposed solutions only add to the magnitude of the problem. Often the "solution" serves only to add to an institutional empire (28).

Almost all proposed solutions to youth problems carry with them further adult interventions. Improved school programs call for more and better trained teachers, preschool training for poor children, more modern plants and more efficient administration, and a better diagnostic system for selecting the educable. In employment programs it is proposed that more trained counselors be retained to help the youth find nonexistent jobs. Similarly, it is argued that poor youth need more correctional officers, more social workers, more police, more recreational specialists, and more psychiatrists and psychologists. All these suggestions, unless offered with markedly new features, militate against youth.

It is not suggested here that all the above services are not needed or that there should be less of an economic investment in youth. Rather, youth should be permitted a say in their own destiny, and further, the roles which they play should be of sufficient importance to command payment. The adult role should be more humble, more compassionate, less tyrannical.

Low-income youth suffer more humiliation from society's institutions than do middle-income youth and have less reason to accept the affront. The middle-class youth must only have patience, for he is on a path to a functioning future. The same is not true for poor adolescents. There is no pay-off to them if they grit their teeth under oppressive conditions. They react more outrageously than middle-class youth because they are more outraged. Although an understanding of the conditions precipitating antisocial behavior does not condone it, such understanding does provide a solid basis for improving the situation.

One of the reasons that the solutions suggested here are not more widely accepted is that youth, to protect themselves, go through elaborate deceptions. Goffman (29) describes the self-preserving mechanisms employed by persons in unequal power positions as "fronts" that youth must present to the establishment as a posture of acceptance of the system. They are given no other choice. If need be, youth are prepared to seem deferential, respectful, apologetic, contrite, dedicated, sincere, loyal, obsequious, and trustworthy. The performance of these roles can reflect self-interest but not commitment. In the confines of their own group, youth are prepared to scoff at all of the above. In the confines of their own groups, in the polarized situation between adolescents and adult authority, the fronts take on a coloration of extreme rebelliousness. Often youths are placed in an intolerable position, a role conflict which happens when the audience contains both peers and adults.

It is in the self-interest of poor youth to pretend to be non-assertive, passive, and dumb, since any other role would disrupt an accepted image. Unfortunately, social scientists accept these attributes to be general traits and, through acceptance, tend to reinforce them without recognizing the relationship of role behavior to power structure.

While youth must submit to overwhelming force, they do this at great cost to self. It seems inevitable that capitulation will bring with it tension that can be resolved only in the interplay of peer groupings. Certainly some of the unsocial and antisocial norms established by adolescent groups stem from lack of opportunity for "pro-social acting out" (30) and by adult insistence upon fronts of conformity to adult authority.

GROUPS AS AGENTS OF CHANGE

A variety of group techniques have been used in rehabilitation and education programs. A detailed analysis of the range and the impact of these interventions transcends the scope of this chapter. It is sufficient to state that there is both empirical evidence and anecdotal suggestion of desirable change occurring as a result of group intervention (31). Much of the change may be illusory, the creation of new fronts for new power structures. Often the change is short-lived and only demonstrable within an institution. But despite limitations, the ability to use the group to change the individual is sound in theory and workable in practice. The issue really is not whether groups can be an effective force but how to maximize the return from group influence.

The most difficult barrier is artificiality. Sherif and Sherif (32) point out the difficulty in maintaining natural group functioning even when the only outsider present is a non-participant observer. Groups that have been contrived by adults for youth are much more vulnerable. The intrusion is greater and more deliberate. The aim of the group is to produce change. As long as the outside influence is maintained, change can be effected in a predictable manner (33), but such groups are not self-sustaining — they depend upon the adult members and institutions to supply the mucilage.

Natural groupings of youths do exist. They exercise an influence on members. These groups take certain forms because other alternatives are nonexistent. In a closed society, the group becomes extremely important to the individual, and as Sherif and Sherif point out: "The greater the importance to an individual member of a natural group . . . the more binding for him is participation in activities initiated by the group. . . . By 'binding for him' is meant the experience of feeling that participation and regulation of his behavior is necessary" (34). The trouble with natural youth groups is that they are irrelevant to future functioning and often tend to prevent development of marketable skills. All too often participation in natural youth groups leads to involvements causing long-range consequences of stigma and forced exclusion from functioning society.

A model has been presented in this chapter for the creation of youth groups which do have a self-perpetuating capacity and also offer continuity to a life career. In a sense, the adult role is to organize and establish a setting and a climate in which youth-run groups can emerge. If the adult can tolerate grouping and refrain from intruding when youth make "wrong" decisions, and if the group has viability for future existence, a natural group can emerge from artificial creation.

In essence, youth in lower-class settings need to be provided an opportunity to form groups which have a link to the future; which permit them to develop marketable competence; and in which they have the right to be wrong, the right to correct wrongs, and mostly, the right to belong.

FOOTNOTES AND REFERENCES

1. W. B. Miller, "Lower-Class Culture as a Generating Milieu of Gang Delinquency," JOURNAL OF SOCIAL ISSUES, Vol. 14, No. 3, 1958, pp. 5-19; O. Lewis, THE CHILDREN OF SANCHEZ. New York: Random House, 1961; A. K. Cohen and M. Hodges, Jr., "Cha-

racteristics of the Lower-Blue-Collar-Class," SOCIAL PROBLEMS, Vol. 10, No. 4, 1963, pp. 303-334; M. Deutsch, "Minority Group and Class Status as Related to Social and Personality Factors in Scholastic Achievement," In Grossack (ed.), MENTAL HEALTH AND SEGRE-GATION. New York: Springer, 1963b.

2. New York State Division for Youth, THE SCHOOL DROPOUT: ROCHESTER, Part II, 1963.

3. A. B. Hollingshead, and F. C. Redlich, SOCIAL CLASS AND MEN-TAL ILLNESS. New York: Wiley, 1958.

4. L. T. Empey and J. Rabow, "The Provo Experiment in Delinquency Rehabilitation," AMERICAN SOCIOLOGICAL REVIEW, Vol. 26, No. 5, 1961, pp. 679-696.

5. U.S. Dept. of Labor, MANPOWER REPORT OF THE PRESIDENT AND A REPORT ON MANPOWER, REQUIREMENTS, RESOURCES, UTILIZATION AND TRAINING. Washington, D.C.: U.S. Govt. Printing Office, 1963.

6. J. I. Snyder, Jr., "The Myths of Automation," AMERICAN CHILD, Vol. 46, No. 1, 1963, pp. 1-5.

7. O. H. Mowrer and P. Viek, "An Experimental Analogue of Fear From a Sense of Helplessness," JOURNAL OF ABNORMAL SOCIAL PSYCHOLOGY, Vol. 43, 1948, pp. 193-200.

8. K. Lewin, FIELD THEORY IN SOCIAL SCIENCE. New York: Harper, 1951.

9. F. Reissman, THE CULTURALLY DEPRIVED CHILD. New York: Harper, 1962.

10. M. Harrington, THE OTHER AMERICA. New York: Macmillan, 1962.

11. J. K. Galbraith, "An Attack on Poverty," HARPER'S MAGAZINE, March, 1964, pp. 16-26.

12. M. Deutsch, "The Disadvantaged Child and the Learning Process: Some Social Psychological and Developmental Considerations," In A.H. Passow (ed.), EDUCATION IN DEPRESSED AREAS. New

York: Teachers College Bureau of Publications, Columbia University, 1963a, pp. 163-179.

13. A. H. Riesen, "The Development of Visual Perception in Man and Chimpanzee," SCIENCE, 1947, pp. 107-108; H.F. Harlow and Margaret K. Harlow, "Social Deprivation in Monkeys," SCIENTIFIC AMERICAN, Nov., 1962, pp. 136-146.

14. J. McV. Hunt, "How Children Develop Intellectually," CHILDREN, May-June, 1964, pp. 83-91.

15. F. Riessman, NEW APPROACHES TO MENTAL HEALTH TREATMENT FOR LABOR AND LOW-INCOME GROUPS. New York: National Institute of Labor Education, 1964.

16. Ibid.

17. Sylvia Ashton-Warner, TEACHER. New York: Simon and Shuster, 1963.

18. U.D. Dept. of Labor, op.cit., 1963.

19. A. Pearl and F. Riessman, NEW CAREERS FOR THE POOR. New York: Free Press of Glencoe, 1965.

20. F.B.W. Hawkinshire, "Training Needs for Offenders Working in Community Treatment Programs," EXPERIMENT IN CULTURE EXPANSION. State of California, Dept. of Corrections, 1963, pp. 27-36.

21. Riessman, op. cit., 1964.

22. F. B. Hubbard, "The Youth Consultant Project of the Program for Detached Workers, Young Men's Christian Association of Metropolitan Chicago," EXPERIMENT IN CULTURE EXPANSION. State of California, Dept. of Corrections, 1963, pp. 65-72.

23. Gertrude Goldberg, "Untrained Neighborhood Workers in a Social Work Program," in A. Pearl and F. Riessman, NEW CAREERS FOR THE POOR. New York: Free Press of Glencoe, 1965.

24. K. B. Ballard, "Offender Roles in Research," EXPERIMENT IN CULTURE EXPANSION. State of California, Dept. of Corrections,

1963, pp. 77-82; D. L. Briggs, "Convicted Felons as Innovators in a Social Development Project," EXPERIMENT IN CULTURE EXPANSION. State of California, Dept. of Corrections, 1963, pp. 83-90.

25. The details of this project can be obtained from THE COMMUNITY APPRENTICE PROGRAM, 1964. (Monograph No. 1, Center for Youth and Community Studies, Howard University, Oct. 1964).

26. E. A. Friedenberg, THE VANISHING ADOLESCENT. New York: Dell Publishing, 1959, pp. 107-108.

27. Ibid., p. 24.

28. S. M. Miller, "Stupidity and Power," TRANS-ACTION, Vol. 1, No. 4, 1964, p. 7.

29. E. Goffman, THE PRESENTATION OF SELF IN EVERYDAY LIFE. New York: Doubleday, Anchor Books, 1959.

30. J. R. Fishman and F. Solomon, "Youth and Social Action Perspectives of the Student Sit-In Movement, AMERICAN JOURNAL ON ORTHOPSYCHIATRY, Vol. 30, No. 5, 1963, pp. 872-882.

31. M. Jones, THE THERAPEUTIC COMMUNITY. New York: Basic Books, 1953; L. W. McCorkle, A. Elias, and F. L. Bixby, THE HIGHFIELDS STUDY: A UNIQUE EXPERIMENT IN THE TREATMENT OF JUVENILE DELINQUENCY. New York: Henry Holt, 1958; M. Epstein, and S. R. Slavson, "Breakthrough in Group Treatment of Hardened Delinquent Adolescent Boys," INTERNATIONAL JOURNAL OF GROUP PSYCHOTHERAPY, Vol. 12, No. 2, 1962, pp. 199-210.

32. M. Sherif and Carolyn W. Sherif, REFERENCE GROUPS. New York: Harper, Row, 1964.

33. M. Sherif, O. J. Harvey, B. J. White, W. R. Hood, and Carolyn W. Sherif, INTERGROUP CONFLICT AND COOPERATION: THE ROBBERS CAVE EXPERIMENT. Norman, Okla.: University of Oklahoma Book Exchange, 1961.

34. M. Sherif, and Carolyn W. Sherif, op. cit., 1964, p. 91.

THE FOXFIRE CONCEPT*

Eliot Wigginton

FOREWORD

The people who were asked to make written contributions to this book were told that they must address themselves to Appalachian high school teachers, many of whom, it was presumed, would be from outside the Appalachian region and hence somewhat unfamiliar with it. This book would help them get started — help them know in advance something of the landscape they would be dealing with.

And in some ways that, I think, is a fine idea. I'm a high school teacher; and if I were going next year to teach in Kodiak, Alaska, I would consider it part of my responsibility as a teacher who sees his job as something more than a job to read as much as I could about the history and environment of Kodiak, the culture and the customs of the people who live there, and the economics of that island. I would also want to make myself familiar, if possible, with the social problems those people face. What's the future of the kids on Kodiak, for example. Is the population stable or transient? What are we to educate the kids *for*?

And at the same time I'd be reading my book on Kodiak, I'd also know that if I accepted at face value all it said, I'd be making a terrible mistake, for I would be accepting at face value the perceptions of other human beings who have their own built-in biases and blinders just as I have, three blind men describing an elephant, as it were. And probably treating it — from what they can feel of its surface texture — as some sort of strange, exotic, very distinctive beast rather than the very normal animal (similar in many ways to all other mammals, though with surface features that make it somewhat distinctive) that it is.

It's a problem of balance, you see. Tell someone to write about Appalachia, and their tendency is to treat Appalachia as a strange and exotic land when in fact there are commonalities here and problems here that all regions share. Accept at face value the exotic stereotypes about Appalachia that you will hear (your kids will all speak Elizabethan English and will come from

* Foreword and Chapter 30 to David N. Mielke (ed.), TEACHING MOUNTAIN CHILDREN. Boone, N.C.: Appalachian Consortium Press, 1977.

tiny picturesque homes that have dulcimers hanging on the walls) and you're going to be in big trouble because that's going to lead you into false assumptions about what kinds of activities these kids will respond to. Face it. Most of them are twentieth century kids who aren't going to take to Chaucer and Shakespeare like ducks to water; who like Marshall Tucker and Led Zeppelin and Paul McCartney more than Jean Ritchie; and who would far rather be driving around town or playing ball or drinking beer than sitting in your classroom.

There. Now I've substituted one stereotype for another. Which do you pick? That's the problem you'll have with a book like this, despite all its good points and its fine intentions.

So what are you to do? I'm not really comfortable cast in the role of the answer man, but my own experiences both in mountain schools and in working with teachers around the country have taught me that:

— Books like this can be helpful — if read in perspective — but they are no substitutes for getting out there yourself in that community in which you're going to be teaching, and making your own observations. Meet everyone, talk to everyone, eat in every restaurant, read every sign, visit every church, shop in every store, go to every community event, rent a little house (and don't put up a no trespassing sign), become a good neighbor; and get to know your kids outside of school as human beings rather than blobs of clay that you must shape into your image of what a youngster should be. Don't criticize, don't judge, don't take sides — not now. Observe, enjoy. Celebrate your community, flaws and all. Spend five years as an apprentice learning *from* rather than teaching. (If you were only going to come to Appalachia for a year or two to sample its strange wares or to do your bit for the downtrodden of the world, you probably shouldn't have come at all.)

— Before the beginning of the school year, make a list of the hard skills your students are supposed to master under your direction, and then figure out ways you can use something in the community itself as the catalyst that will propel your students into the mastery of each skill. (The article I've written for this book explains this further.) Don't rely completely on the texts. You hated them when you were in school, and your kids do too. Use the texts as reference works, but don't rely on them.

— As you become more and more familiar with the community and with the students it is producing, you will come face to face with numerous contradictions. Many of your students will want to remain in that community as adults, but there are few jobs. Some will be more fortunate, and because

274

of their parents may be in line for positions of leadership in the community, but they rarely know anything about the community itself in terms of its needs and the needs of its residents, how the things that must get done get done, how power works and is either used or abused. The other students in the class don't know these things either, but then they're all going to be moving to Detroit, aren't they? And what of those families who provide jobs in the area by virtue of the fact that they own and operate strip mines?

Contradictions abound. Lord knows. But you as a teacher are in a perfect position to make some interesting things happen if you'll use that community (and, by extension, the region as a whole) and let it be one of the vehicles by which your students master the hard skills you're supposed to be giving them. At the very least, they'll come closer to mastering them this way than they would have if you had forced them to stick to the texts. And though they may be forced eventually to move to Detroit, at least they'll go with a firmer understanding of who they are and where they come from — roots — and how any community works and what it must provide to be viable — no matter which one they eventually settle in.

And at best? You may be the catalyst by which some of them become so concerned about and committed to their spot on the globe that they become determined to take its destiny into their own hands and provide a new generation of creative, inspired leadership operating out of informed sensitivity rather than self-serving greed. It's not too much to hope for.

And it's not too much to ask that you, as a teacher, be that catalyst. The creation of an informed, committed, moral, inspired citizenry possessing the hard skills necessary to get the job done is, after all, one of the reasons our schools exist — and one of the reasons, presumably, you were hired.

THE FOXFIRE CONCEPT

In August of 1966, MA in T from Cornell in hand, I began teaching ninth- and tenth-grade English in a 250-pupil high school in the Appalachian Mountains of northeast Georgia. The Appalachians were not unfamiliar territory to me or my family. I was born in West Virginia (one set of grandparents owned the Hitchman Coal and Coke Company outside Wheeling), and after our family moved to Georgia, where my father took a job as a professor at the University of Georgia, we still spent every summer in West Virginia. (That is to say nothing of the large portions of my young life spent in the very county in northeast Georgia where I began my teaching career.)

But despite that familiarity with the region, I soon found as a young teacher that I knew almost nothing about the region at all. It is now 1977, and I am still teaching at that same tiny high school, and I am still about the business of trying to find out what this region is all about, even as I shape and rework an educational philosophy that is constantly being altered by what I discover on a day-to-day basis about myself and my kids and my chosen home.

One part of the philosophy, however, remains inviolate, and that is the conviction that students can do — and must be allowed to do — far more than has been traditionally expected of them in our schools. One of the projects that my students and I began in those first English classes is a magazine called *Foxfire* that still continues today. It has been written about in virtually every publication around, and it is generally acknowledged by educators to be the most visibly successful high school endeavor in this country; and, as such, it has been emulated by hundreds of other high school students coast to coast. In fact, as I write this, one of my tenth grade students (a young man who had never been on a plane before or out of his region until now) and I are on a Delta jet somewhere between Kansas City and Atlanta, returning from a four-day workshop we ran in Portland for thirty Oregon high school teachers, and a speech we made together on the way home to the annual American Association for the Advancement of Science convention in Denver. In a few hours, we will be meeting Herb Kohl in Atlanta and taking him along with us back home to Rabun Gap, where he's going to spend three days with the kids in an attempt to find out what's going on that's causing all the commotion. If you don't know who Herb is, by the way, you got robbed by the college that gave you your teaching degree. They may not have introduced you to Jonathan Kozol or Robert Coles or Jim Herndon or any of those folks either, and so you've some catching up to do if you want to consider yourself a reasonably well-informed, conscientious educator. And I assume you do or you probably wouldn't be reading *this* book.

At any rate, what this preamble has been leading up to is two short points:

1. Despite the fact that the Foxfire idea has now spread all over the country, it is nevertheless useful to remember that it is a concept that was developed in Appalachia by and specifically for people of Appalachian roots in a tiny, extremely traditional and conservative high school that could provide not one penny of financial support.

2. The success of the project is a convincing demonstration by anyone's definition of the tremendous potential that a single teacher has for effecting change. And you must remember that. You and your students to-

gether have far more power than you perhaps imagined; and to believe otherwise is only to provide yourself with a convenient excuse for not doing more
to affect the lives of your students and your community.

This is a good point at which to stop reading if you've decided that this
article is not going to be for you. For the rest of you, well, roll up your
sleeves and dig in. Here's where this article starts.

First, some background. In 1966, I faced 135 kids in six classes who,
for the most part, obviously weren't impressed by the way I was teaching
English. Discipline was a very real day-to-day problem, and the reading and
writing levels of many of my students demanded a radically different approach. The situation finally got so bad that one day I closed the text, told
them to do the same, sat down crosslegged on top of the desk and said,
"Okay, I give up. You know this isn't working and I know this isn't
working. Now what are we going to do to make it through the rest of this
year?"

Several days of discussion followed during which time, in the even-
ings, I also reflected on my own high school days and tried to remember
classroom activities that had impressed me, or moments when teachers had
literally affected my life. There weren't many, but there were some. One
happened when, as a tenth grade student — and a pretty poor one at that
having flunked a couple of courses and so forth — an English teacher read a
composition I had written for him, liked it, and took a few moments of his
time to get it published in our high school literary magazine. When the piece
appeared, with all the words I had had in it originally still there, and my
name spelled correctly at the end, I was jolted in a way I had seldom been
jolted before. Copies of the magazine went to my parents ("See, I'm not
quite as worthless a student as you've been led to believe up until now"); my
grades improved to the point where I graduated near the top of my class, and
I turned an important corner in my life. It had been proved to me in terms I
could understand that I had worth and capability. I could *do*.

Remembering how English finally came alive for me as a direct result
of that experience, and how I finally realized that writing does, in fact, have
some direct applicability to the outside world and perhaps to my life, I suggested to my students that we start a magazine. They shrugged, thought that
sounded as good as anything else I had suggested so far (the school had never
had a publication before so they had no idea what was involved, but anything
was better than what we *had* been doing), and our principal agreed as long as
the school would have no financial responsibility. I proposed it to him as a
six-week unit in magazine production so that the students could see one way

that writing is actually used, and I promised him that all the language arts skills I was being paid by the State to teach would be rigorously observed (how much easier it is to get students to deal with grammatical problems when they know their work is going to be seen by hundreds of people), and that nothing would appear in the magazine that would be slanderous or offensive (from the beginning, articles written about people in the community were read first by those people, corrected, and then formally released for publication).

The students fanned out into the tiny community requesting donations from every individual and business they could find, promising the donors that when the magazine appeared, each would receive a free copy, his name would be listed in the back in a donor's section, and the inside front cover would be personally autographed to him by the students who put the magazine together. In this way, they raised nearly $450. That money was taken to the local printer with instructions to print as many copies of the magazine as he could for that sum when we delivered the camera-ready pages to him.

Meanwhile, students were also shaping the contents. Classroom exercises resulted in poems, short stories, essays, art work and some photographs, the best of which were selected and put aside. At the same time, I was asking each student to do such things as take a mimeographed list of common ailments (asthma, colds, pneumonia, etc.) home and bring back lists of traditional home cures for these ailments. I was also meeting small groups of students after school and taking them on short interviews, using a second-hand reel-to-reel tape recorder I owned, and a 35mm camera my uncle had picked up overseas during World War II. The first tape we made had Luther Rickman, the local, retired sheriff whose grandson was in one of my classes, telling about the time our county's bank was robbed in 1936. Transcribed, that interview went into the magazine almost word for word — an unbroken monologue recounting an experience that was one of the highlights of Sheriff Rickman's career (he captured Zade Sprinkle, the leader of the outlaw band, and brought him to trial).

When the 600 copies of our magazine appeared, that could easily have been the conclusion of our experiment. The magazines were all paid for. They could have been given away (in fact, this is a technique that many high schools are using now, produce one free booklet per year thus avoiding the hassles of subscriptions and deadlines); my classes could have taken on a completely different six-week unit; and that, as they say, would have been that.

But the response to that little magazine from the community and from the kids was so warm that, with the principal's permission, we decided to offer subscriptions. The subscription money that came in paid for the next issue, and now, eleven years and forty-three magazines and five *Foxfire* books later, the project is stronger than ever. And it is stronger not because it remained the same, but because it has constantly evolved — each year being altered or added to in some way in an attempt to meet more successfully the needs of the high school students and the community we work with. Knowing that the magazine itself was not enough to engage the energies of all my students, I directed the royalties from the sale of the *Foxfire* books back into the project using them over the years to:

—hire an additional seven-member staff, each of whom has organized a new division of our project and each of which has become a cluster of elective courses within our public high school. Half of those staff members are former Foxfire students who went on to college like the University of Wisconsin and got their degrees with the hope of some day being able to come back to their home county to work.

—purchase 110 acres of land; then purchase twenty-five 100-year-old log buildings which, with community carpenters and masons and students, we disassembled, could be moved to that land, and then reconstructed and renovated, to form an educational complex that is a supplement to the existing school system, open to community people and our students, but closed to tourists.

—begin a videotape operation that now broadcasts weekly hour-long programs — scripted, filmed, and edited by kids — over the locally-owned cable TV network.

— begin a record company from which come student-produced albums of both traditional music and the work of local songwriters. The students not only do the recording and editing, but also design the albums and handle their distribution.

—begin a publishing company through which we publish a series of books of local and regional interest (such as the recently published *Memories of a Mountain Shortline*, an oral history of the local, now defunct, Tallulah Falls Railroad complete with photographs and diagrams put together by two eleventh-grade girls).

—begin a furniture business that produces fine reproductions of traditional pieces — by students — with the goal of nurturing it into a full-fledged industry in the community that will provide additional jobs (as will the above

279

businesses) for high school graduates who want to remain here.

—begin an environmental division that not only teaches kids, through extensive field work, a respect for their own unique environment, but also engages them actively in research concerning the effects on their environment of such practices as extensive second-home development, highway construction, clearcutting and tourism.

—begin an Appalachian studies department in the high school that for the first time focuses on their own culture and heritage as mountain people, at the same time showing them parallels between our culture and others.

—begin an elementary school division that places high school students in the elementary school in the county as teacher aides with responsibility for helping their students design and build playgrounds out of native materials, create their own learning materials (such as readers) and complete a textbook about the history of our county written by elementary school students *for* elementary school students, and published by our own firm and distributed free to the schools of the area.

—begin a course for seniors to teach them how to begin and run businesses of their own. By *actually creating* some of these businesses (furniture, for example) they create jobs for themselves as high school graduates.

The reason for mentioning all this is not to snatch the opportunity to blow *Foxfire's* horn, but to give others some idea of the tremendous range of activities that can be carried out *successfully* by high school students. There are hundreds more, the only limitation being, essentially, the extent of individual imagination.

That brings me to the core of this article. Nearly twelve years of wrestling in Appalachian classrooms with this thing called education has convinced me of four truths. These form the basis of my own theory of education, and they come not from supposition, but from direct observation — from watching education at work, from seeing sacred cows exploded, from experimentation and tinkering with formulae. They are as follows:

1. Many of the things we, as teachers, assume students cannot do are, in fact, things they are perfectly capable of doing, and will do if given good enough reasons (reasons other than, ''If you don't do this, you will fail my courses'').

I have actually heard teachers from the outside say, for example, that their Appalachian students are incapable of the memorization of large amounts of material, ignoring all the while the mass of evidence that proves them wrong: the fact, for example, that many of their students have already committed to memory a CB language so complex that most of those same teachers wouldn't know much of what their students were saying if they heard them using it; or the fact that one of the favorite games of those same students when on trips is to be the first to call out correctly the make and model numbers of all the large trucks on the road before they are in plain view — GMC, International, Kenworth, Ford, Chevy, White, Peterbilt, Mack — along with all sorts of technical data thrown in on the side just for good measure and added entertainment value; or the fact that the "dumbest" boy in their class probably already has memorized more technical data about guns and automobiles and the habits and habitat of native trout than his teacher will ever know. Whether the information is entirely accurate or not is beside the point. The fact is that a large body of material has been internalized in the age-old ritual of remembering what is relevant for one's life and rejecting the rest.

Similarly, I have heard teachers say that their students cannot write creatively. If that is, in fact, true, then someone is going to have to explain to me why they are able to make up — and memorize — lengthy songs about their school and their teachers, songs which sometimes skewer those teachers so accurately and peg their personality quirks so precisely as to leave no question of who they are talking about if all names are removed; or why it is true that Barbara Taylor, as a senior in our school and an editor for *Foxfire* came within two points of failing senior English, and yet that same year she wrote a long article about *Foxfire* which she sold to Seventeen for $400.00; or why students like Varney Watson, at the same time he is failing English tests, is also writing the music and words for songs so beautiful that twelve of them make up *Foxfire's* second record album (Varney has already performed most of them in public at such events as the Festival of American Folklife in Washington, D.C.).

Similarly, I have heard teachers say, in those terrible rooms called teachers' lounges, that a certain student cannot follow directions from a book and then I have watched that same student, using a manufacturer's manual, tear down an automobile and put it back together again — a feat few teachers in our school could duplicate.

I could go on in this same vein for pages. In most cases, the ability is there. It just isn't being tapped. And the sodden reasons we give students for doing the work we assign are greeted with a skepticism that is all too often absolutely justifiable. We have forgotten, in many of our schools, that students *can* do, and instead of celebrating that fact and building on it and adding to and polishing and extending skills that already exist, we substitute the belief that there is a tremendous amount that students *cannot* do, and therefore they must be educated. . . .

2. We, as adults, know for a fact that we are the sum total of our past experiences. These experiences have determined almost completely not only the way we feel about ourselves, and what we know about ourselves, but also our attitudes about the world around us, our perceptions of what tasks need to be done to make this world more habitable; and whether we will be the ones to accomplish these tasks or will be the ones content to sit on the sidelines sniping at or rooting for or ignoring those who try. Confident or timid, self-assured or insecure, positive or negative, optimistic or cynical — these attitudes are the results of our testing ourselves against the world and drawing conclusions about ourselves and our abilities from those experiences. Many of these attitudes are formed when we are young. I am still insecure about the game of basketball, for example, and avoid faculty/student games like the plague because, as an awkward youngster, I was always the last boy chosen for a team, was only rarely given the ball, and never learned how to dribble or shoot. On the rare occasions when I did get a chance to shoot, I always missed — an error which was exactly expected of me and which simply served to perpetuate the cycle and the series of assumptions that were being made by others (and consequently by myself, others being the only yardstick I had by which to measure myself) about my ability. I cannot play that game to this day. Math is torture for basically the same reason. Fail a few tests, misunderstand a few assignments, get criticized a few times and the dye is cast. It doesn't take any kid long to find out which parts of a stove burn.

Other experiences went better for me, luckily. I remember being entranced one day when, in elementary school, a white-haired gentleman who used to be a high school principal brought in some of the pieces from his Indian artifact collection and talked to us about them. Later, I was astounded to find that my family knew this man, and that he and my grandmother actually hunted for arrowheads together from time to time. I wrangled an invitation, found a couple of points that were exclaimed over, and almost became an archaeologist in college. To this day I love that field, and I intend soon to add a professional archaeologist to our staff to do digs with our students.

Similarly, I know I am a more observant person because, when I was young, my father, who is a landscape architect, used to take me along when he went sketching. I had my sketchbook, and he had his, and together we sketched and studied details of trees, houses, landscapes. He criticized my work, but always positively and with love, and I still sketch to this day, and encourage my students to do the same.

Because my father helped me build a doghouse for my dog, and assorted furniture for my bedroom, and taught me how to use tools in the process, I had enough self-confidence to build the house in which I now live. And I never fail to be astounded, when I sit alone in that two-story house with its thirty-foot-high stone fireplace, by the fact that I ever attempted it at all. Why did I? Because I knew, from past experiences, that I could pull it off.

The interesting thing about these experiences (called "peak experiences" in the jargon of the trade) is that despite the fact we *know* their importance (one has only to go painstakingly over his own life to have the truth come rushing in) we only rarely, as teachers, make them happen in the context of schools. We hand out plenty of defeats and precious few victories — precious few experiences *at all* — beyond those texts we have allowed to totally dominate the lives of our students.

Now that fact strikes me as being not only tragic, but immoral. The young men and women in our charge will cling desperately to their triumphs and turn their backs on their defeats. And who can blame the student who, finding success and acceptance and a sense of accomplishment *only* in drinking beer late at night on lonely roads, drops out of school to make that one of the central activities of his life?

Do I stretch the point? Consider this: I said earlier that Jack Tyrer's act of generosity in getting that composition of mine published when I was in the tenth grade jolted me in a way I had seldom been jolted before. In fact, it is probably because he took the time to do that that I wound up eventually becoming a tenth-grade English teacher and starting a magazine.

Ask yourself this: how many students hate my subject now because of me?

I don't hate math and basketball because it was genetically predetermined that I should. . . .

3. It is a simple fact that most of the peak experiences I speak about take place not in the classroom behind a text, but in, or in association with, the world outside that classroom. The extent to which we, as teachers, can

meld the two together into one powerful learning force is the extent to which school, I believe, begins to make some sense.

Foxfire, at its most elementary level, worked in that tenth grade English class because the hard skills the students were learning were being learned not simply so they could pass a test or complete a text-related homework assignment, but because — through the vehicle of their own community — the applicability of those skills had suddenly become clear, and the skills came to life. They were useful. They had reason for being. Their use made sense. Community as *vehicle.* And as that imaginative, forceful description of Aunt Arie Carpenter living alone in her log house with no electricity, plumbing or TV (and surviving on $48 a month in social security payments) became important, so too did the ways that other writers had found to describe their own surroundings and their own communities become important. And as a concise, clean description of how Aunt Arie carried out a particular survival task became important, so too did the ways other writers dealt with the same problem become worthy of a second look. And to the extent a student became the medium through which Aunt Arie could express, in her own words, her own insecurities and trials and victories and her own particular philosophy of life; such was the extent to which that same student became sensitive to and curious about the philosophical wrestling of others as expressed in texts, or in the neighborhood, or in the family — or even in plays by Shakespeare.

Linkages.

Community as vehicle. I can't say it any more clearly than that.

And in the act of using the community in that way, some wonderful things happen. One of them, of course, is that the student begins to understand who he is and where he's come from in terms of ancestry, past, heritage, roots. At the *very* least, he is exposed to a variety of lifestyles and philosophies he had probably not considered previously. And a sensitivity to his own roots and culture awakened, there is always the possibility that he can then be equally sensitive by extension to the culture and roots of other considerations.

But there's more. One of the ultimate absurdities of our high school system is that we expect our students to walk out the doors of our high schools at graduation, ready and able to take some kind of a responsible role inside either our own community or some other community of their choice, and yet we never, during their high school years, take the time to *show* them what a community is. They don't know what kinds of people make it up, what services it must have (and provide) to survive, where power lies and how it is attained and then either used or misused — and what to do about that. Their not knowing what jobs exist and how to apply for them and what they're like on a daily basis (most haven't even been able to work with a parent for a day to see what his job is all about) is only the tip of the iceberg. Beyond that, they don't know enough about what the community *could be* to know, for example, what industries they themselves might *create* and run, much less how to do that. They often go out of our schools as ignorant of their surroundings (both ancestral and environmental and economic and architectural), the human condition, and the workings and the needs of the world as the day they entered them. And that is a fact. Not only do they not know what their options for action are, but they know so little about "community" that they couldn't possibly have any commitment to the idea, and so they couldn't care less about that action. You can't care deeply about something you're not personally acquainted with. Victims, they fit in wherever it's expedient for the powers that be *to fit them.*

That is our newest American tragedy, the most recent symbol of which is schools purposely so isolated from the community surrounding them that they don't even have windows.

4. On top of all this, we know for a fact that there are crucial needs that, universally, adolescents face. We tend to ignore these in our classrooms, but they are there nevertheless. And they are true no less in Appalachian schools than in any other schools in the world.

Most child psychologists agree that there are two distinct phases of adolescence, each with its own particular emotional demands:

In the first phase, called early adolescence, the most important single need the child has is a need for self-esteem; and this is satisfied most effectively by the praise, affection, attention — the sense of belonging — he receives from others. In an atmosphere — a classroom, for example — where this need is not addressed, and where the child (perhaps because of the possibility of failure) feels threatened, frustrated, cast out, powerless, *no learning will take place.* The attention and praise he needs will, more often than not in this situation, be sought from peers via antisocial behavior. In our vocabulary that's discipline problems.

It's a crazy cycle. Our mountain classrooms are filled with students who don't feel very secure about their academic abilities, and consequently don't feel any too good about themselves in our classrooms. They have been led to believe they can't read well, or write well, and we continue, through our ignorance (and through an endless series of assignments that are culturally inappropriate and hence seen as boring and irrelevant) to make these tasks so unpleasant for them, and to make them feel so uncomfortable that we often give them no choice but to reject us and the academic discipline we stand for. And so they fail, or get passed indifferently on up the line, having learned nothing from us but a series of evasive maneuvers; the cycle repeats itself, and they go elsewhere for their sense of accomplishment and self-esteem leaving us to wonder why they would rather hunt deer or play football or rebuild a '56 Chevrolet than read *Evangeline* or *A Tale of Two Cities,* or write a term paper about the Yangtzee River. Face it. At this stage of their lives they will put their hearts into only those things they feel they *can do,* and can get some sense of satisfaction and achievement out of the doing through the praise of others.

(Don't misunderstand me. I'm not saying that a term paper about the Yangtzee River shouldn't be done. I'm only saying that this may not be the best time for it. Perhaps first should come some intimate first-hand knowledge of a river in the student's community, researched fully in terms of its value *to* the community and the use to which it is put *by* that community. Then, as the student sees how that river affects *his* particular culture and what role a river plays in society, *then* perhaps the teacher can move him with some hope of success one step further.)

This phase is outgrown as students zero in on things they are good at, and they move into a second phase called late adolescence where self-worth is defined not only in terms of how others respond to him, but also in terms of actual accomplishment — in the words of John J. Mitchell in the Department of Educational Psychology at the University of Alberta, Canada, "what he *does* and what he *represents*" (1).

In this phase, it is essential that students be engaged in activities which they see as being important — as *making a difference,* for, as Mitchell says, "All healthy humans, universally and without fail, abhor not making a difference. It is the closest thing to nonexistence man can experience" (2). If a student feels he is not making a difference, a number of things happen to him, not the least of which is his questioning whether or not he will be able to make a difference *at all* as an adult. Stalled, the student begins to lose self-confidence, and falls back into a pattern of conformism (needing the constant reassurance of others) at the expense of individually initiated and self-motivated action.

Mitchell is strong in his criticism of society in general here: "For the majority of youth, little opportunity exists to *do* things which generate feelings of self-importance. Little opportunity arises to build or construct useful products which contribute to the improvement of the environment; little opportunity emerges to assert oneself in a positive and wholesome manner because the areas of life in which youth actually make a difference are minimal'' (3).

It was not always so in the Appalachians, but too often it is now. What can we do about it?

I have had teachers argue that in the schools it is almost impossible to create a situation where all students have a chance to *do* important work in the context of their classroom obligations. A student body president may, in an extraordinary school, have an outlet by which he can do work he perceives as making a difference, but few other students can have these outlets simply because they can't be provided in schools. They aren't set up that way.

True enough. Our schools often aren't set up that way. But they can be. At the very least, our classes can be. Granted, the task is made immeasurably more difficult if a student's past experiences in school during early adolescence have left him angry and frustrated and crippled — convinced already that he is hopeless in English or history or math. But it can still be done (4).

In fact, the precise reason why *Foxfire* worked as well as it did in English classes, above and beyond the fact that through the use of culturally approved activities and positive energy it proved to all the kids that they could read and write better than they had ever thought possible, was that they perceived the work they were doing as making a difference — as *being important*. The fruits of their labor were not simply busy-work exercises destined for a teacher's indifferent sigh and eventual destruction, but they were going to be *used*. And without the students (who had the community contacts and the automatic entree that I did not have) the work would not have been done at all and the magazine would not exist. They *mattered*. And they still do.

These four truths are at the heart of the reason why *Foxfire* magazine worked in those language arts classes. The list of hard skills I was being paid by the State to teach (grammar, composition, composing a business letter, talking on the telephone, etc.) was being rigorously adhered to — albeit with the text used only as a reference manual in just the way that I believe it was originally intended to be used before it took over our lives; the basic competence already in most of the students was being taken advantage of and built upon; the students were being provided with far more peak experiences than the two or three I can point to as being vital in my five years of high school; the community was integrated fully into the life of the classroom both as a motivating force and as an aspect of life in itself worth serious attention; and the basic emotional needs of the adolescents were being addressed via classroom experiences leading to the production of an end product in which all could take justifiable pride. They owned the end product, ran the activities (read business) that produced it, and were essential to its growth and survival.

Once the staff members and I had the language arts under control, we began to plot ways to infiltrate and influence other areas of the curriculum — the four truths always being held foremost — adding a community-based, experiential component to each. Our new Appalachian studies class, for example, became part of the social studies offering of the high school, the end product being additional articles for the magazine (focusing not only on folklore but also on pressing social problems) as well as a new understanding of history and its influences on this piece of the globe (a study of the Depression, for example, would *begin* with the first person testimony of mountain visitors to the class who would tell the kids what that period in their lives was like). Appalachian music, with its end product of record albums produced, edited, designed and marketed by kids, became a part of our high school's art offering (as did a creative photography course that resulted in regular student exhibitions in the halls of the school building and the cafeteria). Environmental education, with its end products being a continually revised, mimeographed field manual written by kids as well as written studies which looked objectively at both sides of environmental problems such as clear-cutting, and environmental controversies such as seed gardens, experiments with American chestnut trees and planting by the signs, and nature trails, was integrated into biology. Furniture making, with the potential of creating a new industry in the County, dovetailed into industrial arts. Complex diagrams required to explain the workings of various material artifacts such as banjos and hog rifles found a home in the drafting classes. The television shows our kids began to script and produce for the local cable TV network earned for them credit in the media sciences. Our bookkeeping division gave students in the accounting classes genuine experience. Our course in creating businesses tied into both economics and career ed. And all of these additions, rather than taking the place of the existing curriculum, simply became adjuncts to it — activities that brought these areas of the curriculum to life and engaged the energies and the capacities of the kids in ways they had seldom been engaged for. Education became, and is still becoming, real. Future targets for the insertion of culturally relevant — and thereby motivating — activities include physical education, home economics, chemistry and physics.

That sounds like a lot — maybe too much. But I think we can do it. Remember that this whole project was started — quietly and without rocking boats — in ninth and tenth-grade English classes eleven years ago with $440 in donations. You've got to start somewhere.

In *The Watches of the Night*, Harry Caudill, with a good deal of justification, blasts Appalachian schools. On page 226, he says,

> . . . *It is apparent that improved physical plant and increased pay do not automatically equate with more learning. After twelve years in the classroom — two thousand, three hundred and twenty days of teaching — mountain youths are unlikely to know from memory a single paragraph of Shakespeare, to have memorized even a couple of poems, or to be able to solve such simple problems as will determine, for example, the quantity of water within a tank of specified size. Furthermore, they are rarely able to punctuate or spell with accuracy or display more than rudimentary knowledge of the history of their country, state or nation. Such remote places as China are unknown. The philosophers and their teachings are as off limits as Shakespeare and Gibbon. Almost none knows anything about the botany of the age-old forest that now cloaks the region as second or third-growth timber. Most tragic of all, few leave the schools with the habit of reading or reflection, a lack which promises few innovations in confronting and solving the jarring problems that are bearing down on the Cumberland Plateau with the velocity and finality of an avalanche.*

I agree with most of that. I also know, for a fact, that something can be done about it. You and I as Appalachian teachers will probably never be able to make even our own solitary schools all that Harry Caudill would like them to be, but each of us, in his own way and on his own chunk of turf, can roll up his sleeves and pitch in and give it a hell of a go. To do less than that is inexcusable, for if the future of our mountains does not get taken up by the hands of those we sensitize and equip for the long fight ahead, then into whose hands does it fall?

FOOTNOTES AND REFERENCES

1. "The Nature of Adolescence: Some General Observations," a paper written for The National Commission on Resources for Youth, New York City, 1976, p. 11.

2. Ibid., p. 16.

3. Ibid., p. 13.

4. For teachers interested in implementing Foxfire-type projects in their schools, the following books are recommended: Eliot Wigginton, MOMENTS, THE FOXFIRE EXPERIENCE; Pam Wood, YOU AND AUNT ARIE, A GUIDE TO CULTURAL JOURNALISM. The first is a guide for teachers and the second is a handbook for kids. Both are available from: IDEAS: 1785 Massachusetts Avenue, N.W., Washington, D.C. 20036.

TOMORROW'S EDUCATION: MODELS FOR PARTICIPATION

Ernst Wenk

Recent years have witnessed a fundamental political shift within our society. It appears to press toward more direct citizen participation in the democratic process — a development that could transform our basic political structure. Education emerges as a guiding force in this development and a redefinition of the varied roles of education in our society seems inevitable. Educational approaches to social problem-solving seem to have greater potential than some other models that have been tried. Legal and medical models, for example, have been proved inadequate in dealing with alcoholism, drug abuse, crime, and delinquency. Educational approaches do not prescribe solutions but rather provide a process through which solutions can be found or created. Ideally, the educational process draws its energies and its directions from the involvement of active participants. Such problem-solving approaches contain the ingredients needed for interactive (democratic) government, but they also foster individual growth and improved mental health. Education, in this model, is the central force for community development as well as a key to personal development and well-being.

We have neglected community participation in problem-solving. For too long we have looked outside our communities for solutions to social problems. Federal and state aid available for help in improving education, reforming criminal and juvenile justice, providing welfare and better health services, have led us to believe that the roots of our social problems and their solutions lie outside the community. It has become fashionable to rely on distant, impersonal government bureaucracies, to see ourselves as neither part of the problem nor part of the solution. We appear to have forgotten that many social problems are rooted in families, and local communities and that actions aimed at problem-solving must originate in the community and neighborhood if they are to have maximum impact.

No doubt there is a need for federal and state programs to bring about some equalization in the distribution of resources or to stimulate new and innovative programs which, after an initial period, can be supported from local sources. But if our communities are to be revitalized, and if we are to find better solutions to problems that manifest themselves in the community, the *initiative* for change must come from the communities themselves. Communities must design, implement, and maintain community-based problem-solving structures that are controlled by local residents and involve a reasonable cross-section of all those affected by their decisions and actions.

Unfortunately, most communities are ill-prepared for such an undertaking. The present paper presents two educational innovations that may be helpful in working toward the goal of interactive community development. Neither program has been designed specifically to prevent juvenile crime or other misbehavior in school and in the surrounding community. Both, however, could have considerable impact on juvenile delinquency and youth crime. Each is supported by a significant body of theoretical literature and practical experience indicating that its assumptions are sound and its methods generally effective in preventing delinquency and in interrupting what appears to be a causal chain leading from school failure to school crime. Some of the areas that are relevant in this regard are curriculum tracking, perceived lack of linkage between schools and communities, perceived irrelevance of the schooling process by many students, low student commitment to school, lack of involvement by students in educational planning and decision-making, and lack of many peer teaching opportunities for students.

Partnership in Research, tested in New Hampshire and further developed following initial evaluation, is essentially a youth involvement strategy. It also has roots in one branch of social action theory, particularly in that reflected by what Donald T. Campbell has called the "experimental society" — a society in which progress is made by integrating the best of science and democracy (1). The Integrated Community Education System is basically a community involvement strategy. It envisions a radical restructuring of the educational system to provide for flexible and largely self-initiated programming for people of all ages and an open-ended school system which allows for life-long experiential learning.

PARTNERSHIP IN RESEARCH

The Partnership in Research strategy assumes that knowledge acquired through active learning has a more significant impact than learning by passive acceptance. The transitory nature of knowledge is also imparted by this approach: knowledge gained through activity is experienced as a time-bound, situation-bound phenomenon requiring constant updating to be continually relevant. Partnership in Research is designed to keep the individual sensitive to an inquiry type of knowledge that encourages self-discovery, adaptation, and personal development — a basic mental posture that it is hoped will be adopted as a life-long strategy of learning and growth.

The PIR strategy was tested in spring 1972 in a New Hampshire senior high school (2). The prime interest was to involve as many students as possible in defining some of the major concerns with respect to the school setting. It was hoped the increased understanding of the educational setting might lead students to learn about school-related factors that contribute to social problems, such as juvenile delinquency and youth crime, school non-involvement, and dropping out. The high school, situated in a medium-large New England city, had a student population of close to 2,000 students in grades 9 through 12. Like most schools in the United States, it was co-educational.

During meetings between the vice-principals and research staff, a decision was made to initiate the project during the school's English periods. This ensured that practically all students would be reached initially. English classes remained the major source of communication between the project and the students, but the actual work of the project was an extracurricular option for the students.

PHASE 1: PLANNING AND INITIATION

Project staff made preliminary contacts with some students and teachers and prepared a questionnaire asking students to name three of the most pressing concerns or problems they felt needed attention in the school. The questionnaires were presented and the study explained to each English class by project staff, starting with the senior classes and recruiting and instructing volunteer senior students, who then acted as assistants, administering questionnaires and introducing the study to the junior, sophomore, and freshman classes. This completed the first step in turning the study over to the students.

Besides the initial questionnaire, each student in grades 9 through 12 received a questionnaire to give to his parents. Parent questionnaires asked about priorities of concerns and whether or not parents should be involved in this kind of study. Teachers received a similar questionnaire, as did the janitorial staff and the food services staff. Also, each student who had dropped out during the current school year received a questionnaire and was asked to designate a student still in school who would act as a liaison between himself and the study.

PHASE 2: FORMING STUDENT TASK FORCES

The return rate of the questionnaires filled out by the students was close to 100 percent. One-third of the teaching staff and approximately 5 percent of the parents returned the questionnaires. There were practically no responses from the janitorial and food services staff or from students who had dropped out earlier in the school year (which may suggest a feeling of alienation predominant in these groups).

Eight major topics surfaced that led to the formation of student task forces or study groups to look into the following student concerns:

1. *School Rules*. This group was to study school regulations and measures taken at the school, as well as the relationship between school, police, and the courts.

2. *Race Relations*. This group was to study ways to improve race relations among students. Concerns were particularly expressed by students who experienced during the previous school year serious disruptions in school because of racial conflicts.

3. *Drug Misuse*. This study group was interested in looking into student involvement in drug misuse and presenting some suggestions for coping with this problem.

4. *School Programs for the Non-College-Bound Student*. This study group was to investigate problems available to the student seeking a vocational career and needing preparation to enter the labor market.

5. *School Programs for the Academically Inclined Student*. This study group was to look at programs for the college-bound student.

6. *Student Roles*. This group was to study the roles of the high-school student, his rights and responsibilities. They were to focus on the way students can be involved in curriculum planning and other aspects of the administration of the school. This group's emphasis was central to the major study objective of mobilizing untapped student resources.

7. *School and Community*. This group was to study the relationships of the school to the community, the voters, the taxpayers, and the authorities (such as the School Board), and to come up with suggestions to improve these relationships.

8. *The Drop-out Problem*. This study group was to interview school drop-outs and planned to develop alternative educational programs for students who feel alienated from most current educational programs.

All groups began with a nucleus of a few students who were highly involved in the particular issue and who volunteered to recruit additional students to help with various study tasks. Special efforts were made to keep established student leaders from taking over the study group by assigning traditionally active students, already in leadership roles in the school, to individual assignments in the project that were independent of the study groups. Leadership positions in the study groups thus were open to students who previously had little opportunity to express themselves or take leadership. This gave the project the opportunity to mobilize untapped student resources while still making use of active student leaders for important tasks outside the study groups.

PHASE 3: STUDY GROUP PROJECTS

During Phases 3 and 4, a recently graduated college student, who had experience in working with groups, was the resident project staff at the school. She acted as advisor and liaison among the project, the teaching staff and the school administration. While the initiative was left primarily to students, coordination and assistance were actively provided by giving support as soon as the need was perceived.

With the help of the director of the business department, the research assistant set up an office space for the project. Two students from the business department were employed part-time by the project under a student work program. This project office provided services to the various study groups and maintained contact with the students.

The various study groups of volunteer students went about their business in their own ways. One group decided to interview local citizens about their attitudes toward smoking, alcohol, drugs, open campus, or school rules. Another group interviewed drop-outs. One group, after several meetings and uncomfortable discussions, got scared and disbanded, but not before they had designed and administered a questionnaire probing racial attitudes. The group studying academic programs designed a questionnaire and administered some, but the group lost interest generally.

Two groups were quite active and involved, and carried out productive programs. The vocational program group presented plans for students, in conjunction with staff, to run the cafeteria on a business-like basis in order to learn the food services trade. They also proposed to develop and operate a school-based communications center with its own 5-mile radius radio station, video studio for intramural T.V., and a student newspaper. They made a field trip to a neighboring state to visit a student-operated radio station and reported back to the project.

The drug abuse group probably was the most active and most involved.

295

Each student had a good reason to be part of this group. One was a former heroin user who returned to school after treatment to finish his requirements for a high-school diploma. Others had had experiences with drugs or had brothers, sisters, or friends who used drugs, or parents with an alcohol problem. Some were just deeply concerned about what they saw happening around them. This group visited local facilities for drug prevention and treatment, designed and administered a questionnaire, compiled some of the results, and conducted a workshop at the end of the project.

PHASE 4: WORKSHOPS

Four groups conducted workshops during the last week of the project. These included the groups studying drug use, school rules, vocational curriculum, and student roles. The panels were composed of students, while other students and teachers were the participating audience. These meetings were videotaped and replayed for students at the school to pass on some of the information and ideas generated by these activities.

SUMMARY RESULTS

This peer-conducted research effort demonstrated that high-school students, working under their own volition, can develop questions and identify issues that are highly relevant to their own interests and development. The collection of data actually was secondary to the real goal of this endeavor, which was to involve students in observing and evaluating issues that have a significant impact on their lives.

The project was exploratory and had only limited financial backing. These restrictions were offset by the enthusiastic support the study received from students and from some of the school staff. It is recommended that future attempts to carry out PARTNERSHIP IN RESEARCH projects be made part of the regular school curriculum, rather than appended to the school program as an extracurricular activity. This kind of scientific inquiry could then develop a tradition of its own and become, for certain research projects, more sophisticated in research methodology. Projects then might focus on other problems, not directly related to the school, that are of special interest to students.

The findings of the study groups were modest and the methods employed were relatively unsophisticated. Yet, the method and the findings are valuable from several points of view:

1. Interesting facts were uncovered.

2. The project gave students the opportunity to make a deep, personal commitment to an activity that was aimed, in part, at learning more successful coping strategies.

3. The project provided an example of a democratic educational experience by giving students the opportunity to act as independent participants and by showing respect for their critical insights.

4. The sharing of decision-making gave the students the opportunity to experience an existential equality with the adults involved.

5. The open, honest, and objective confrontation with social problem issues provided a learning experience that seemed to enhance personal growth.

6. The learning that resulted from participation in the process of research seemed to produce a much deeper understanding than could be expected from the final reading of a final report and listening to a lecture. The existential approach seems to facilitate acquisition of the learning and adaptive skills necessary for survival. The focus of this method of self-evaluation, self-help, self-development, self-growth, within both the individual and the group, should lead to continuing growth.

For many kinds of behavior, such as drug abuse, alcohol abuse, juvenile delinquency and youth crime in school and the community, legislation appears to be highly ineffective as a control mechanism. In fact, some laws and the difficulties inherent in their enforcement may simply aggravate the problem. Educational methods, such as PARTNERSHIP IN RESEARCH, may offer a more effective means of prevention and intervention. The study in New Hampshire was intended to provide exploratory material in support of this thesis.

THE INTEGRATED COMMUNITY EDUCATION SYSTEM

Partnership in Research might be particularly effective if it were part of an Integrated Community Education System (ICES) (3, 4). To the general public, research is not an ally. The average citizen often perceives research as a tool of government or under the control of large corporate interests that tend to exploit the consumer. Until very recently, research has been preoccupied with peculiarities and deficiencies of individuals and little attention has been paid to deficiencies and injustices in government-provided services or to corporate actions that are in conflict with public interest. Specifically, social science has focused on individual "deviants" and their characteristics, almost totally neglecting environmental and social factors and their impact on individual behavior.

All this is changing. Science is beginning to serve more directly the public interest and may become a powerful tool for communal problem-solving. Donald T. Campbell proposes to create an "experimenting society" that makes science its servant and takes as its values the best of those of both democracy and science: honesty, open criticism, and a willingness to change in the face of new evidence. He calls for actions that integrate science and social concerns by adopting rigorous, rational, and scientific evaluations of new programs and ideas that allow further development of the best and modification or discontinuation of those that prove ineffective. Campbell suggests that we develop such evaluation research into a "folk science" that can be applied in a do-it-yourself fashion with voting-booth consequences.

The Integrated Community Education System (ICES) seems to hold promise for the creation of an informed and involved citizenry that can deal constructively with both the scientific aspects of social program development and the political constraints and consequences associated with responsible program decisions. The ICES is distinguished from other educational models in that it incorporates all of the following major features:

1. The system is planned, administered, and controlled by the community. ICES is created through intensive community participation and responds in part to changing community needs.

2. ICES is based on the concept of life-long learning for all interested persons.

3. Most learning environments are multi-age.

4. Educational opportunities are flexible to meet individual objectives of students.

5. Two substantially different structures are the basis for all instruction:

   a. The General Education Structure operates learning environments that emphasize success and personal development while exploring subjects in a non-threatening way to broaden one's knowledge without the possibility of failure; and

b. Career Education Structure operates learning environments which demand strict, disciplined learning that allows for serious and hard work toward skill development in the particular subject area.

6. Because of the multi-age learning environments and involvement of the community in their planning, administration, and control, ICES programs are envisioned as year-round educational programs.

The Integrated Community Education System has no narrowly defined educational programs or schools such as junior high, senior high, adult education, community college, or extension programs. Instead, a conceptually-based mode of instruction is offered for each of three different groups or levels:

Level I: Children, from birth to seven years of age

Level II: Children and youth, eight to fourteen years of age

Level III: Young adults and adults, fifteen years of age and older.

LEVEL I PROGRAMS

For children from birth to seven the mode consists of services directed toward need fulfillment and motivational, social, psychological, and physical development. This level, Comprehensive Children's Services, utilizes extensively students of all ages enrolled in level II and III programs, applying cross-age tutoring to its fullest with all the benefits that accrue for the student volunteer. At this level, services also are provided to parents directly. All level I programs are voluntary.

LEVEL II PROGRAMS

For children from eight to fourteen years, educational strategies are directed toward the further development of social and communicative skills as well as instruction in basic subjects. For this age group attendance is mandatory and students and teachers are held accountable for meeting certain educational standards.

LEVEL III PROGRAMS

For the young adult and adult group, participation is again voluntary and the individual selects his own educational objectives with the help of an educational guidance counselor. The educational opportunities available at this level, including personal development as well as academic, vocational, and social skill development, permit any number of combinations of these different programs at any one time. Education for the young adult and adult consists of a life-long process of learning and teaching, since teaching and tutoring others at any of the three levels becomes a part of the individual's own learning and growth.

MAJOR ICES PROGRAM FEATURES: COMPREHENSIVE CHILDREN'S SERVICES

Noting the results of recent educational, psychological, and medical research documenting the crucial importance of the first eight years of life (5), Wilson Riles, Superintendent of Instruction for the State of California, sought and received benchmark legislation that allows for the development of comprehensive plans for early childhood education. Early childhood education is one of the principal components of the Integrated Community Education System, but the latter goes beyond the early childhood education concept to include Comprehensive Children's Services for the youngest target group — children from birth to seven years of age. These services would be provided on a community basis through neighborhood children's centers operated by professional child care staff who receive maximum support (professional services and student participation on a voluntary and paid basis) from other components of the Integrated Community Education System.

Neighborhood children centers would be numerous, well-equipped, and prepared for quality service to children and their parents. Parents could bring their small children any time to the neighborhood children's center where professional services would be available. The emphasis would be on making them content while they are there, to provide them with comfortable shelter and food, to play with them, and to give them attention and love regardless of their background or home environment. All these services would be provided by students from the Integrated Community Education System, working under the supervision and guidance of professional staff.

Everyone involved would benefit from such a system of children's centers. The children would experience warmth and comfort and over the years would develop a strong positive attitude toward the community. Parents would utilize these centers as a welcome resource. They would be offered opportunities to take part in in-service education to learn child-rearing and child care, thus enabling them to become more effective parents. Student employees or volunteers would derive great satisfaction from the service they provided and would themselves learn a great deal from their participation in in-service education in child care and development. The community would benefit from the early identification and fulfillment of the needs of children and youth.

In our preoccupation with machines, we have come to expect a gas station on almost every street corner. If service stations are not abundantly available to take care of our cars, we feel that vital resources are missing. It is time that we perceived the critical lack of resources to serve children and young people and to insist that these resources be provided and developed.

ICES PROGRAM STRUCTURES: GENERAL AND CAREER EDUCATION

Under the ICES model, the student aged seven or older has the option to choose programs in two basic education structures: general education or career education. Students who successfully complete certain career education requirements have the further option of entering higher education through the professional education structure, which is equivalent to our present college-level instruction. The term "career education" as used in this paper should not be confused with vocational training or trade training. As used here, the term refers to any disciplined learning that has clearly defined objectives. These basic structures, with their differing educational objectives and methods, provide the depth and diversity that give the individual the freedom to construct his own educational program to fit his particular needs. The teacher also is provided with a variety of teaching environments, enabling him to express his own teaching style and pursue his own interests.

The core of both the general education structure and the career education structure is the classroom or a class module. As the educational pioneer Pestalozzi put it, "a country's future is decided in its classrooms." It is equally true that the individual's future is decided in the classroom. In our culture, the classroom is — potentially, at least — the most universally available environment for learning, thinking, and exchanging ideas, for maintaining perspective, for practicing equality and justice, and for encouraging respect and love for others. The classroom should be a "laboratory of life" in both a personal and communal sense.

GENERAL EDUCATION

General education provides for learning activities designed primarily to enrich and to motivate without fear of failure. Activities are exploratory, and structured to encourage the student to seek out, for as many subjects as he wishes, the more demanding educational programs offered in career education. It should be possible to fulfill minimum educational requirements by attending general education classes and achieving a level of reading, writing, and arithmetic that fulfills the requirements set by the state. Most individuals probably would combine general classes with career education classes; the teacher of general education classes would place primary emphasis on the general welfare of the student as an individual. In addition to presenting subject matter in a nonthreatening and collaborative manner, the teacher in this educational environment would pay a great deal of attention to the personal needs of his students. The subject matter or class focus becomes a means of achieving multi-faceted goals related to personal development and individual growth.

A concrete example of how these general education classes are envisioned is shown in the foreign language module, such as French. In general education, individuals of varied backgrounds meet for an introduction to the French language and culture. A variety of aspects related to the French culture such as music, philosophy, politics, cooking, and sports are explored. Exposure to the language would be provided through records, tapes, films, and conversation. No specific learning objectives would be set because the education structure of general education is motivational and enrichment-oriented rather than achievement-oriented to meet preconceived objectives.

Naturally, this multi-age, multi-background student group may learn a limited amount of French that would be useful in travel abroad or in future professional work. However, students could expect to have a pleasurable educational experience that widens their horizons. For some, the program may prepare them for a more demanding program in French under the career education structure. Similar exploratory treatments of other subjects, such as science, mathematics, history, homemaking, or vocational skills, would be presented in learning environments conducted by competent teachers who are primarily motivators and facilitators of growth for their students.

Another example of a general education class module is the physical education program. Within the general education structure traditional team-based competition would be discouraged. Exercises and sports would be undertaken for enjoyment. Individuals of all skill levels would be accommodated, and teams necessary for certain games would be frequently reconstituted to provide variety in team composition and to foster non-specific competition.

There is much to be learned from the non-competitive educational structure in which, while the individual is not graded, the class as a whole may develop its own "grading" system to address questions of the benefits and relevance of the learning activities on a class-wide basis. They may consider the contribution not only of the teacher but of the students as well.

CAREER EDUCATION

The learning environment within the career education structure is substantially different from that of the general education structure. Career education classes have specific learning objectives that will be met throughout the class sessions. Students of differing backgrounds and ages are grouped together by virtue of their common educational objectives. Participating students voluntarily subscribe to disciplined and specifically goal-oriented activities that can be carried out only if efforts by the students and the teachers toward reaching class goals are consistently maintained. The pay-off for these efforts are the skills learned as specified in the class objectives. Therefore, students and teachers are highly motivated to achieve in the particular subject chosen. Career education courses lead to higher education or professional education as higher education is an extension of the strict, disciplined career education structure.

In contrast to the French class in the general education structure, a career French class is clearly devoted to teaching specific language skills. For example, French I has a clearly defined beginning and a clearly defined end. French II builds on French I with its own clearly defined objectives. The career education structure with its career credit system allows a person to pursue particular skills throughout the career structure and beyond by moving into the professional education structure that is represented by our university and higher education system. The professional education structure, for example, would provide an individual with qualifications as a French teacher or certified interpreter.

In physical education, career education would include the highly competitive team membership or individual athletic achievement that in today's schools, where few general education opportunities exist, excludes unfortunately many students from sports activities.

Vocational training provides another example for contrasting the two basic education structures. In auto mechanics the general education structure would offer programs that expose the students in a disciplined way (no education can proceed without discipline with respect to the educational environment and the maintenance of equipment and tools) to auto mechanics. These courses would be motivational and exploratory, but might also include arrangements for the student to get work experience in an operating auto mechanics business in the community. Then, when the individual is ready to accept the challenge of career training, and is willing to expend the effort to acquire professional auto mechanic skills, he must either enroll in a career education class with specific educational objectives in this field, or he must enter into a formal apprenticeship agreement with an operating business in the community.

These two educational structures complement each other. They replace tracking students by allowing the student to tailor his education to his own needs through a combination of components from both educational structures. The opportunity for the individual to participate in the design of his own educational plan (including any combination of exploratory general classes and strict career classes) and the opportunity to keep educational options throughout life are the main features of the Integrated Community Education System.

Many of the alternatives available in traditional schools appear limiting and often degrading. Continuation high school, low-achiever tracks, and special programs for the educationally handicapped provide little variety or flexibility. An appropriate combination of general education and career education would allow a person to escape labeling or identification as a member of a low-status program. Most slow learners are not slow in all subjects. This approach gives the youth who needs primarily general education classes the opportunity to explore in greater depth an area in which he feels the greatest motivation and competence. He may enroll in the career class in auto mechanics or physical education, for instance, while remaining in the general education structure for other subjects.

EDUCATIONAL REFORM AND DELINQUENCY PREVENTION

Both Partnership in Research and the Integrated Community Education System concept are directed toward the broader goals of revitalization of the community and its educational institutions. There are, however, some important implications for the prevention of youth crime and misbehavior which arise indirectly from such factors as: involvement of youth in their communities and in their own education; reduction of the artificial barriers which isolate young people from persons of both younger and older age groups; elimination of low-status educational groups (tracking, continuation schools, underachiever programs, etc.); involvement of youth and community residents in studying such problems as student crime and in designing solutions based on their own observations; increasing the importance of the student role within the school; improving the fit between the student and the learning environment; and reducing the split between student and teacher roles, and between the functions of teaching and learning, by combining each individual's own education with the tutoring of others.

If the strategy is to be set with a typology of "prevention" approaches, it can be viewed as *educational*, as opposed to the more common medical and legal models. In contrast to medical and legal approaches, the educational strategy assumes a basic outlook of growth and development and perceives the individual to be helped as student or "learner," a role that is maintained throughout life by many educated persons. The requirement of the medical approach that the person to be helped adopt the role of "patient" and the requirement of the legal approach that the person adopt the role of "criminal" or "delinquent" are viewed as detrimental to individual growth and maturation. These two requirements, and the stances generally adopted by mental health, criminal justice, and law enforcement professionals, tend to have stigmatizing effects and often are counterproductive by preventing social readjustment. The educational strategy does not need to apply negative labels (although frequently it too falls into this trap), but instead applies the supportive label of "student" that can enhance self-esteem and facilitate growth.

It is suggested that these and other learning models can be successfully applied in social problem-solving, particularly before sanctions based on medical models and legal models are employed. Such an approach may prevent a great many individuals from becoming "patients" or "convicts" by keeping them in a learning role as involved and motivated students. Education, then, might largely replace treatment, therapy, and correction, which could be reserved for less responsive persons and persons who present a serious danger to themselves and to others.

Partnership in Research, which involves public school students in the scientific examination of issues important to them, and the Integrated Community Education System, which anchors the public school to the local community, offer a unique opportunity to build a strong foundation for the experimenting society required for responsible change and problem-solving.

By bringing young people and other community residents into the process of experimental problem-solving, we can benefit from the utilization of as yet untapped human resources in our efforts to control delinquency and crime, alcoholism, drug addiction, and other social problems. By providing citizens with a means of effecting change through active participation in the democratic process of government, we also can offer a viable alternative to apathy and irresponsible behavior. At the same time, we can move in the direction of an experimental society with local responsibility for and interest in the quality of its social programs and their rigorous evaluation.

FOOTNOTES AND REFERENCES

1. Tavris, Interview with Donald T. Campbell, PSYCHOLOGY TODAY, 1975.

2. This research was supported in part by a grant from the New Hampshire Governor's Commission on Crime and Delinquency to the Research Center of the National Council on Crime and Delinquency and by General Research Support Grant ISOL RR-05693-02 from the U.S. Public Health Service; E. Wenk, PEER CONDUCTED RESEARCH: A NOVEL APPROACH TO DRUG EDUCATION. Paper presented to the First International Congress on Drug Education, held at Montreaux Vd., Switzerland, October 14-18, 1973.

3. Ernst Wenk, "Schools and the Community: A Model for Participatory Problem-Solving," in E. Wenk, (ed), DELINQUENCY PREVENTION AND THE SCHOOLS: EMERGING PERSPECTIVES, CONTEMPORARY SOCIAL ISSUES, Vol. 29, Beverly Hills, CA: Sage Publications, 1976.

4. Ernst Wenk, "Juvenile Justice and the Public Schools: Mutual Benefit Through Education Reform," JUVENILE JUSTICE, 1975, Vol. 26, pp. 7-14.

5. California State Department of Education, EARLY CHILDHOOD EDUCATION: REPORT OF THE TASK FORCE ON EARLY CHILDHOOD EDUCATION. Sacramento: Department of Education, 1972.

PART IV

DIMENSIONS OF A
NATIONAL YOUTH POLICY

DEVELOPING A POSITIVE NATIONAL YOUTH POLICY

Dennie Briggs
Douglas Grant

The times have seldom been so opportune for the development and implementation of a national youth policy. There is a growing interest in preventive approaches to social problems. This focus on prevention derives in part from the need for efficient use of dwindling resources. It is spurred as well by the decline of the "medical model" and disenchantment with efforts to treat individuals for deficiencies generated by their social environment.

Cross-agency collaboration and citizen/client participation also are moving to center stage. Interagency collaboration signifies a movement away from providing services to isolated categories of problems and toward program development for more broadly-defined target groups. Such collaboration, along with client participation tends to decrease the costs of service delivery and make programs more relevant to the consumer.

Opportunities for developing a positive national youth policy also are forecasted by such varied events as:

— the taxpayer revolt
— the United Nations' International Year of the Child
— the White House Conference on Children and Youth.

Cutbacks in local government spending necessitated by a reduced tax base can force long-needed re-evaluation of all basic services. Rather than seeking alternate funds to prop up existing systems, citizens can participate in the planning of viable ways to cope locally with local problems.

The International Year of the Child, planned for 1979 by the United Nations, offers a chance to realize the enormous potential of youth in the development of global policies and programs. The U.N. has allotted $1.4 billion for a five-year program. The possibilities are staggering. Cross-cultural interchanges on a massive scale, as one example, could enhance the role of young people while contributing materially to world peace.

The following year, in this country, the 1980 White House Conference on Children and Youth will provide a focus and a means for implementing a positive national youth policy.

The simultaneous occurrence of such opportunities is rare — it should be taken advantage of quickly. In the late 1960's, valuable opportunities were lost because of our repeated failure to listen to the nation's youth and collaborate with them in their efforts to promote social change. This time around, the opportunity must be seized to work with American youth, capitalizing on their immense energies and latent talents. Encouragement must be given to their genuine participation in meeting emerging national priorities. To do anything less would be a shocking waste of a vitally important national resource.

KEY ELEMENTS OF A NATIONAL YOUTH POLICY

During the years before 1970, the nation lacked a coherent youth policy. Government policy at all levels concentrated on suppressing dissidents and treating deviants through changing behavior — variations of the so-called "medical model." The time has come to discontinue such practices and to design a new national policy on youth. This policy must concentrate on seeing youth in a positive light — not as dropouts, drug users, or delinquents. Youth instead can be facilitators in the effort to bring about social change — an asset to society rather than a liability. Seven additional elements of an effective national youth policy are identified here.

1. A national youth policy requires youth involvement. The policy must provide for direct youth involvement in contemporary social problems — not only in identifying the problems, but in carrying out solutions. We have had little success in dealing with youth in a variety of client roles. A more promising approach would be to engage youth in changing their own behavior, making them active and responsible participants in solving their own problems. This stance is in sharp contrast to the passivity of being a recipient of services provided by experts.

2. A national youth policy must integrate youth programs. Youth programs tend to be isolated, fragmented, and concentrated on categories of specific problems (e.g., drug abuse, delinquency, school failure). They address individual problems without attacking the larger one: the need to view youth in a positive light. Society excludes some young people from its affairs and generally views them as a liability rather than a resource.

3. A national youth policy must be concerned with all youth. At one level there is a need for new ideas, the elimination of overlap, and the shoring up of existing programs. At another, there is a need to develop programs which the participants themselves believe are necessary and worthwhile. Currently, governments at all levels are trying many different kinds of programs to meet many interests and needs. Their efforts do not seem successful — perhaps because all are based upon a negative picture of young people and concentrate primarily on "problem" youth. These programs, some more than others, ignore the institutions which breed the problems — and the fact that those problems are faced by *all* youth.

A positive national youth policy — concerned with prevention rather than treatment — would benefit all young persons by recognizing both their needs and their rights. It would change the institutions' responsibility, thereby attacking the problem at the source.

4. A national youth policy must be directed toward opening up opportunities for productive participation in society. Such a strategy represents a tangible commitment to grass-roots democracy, while assuring more effective program development. Youth involvement implies more than their participation in the activities of adult society. It also suggests a need to permit and encourage young people to take an active part in planning their own futures and accepting responsibility for them. Experimentation with alternate self-perceptions, lifestyles, and ways of interacting with others must be recognized as necessary and useful. At the same time, young people must be involved in, and have substantial control over, the process of their own transition to adulthood.

5. A national youth policy must serve national goals. We have many identified national needs (e.g., school improvement, welfare reform, employment development, preservation of the environment, senior citizen concerns, teenage pregnancies, to name but a few). There are also innumerable programs to deal with these needs. Lacking is a common focus.

The nation can take advantage of youth as a resource in responding to a multitude of pressing needs only by drafting an updated youth policy. This policy must not only upgrade unmet needs to a higher priority but also utilize youth in meeting these needs. The goal is to merge youth involvement with those priorities to which the nation is prepared to direct its attention and its best efforts. Involving young people in the definition of national problems — plus the design and implementation of solutions — not only opens meaningful opportunities to youth but permits optimal use of national resources in addressing priority problems.

6. A national youth policy must break down the barrier between work and education. Work must become an opportunity for learning and education must contribute to work effectiveness. This fusion is demanded by the need to make informed and responsible decisions on rapidly changing social and technological problems. The merging of education and work also decreases the perceived irrelevance of education. It eases the transition from youth to adulthood and can minimize the problems such transition often brings in its wake. This element will require some restructuring of the educational system, which is already underway in some areas, both here and abroad. The United Nations Educational, Scientific, and Cultural Organization has reaffirmed that education everywhere is undergoing a revolution. The Deputy Director of this international body reports: "When we say 'education' today, we include work as part of the process of education" (1).

Two existing approaches which include work as a part of education are independent study and individualized learning. The emphasis of both these means is on active learning. Active learning concentrates on knowledge-building rather than passive storage of information.

A related theme to be incorporated into the national policy is represented by programs which enable young people to learn and to use the skills associated with studying problems and designing, implementing, and testing their solutions. An HEW task force recommended that America become an "experimenting society" in which everyone takes part in redesigning their jobs (2). Young people as well as other citizens could participate in the definition of problems and the development of programs to deal with them. Such citizen-conducted studies could be focused on any local, state, or national program—not only employment, but energy conservation, environmental protection, inter-cultural relations, etc. For youth in school, participation in such studies would bring the added benefit of course credit applicable toward graduation.

7. *A national youth policy must treat youth as a resource, not as a collection of problems to be solved by adults.* What is needed, then, is a policy which promotes youth development through participation in resolving social problems — both those that concern them as young people and those that they will inherit as adults. There is an overwhelming array of national needs which are still unmet. Such a merger of social problem-solving with productive work would contribute to their own and the nation's development.

MAKING IT WORK

The development and promotion of a national youth policy will require immediate action to develop enabling legislation and to foster nationwide awareness of the need for youth development. A resource and support entity is needed. There must be formal mechanisms for coordinating efforts and generating support for change in the opportunity structure and roles of youth. And we must identify and amplify exemplary projects and program models.

Legislation. The 1965 Older Americans Act provided a basis and an impetus for policy and program development to benefit the "senior citizen" population (3). In like manner, new youth policy could be coordinated through federal, state, and local organizations and agencies created for the purpose. New programs could be carried out using the combined resources and expertise of existing agencies now responsible for services to specific problem groups such as health, welfare, education, employment, and juvenile justice (4). There already exists federal legislation urging interagency collaboration in program development and some states (e.g., California) have enacted parallel legislation at the state level (5). Additional legislation could further define the cooperative roles of new and existing agencies with respect to youth development, as well as provide for specific youth programs that fit within a comprehensive youth policy (6). Legislation also may be needed to establish the procedures for implementing new youth policy.

Public awareness. To support passage of enabling legislation and to insure effective implementation of any national youth policy, deliberate and coordinated efforts will have to be made to generate public awareness (7).

Changing the image of young people will require the cooperation of the media as well as the efforts of youth and their advocates. Journalists, film-makers, television directors, and newscasters are in a position to significantly shape public perception of youth. Young people themselves will have to do much of the work to change their public image. Projects in which youth work with adults in resolving local issues will accomplish a great deal. Responsible and ongoing participation of youth in ecology, civil rights, and human service programs will have both immediate and long-term effects. The public will form a new image of youth only through the deliberate coordinated efforts of the media, youth advocates, and youth themselves.

Resource and Support Center. The implementation of a comprehensive national youth policy and the generation of broad-based but focused public support will require the establishment of a Resource and Support Center. Existing facilities concentrate on the storage of historical information rather than its use. More than a library or clearinghouse, this new Center would have overall responsibility for the promulgation of a national policy on youth. In addition to the collection and dissemination of information, the Center would be responsible for the organization and analysis of information, preparation of position papers, development of recommendations for legislative or policy changes, and interpretation of existing legislation and evaluative data. As such, the Center not only would serve as a central source of up-to-date information, but would contribute directly to implementing, evaluating, and publicizing youth policy.

Supporting networks. Working with the national Resource Center would be networks of political, professional, and citizen groups and organizations with an interest in promoting a national policy for youth development. Many such networks already exist:

— the Collegial Association for the Development and Renewal of Educators (CADRE), a Denver-based nationwide association of educators dedicated to school improvement

— the community work/education consortiums of the National Manpower Institute

— the National Association of Secondary School Principals

— the National Institute of Education's National Diffusion Network

— Youthwork, Inc. (a private, nonprofit agency in Washington, D.C. that funds exemplary projects linking work and education)

— the National Child Labor Committee

— the National Commission on Resources for Youth

— the National Council on Crime and Delinquency Youth Development Center

— the National Network of Family and Youth Services (formerly the National Network of Runaway Youth Services)

— the Office of Education's Division of Alcohol and Drug Abuse Education Programs which operates five training centers that work with schools nationwide to reduce drug and alcohol abuse and, under current Office of Juvenile Justice and Delinquency Prevention funding, to deal with the problems of school crime and disruption

These networks represent only a very few of those that could be enlisted to support a comprehensive national youth policy, operating as a coalition of networks to meet common objectives. New networks, of course, can be created by developing formal or informal coalitions.

There even exists a prototype for a national effort to develop policy — and a network system to insure its implementation. In a project supported by the Office of Juvenile Justice and Delinquency Prevention, a network of task forces involving policy-makers at state, county, and city levels is being created to develop and promote programs that combine education and work, focusing on reform of public education. The task forces, representing youth-serving agencies (education, employment, justice, mental health) will devise action plans for the promotion of student-initiated research and evaluation of school-related issues. Students will be employed to study the educational system and will receive academic credit for knowledge gained in the process. A resource center will provide technical assistance to the task forces through local and national workshops and dissemination of resource materials. The resource center has an action team of youth (ages 12 to 21) who conduct projects, locate and assemble resource materials for use by the task forces, and publish a newsletter on education and employment. Members of this team are paid a regular wage in addition to receiving academic credit for their work (8).

Building an effective networking system is complex and the effort must be sustained. The first task is to bring together individuals and groups with a common interest in youth development. In creating a network of independent coalitions, it is important to coordinate but not to control. Keeping the network functioning, then, requires continuous communication through such means as dissemination of publications, meetings, audio-visual presentations, and personal contacts by telephone or mail (9, 10, 11).

IDENTIFYING AND DEVELOPING PROGRAM MODELS

In addition to enabling legislation, and the establishment of the network system, there must be developed a body of knowledge and experience relating to programs and services for youth. Exemplary projects and model programs already exist and, based on experience gained from these, many others could be designed and tested. Promising models for replication or adaptation are found throughout this country. A number are described in this volume. They deal, in quite different ways, with participatory learning, the integration of work and education, and involvement of youth in community problem-solving.

There are, for example, over 1200 "alternative schools" now in operation. Some, like the St. Paul Open School (see page 219), are exemplary models of youth participation in the education process. Far West High School, in Oakland, California, is another such model (see page 197). Operated within the public school system, Far West is based entirely on "contract" learning. Situated in a downtown office building, this unconventional school helps students to take advantage of community resources rather than duplicating services within the school system. Another prototype is found in Palo Alto, California where secondary school students are studying issues and problems and helping to develop action plans to deal with school-related topics of interest to them (see page 169). The National Institute of Education's Experience-Based Career Education (EBCE) program, discussed in several papers in this book, represents a significant departure from traditional educational approaches: students are involved in designing their own educational program, teachers function as "resource consultants," and the learning process occurs, to a large extent, in the community.

Related to school-based programs, there are opportunities for youth participation in the field of work. The new focus will be on the integration of school and work and the involvement of young people in adult society. A proposed agreement among the Departments of Labor, Justice, and HEW would make federal youth employment and delinquency prevention funds available for job development. A development component would be added to the more than 150 runaway youth programs funded by HEW's Office of Youth Development. This interagency agreement would provide for paid jobs for youth, integrated with education. In addition to providing community services (e.g., outreach, community education, and crisis intervention), youth would be hired to help in defining program objectives, identifying obstacles and resources, and developing strategies. For such work, youth not only would be paid but would receive educational credit for knowledge gained through community service.

These are but a few of the existing program models on which a national youth policy might be based. Many more are already in operation or are in the planning stages. Implementation of a positive youth policy will require the identification of a range of these program models, the accumulation of experiential data on such programs, and the transmission of successful models to others.

In contemporary American society, two sizeable groups are largely excluded from productive work: the young and the elderly. While most of the elderly are out of the work force, most young people hope to enter it. Although the majority make the transition to the world of work, many do not. The alienation of those youth from society is not only an important youth problem, but also a problem of society.

Society has many other problems and urgent needs. The price of health care is astronomical and rising. Alternatives to traditional medical treatment of disease and disability are greatly needed, and greater personal responsibility for health maintenance should be encouraged. We also need to increase cross-cultural and cross-national understandings, and to find more effective ways to protect the environment. Most importantly, solutions to all these problems must be energy efficient and labor intensive.

The alienation of youth and the need for labor intensive solutions to social problems can be approached by creating participatory work opportunities, integrated with education, for all. Through such a merging of learning and doing, young people will become more directly involved in community problem-solving. Youth will thus gain the experience that they will need as adults to deal with the complex problems of a changing world.

FOOTNOTES AND REFERENCES

1. John E. Fobes, in "Symposium of Young Workers on the Quality of Work and Work Prospects." Paris: UNESCO Document ED 76/CONF 816/4, November 1976.

2. WORK IN AMERICA, Report of a special task force to the Secretary of Health, Education and Welfare. Cambridge, Mass.: MIT Press, 1973.

3. Public Law 89-73, "Older Americans Act of 1965."

4. For example, demonstration programs in youth development could be carried out within such existing HEW entities as the National Institute of Drug Abuse, the National Institute on Alcohol Abuse and Alcoholism, the National Institute of Mental Health, and the Office of Youth Development, relying on their component legislation and existing funding. Their extensive training systems also could be used to build local youth development capabilities.

5. Public Law 93-510, "Joint Funding Simplification Act of 1974;"

California Assembly Bill Number 965, "Multiservice Youth and Family Programs."

6. Examples of the latter include current youth employment legislation which makes an appreciable amount of funding available for youth participation through paid jobs, offering an opportunity for the constructive blending of work and education, as well as modifications of education codes to provide for independent study to supplement or replace traditional classroom education.

7. "Building Capacity for Renewal and Reform: An Initial Report on Knowledge Production and Utilization in Education," Task Force report on Resources Planning and Analysis, Office of Research and Development Resources, National Institute of Education, 1973.

8. Grant Award #78-JN-AX-0013, "Training for Youth Participation in Program Development," awarded to the Social Action Research Center, San Rafael, California, by the Office of Juvenile Justice and Delinquency Prevention, of the Law Enforcement Assistance Administration.

9. W.N. Dunn and F.W. Swierczek, "Planned Organizational Change: Toward Grounded Theory," J. APPLIED BEHAVIORAL SCIENCE, 1977.

10. E. Katz, "The Social Itinerary of Technical Change: Two Studies on the Diffusion of Innovation," in W.G. Bennis, et al., THE PLANNING OF CHANGE, Second Edition. NY: Holt, Rinehart and Winston, 1969.

11. Seymor B. Sarason, "Community Psychology, Networks, and Mr. Everyman," AMERICAN PSYCHOLOGIST, 1976, Vol. 31, pp. 317-328; S.B. Sarason, C. Carrol, K. Malton, S. Cohen, and E. Lorentz, HUMAN SERVICES AND RESOURCE NETWORKS. San Francisco: Jossey-Bass, 1977.

DIALOGUE BOOKS®

A persistent and frustrating problem for both the human service professional and the social action advocate is the fragmentation of information on important social topics. Most social science information is scattered throughout a vast publication system, a fact which seriously obstructs the development of effective approaches to social problems.

RESPONSIBLE ACTION brings together a wide range of opinion and information on timely and important topics in its DIALOGUE BOOKS series. DIALOGUE BOOKS are written for people in education and the human services, or others who care about social progress generally; but they also depend on the interest and support of this varied readership. A dynamic interchange — an ongoing dialogue — with people who work within the many disciplines in this field is essential if these publications are to remain current, relevant, and based on practical experience.RESPONSIBLE ACTION attempts through its ASSOCIATE PROGRAM to form the foundation for such a productive dialogue.

1978 DIALOGUE BOOKS

STRESS, DISTRESS, AND GROWTH
MORAL EDUCATION
PARTNERSHIP IN RESEARCH
THE VALUE OF YOUTH
DELINQUENCY PREVENTION: Educational Approaches
SCHOOL CRIME AND DISRUPTION: Prevention Models
DROPOUT
THE YOUNG ADULT OFFENDER

DIALOGUE BOOKS are quality paperback editions.
Price: $ 5.75   Student Manuals and Workbooks $ 3.75

Order your books through your local bookstore or through RESPONSIBLE ACTION.

6413
RESPONSIBLE ACTION, P.O.Box 924, Davis, California 95616